STANDARD LOAN

The Church in the Modern Age

THE I.B.TAURIS HISTORY OF THE CHRISTIAN CHURCH
GENERAL EDITOR: G.R. EVANS

The Early Church
Morwenna Ludlow, University of Exeter

The Church in the Early Middle Ages
G.R. Evans, University of Cambridge

The Church in the Later Middle Ages
Norman Tanner, Gregorian University, Rome

Early Modern Christianity
Patrick Provost-Smith, Harvard University

The Church in the Long Eighteenth Century
David Hempton, Harvard University

The Church in the Nineteenth Century
Frances Knight, University of Wales, Lampeter

The Church in the Modern Age
Jeremy Morris, University of Cambridge

THE I.B.TAURIS HISTORY OF THE CHRISTIAN CHURCH

The Church in the Modern Age

Jeremy Morris

I.B. TAURIS
LONDON · NEW YORK

Published in 2007 by I.B.Tauris & Co. Ltd
6 Salem Road, London W2 4BU
175 Fifth Avenue, New York, NY 10010
www.ibtauris.com

Vol 1: *The Early Church*   978 1 84511 366 7
Vol 2: *The Church in the Early Middle Ages*   978 1 84511 150 2
Vol 3: *The Church in the Later Middle Ages*   978 1 84511 438 1
Vol 4: *Early Modern Christianity*   978 1 84511 439 8
Vol 5: *The Church in the Long Eighteenth Century*   978 1 84511 440 4
Vol 6: *The Church in the Nineteenth Century*   978 1 85043 899 1
Vol 7: *The Church in the Modern Age*   978 1 84511 317 9

A full CIP record for this book is available from the British Library

Typeset in Adobe Caslon Pro by A. & D. Worthington, Newmarket, Suffolk
Printed and bound in Great Britain by CPI Bath

THE I.B.TAURIS HISTORY OF THE CHRISTIAN CHURCH

Since the first disciples were sent out by Jesus, Christianity has been of its essence a missionary religion. That religion has proved to be an ideology and a subversive one. Profoundly though it became 'inculturated' in the societies it converted, it was never syncretistic. It had, by the twentieth century, brought its own view of things to the ends of the earth. The Christian Church, first defined as a religion of love, has interacted with Judaism, Islam and other world religions in ways in which there has been as much warfare as charity. Some of the results are seen in the tensions of the modern world, tensions which are proving very hard to resolve – not least because of a lack of awareness of the history behind the thinking which has brought the Church to where it is now.

In the light of that lack, a new history of the Christian Church is badly needed. There is much to be said for restoring to the general reader a familiarity with the network of ideas about what the Church 'is' and what it should be 'doing' as a vessel of Christian life and thought. This series aims to be both fresh and traditional. It will be organized so that the boundary-dates between volumes fall in some unexpected places. It will attempt to look at its conventional subject matter from the critical perspective of the early twenty-first century, where the Church has a confusing myriad of faces. Behind all these manifestations is a rich history of thinking, effort and struggle. And within it, at the heart of matters, is the Church. *The I.B.Tauris History of the Christian Church* seeks to discover that innermost self through the layers of its multiple manifestations over twenty centuries.

SERIES EDITOR'S PREFACE

Against the background of global conflict involving interfaith resentments and misunderstandings, threatening 'religious wars' on a scale possibly unprecedented in history, Christians and the Christian Church are locked in internal disputes. On 2 November 2003, a practising homosexual was made a bishop in the Episcopal Church in the United States, America's 'province' of the Anglican Communion. This was done in defiance of the strong opinion in other parts of the 'Communion' that if it happened Anglicanism would fall apart into schism. A few years earlier there had been similar rumblings over the ordination of women to ministry in the same Church. A century before that period, the Roman Catholic Church had pronounced all Anglican ordination to the priestly or episcopal ministry to be utterly null and void because of an alleged breach of communion and continuity in the sixteenth century. And the Orthodox Churches watched all this in the secure conviction that Roman Catholic, Anglican and all other Christian communities were not communions at all because they had departed from the truth as it had been defined in the ecumenical Councils of the first few centuries. Orthodoxy alone was orthodox. Even the baptism of other Christians was of dubious validity.

Those heated by the consecration of a 'gay' bishop spoke on the one side of faithfulness to the teaching of the Bible and on the other of the leading of the Holy Spirit into a new world which knew no discrimination. Yet both the notion of faithfulness to Scripture and the idea that Jesus particularly wanted to draw the outcasts and disadvantaged to himself have a long and complex history which makes it impossible to make either statement in simple black-and-white terms.

One of the most significant factors in the frightening failures of communication and goodwill which make daily headlines is a loss of contact with the past on the part of those taking a stand on one side or another of such disagreements. The study of 'history' is fashionable as this series is launched, but the colourful narrative of past lives and episodes does not necessarily make familiar the patterns of thought and assumption in the minds of those involved. A modern history of the Church must embody that awareness in every sinew. Those embattled in disputes within the Church and disputes involving Christian and other-faith communities have tended to take their stand on principles they claim to be of eternal validity, and to represent the will of God. But as they appear in front of television cameras or speak to journalists the accounts they give – on either side – frequently reflect a lack of knowledge of the tradition they seek to protect or to challenge.

The creation of a new history of the Church at the beginning of the third millennium is an ambitious project, but it is needed. The cultural, social and political dominance of Christendom in what we now call 'the West' during the first two millennia made the Christian Church a shaper of the modern world in respects which go far beyond its strictly religious influence. Since the first disciples were sent out to preach the Gospel by Jesus, Christianity has been of its essence a missionary religion. It took the faith across the world in a style which has rightly been criticized as 'imperialist'. Christianity has proved to be an ideology and a subversive one. Profoundly though it became 'inculturated' in the societies converted, it was never syncretistic. It had, by the twentieth century, brought its own view of things to the ends of the earth. The Christian Church, first defined as a religion of love, has interacted with Judaism, Islam and the other world religions in ways in which there has been as much warfare as charity. We see some of the results in tensions in the modern world which are now proving very hard to resolve, not least because of the sheer failure of awareness of the history of the thinking which has brought the Church to where it is now.

Such a history has of course purposes more fundamental, more positive, more universal, but no less timely. There may not be a danger of the loss of the full picture while the libraries of the world and its historic buildings and pictures and music preserve the evidence. But the connecting thread in living minds is easily broken. There is much to be said for restoring as familiar to the general reader, whether Christian or not, a command of the sequence and network of ideas about what the Church *is* and what it should be *doing* as a vessel of Christian thought and life.

This new series aims, then, to be both new and traditional. It is organized so that the boundary-dates between volumes come in some unexpected places. It attempts to look at the conventional subject matter of histories of the Church from the vantage-point of the early twenty-first century, where the Church has confusingly many faces: from Vatican strictures on the use of birth-control and the indissolubility of marriage, and the condemnation of outspoken German academic theologians who challenge the Churches' authority to tell them what to think and write, to the enthusiasm of Black Baptist congregations in the USA joyously affirming a faith with few defining parameters. Behind all these variations is a history of thought and effort and struggle. And within, at the heart of matters, is the Church. It is to be discovered in its innermost self through the layers of its multiple manifestations over twenty centuries. That is the subject of this series.

Contents

To Alex
With love and gratitude

Preface

A short, one-volume history of the worldwide Christian Church in the twentieth century is a tall order. If the Christian faith had at last become a truly global religion in the nineteenth century, in the twentieth century its conflicts, divisions and political contexts multiplied dramatically. So much material is available to the historian, with so little time yet for hindsight and the chance it brings for sifting the significant from the mundane or inconsequential, that he or she is likely to be overwhelmed. It was tempting to take one of a number of possible short cuts – to rely on a few carefully chosen themes, for example – in order to keep the material under control. I avoided short cuts, however, in the belief that what will be most useful to the student or general reader coming fresh to contemporary church history is a comprehensive overview of the field, paying attention to relevant political events, focusing on the major theological divisions of the Christian Church, and giving some flavour of local (or, rather, regional) developments – a tall order indeed.

A few words of explanation about my general approach may be useful. A number of people have asked me what my interpretation would be. My response has been puzzlement – *one* interpretation? There are too many trends, churches, contexts and controversies to make one general interpretation convincing, especially when so many of the issues Christian churches faced towards the end of the century are still working themselves out. To produce such a general view would require a general theory of religion, and there is no space here for that. I can pick out a few elements of the story that I regard as especially significant, including the fall of the European empires, the rise and fall of Soviet communism, the faltering of the churches in Europe, the rise of Pentecostalism, and above all the shift of Christianity's centre of gravity towards the Global South – this last a trend that almost obliterates many of the generalizations about religion that Western social commentators were making for much of the century. I hope I have given due to weight to all these phenomena. But above all my aim has been to present an outline history of the main sub-divisions of the Christian

Church within a chronological framework that makes sense of the major crises of the century in political order and international relations. And so I have divided the century into three sequences of events: 1914 to 1945, an era framed by the two world wars; 1945 to 1973, the beginning of the Cold War and the era of decolonization; and 1973 to 2000, when the oil crisis of 1973, and later the collapse of the Soviet Empire, marked the beginning of a new period of confusion and instability in international relations. Within each period there are chapters on political events, Catholicism, Eastern Orthodoxy and Protestantism. Additionally each period also has a thematic chapter attached dealing in turn with three subjects which require a longer timescale – ecumenism and mission, independency and Pentecostalism.

To some extent this is an arbitrary division of the century, and church history does not always fit neatly around it. But it makes broad sense as a way of describing, firstly, the conflicts and major templates in international relations in which Christianity had to operate in the course of the century, and, secondly, the widening circle of consequence by which a world run by a handful of European powers became one in which – in theory at least – there is a true world community of 191 sovereign states. At the same time as trying to give due weight to Christianity in all parts of the world, I have also tried to give proper attention in my narrative to the diminishing influence of Western Christianity and to the rise of post-imperialist, non-Western Christianity. For that reason, the fall of empires and the process and effects of decolonization are the lynchpins of this book.

I should also like to add a few comments about terminology. I have written for an English-speaking audience and have generally used the most familiar Anglicized spellings of place names. I have also generally translated non-English titles of churches and other organizations, except in those instances where a title is likely to be so well known in its original language that it needed no translation. I have not translated commonly used terms from other languages, nor technical ecclesiastical terms in reasonably common use – I have assumed the reader can consult a dictionary if need be. More controversially, I have been a bit slippery about regional terminology. Sometimes 'America' refers to North America as a whole, and sometimes to the USA – I hope the context makes clear which is which. Sometimes 'Asia' has included countries of the Pacific Rim, since I was always taught that the continents are Europe, America, Asia, Australasia and Antarctica; but sometimes I have also specifically referred to the Pacific Rim. My own British identity is probably evident in occasional use of the term 'the continent of Europe' as if it was a separate entity from Britain. I expect a particularly controversial usage is 'Third World', which is still frequently used in the Western world, though interchangeably with 'Global South' or 'the developing world' – both of which also appear here. My only defence is that there is no pejorative intention here: the term 'Third World' was introduced originally as much as a geographical and economic category, distinguishing the rest of the world from the capitalist 'First World' and from the Soviet communist 'Second World', and that is simply what I have intended here. Similar difficulties attend the use of 'Middle East' and 'Far East'. Again, most English-speaking Westerners will know what I mean by these terms, but I am well aware of the dangers of Orientalism, and I have used these terms only in a sense which is geographically convenient.

One final comment is about reading and sources. Since this is intended as a textbook for those coming new to the field, the aim has been to present a text unencumbered by long sequences of footnotes. Where the opinion of a particular scholar is specifically quoted, I have provided a reference, but that is all. The bibliography features books I would recommend for those who want to pursue particular subjects in more depth, but it is not a detailed list of sources for this book.

I would like to record my thanks to a number of people whose insights and advice were extremely helpful in the course of writing this book – especially Ben de la Mare, John Clarke, Peter Clarke, Valentin Dedji, David Galilee, Paula Gooder, Douglas Hedley, Kaisamari Hintikka, Graham Howes, Clare Jackson, Peter McEnhill, John Nurser, John Pollard, Nicholas Sagovsky, Mark Santer, Sheila Watson, Jane Williams, and members of AngPol (you know who you are). Thanks too to Alex Wright, the commissioning editor, for his patience. My own experience of the world church has broadened immensely over the last few years through various ecumenical commitments, and there any many people I could name whom I have met around a table talking about Christian differences and church unity, but this general acknowledgement will have to suffice. I would also like to thank the Master and Fellows of Trinity Hall for the study leave which enabled me to write the book, and above all my wife Alex and my children Isobel, William and Ursula for all their support.

The Church and the World on the Eve of War

A false dawn?

'Never such innocence, never before or since,' wrote the British poet Philip Larkin of Britain on the eve of the First World War, looking back caustically from the 1960s – 'Never such innocence ... as changed itself to past without a word.' Larkin's words could be applied almost without exception to the spirit with which the European nations embraced war in 1914. By the end of the twentieth century, people in Western Europe thought of their age as born in catastrophe, when the most powerful nations of Europe stumbled unthinkingly into war in August 1914. It is hard to conceive of any other coherent starting point for a history of the worldwide Church in the twentieth century. From conflict in Western and Eastern Europe in August 1914, the war spread to engulf parts of Africa and Asia, and the oceans of the world. Some 15 million people, combatants and non-combatants, were killed, and many millions more were wounded. The war triggered revolution in Russia, and the fall of the German, Austro-Hungarian and Ottoman empires. It marked the emergence of the United States as a major global power. It stimulated movements for national independence in European colonies throughout the world. Culturally, in the West, it brought an end to a climate of optimism. Never such innocence again.

The notion of 'crisis' is a very convenient one for historians. It enables them to cast a sharp, clear light on movements, ideas and people in history. Crises become motors of explanation, tidying up awkward facts and tying together seemingly disparate material. The worldwide scale of the conflict of 1914–18, with its unprecedented enormity of suffering and loss, naturally lends itself to the language of 'crisis'. Certainly even for the Christian churches it brought about significant long-term changes. And yet, look closely at the Christian churches before, during and after the war, and you can find at once continuity where you expected to find disruption, and alarm and apprehension where you expected to find complacency. Theologians and church leaders in the Christian West did not sleepwalk into the war, supremely confident in their own inherent supremacy, as historians would sometimes have us believe. Already, in the years before 1914, they were voicing concerns about the deteriorating international situation. They were highly conscious of their own internal divisions, and accustomed to speaking of the imminent 'crisis' of Christianity in the West. Yet the political dominance of the European empires worldwide, and the continuing influence of the European churches, also gave church leaders an immense confidence in the possibilities ahead. They did not seriously conceive what a future without European colonial empires would look like. They assumed that, however critical of imperialism many of them might be, nevertheless the world would dance to the West's tunes.

The complexity of the churches' outlook on the eve of war can be caught above all from the great World Missionary Conference held in Edinburgh in 1910. The largest ever gathering of Western missionary representatives, Edinburgh was the symbolic apogee of the Protestant missionary movement. It was an overwhelmingly Anglo-American and German affair, but the Germans were a definite second string. When the conference gathered in the Assembly Hall of the United Free Church of Scotland in June 1910, of its 1,200 delegates only 170 were from the non-English-speaking missionary societies of mainland Protestant Europe. The semi-official report on the conference, written by the missionary William Temple Gairdner, prided itself on the presence of indigenous representatives from Africa and the East, but there were only 17 of them.[1] All the rest of the delegates were British or American. There could not be a clearer statement of Anglo-American dominance. This was itself politically realistic, however, at least in the sense that it was far and away the British and American missionary societies that were most numerous in Africa and Asia. The catchphrase of the conference – 'the evangelization of the world in this generation' – masked the fact that conversion was to proceed by the medium of English, and according to Anglo-American ideas of Christianity.

Taking their cue from this Anglo-American ascendancy, some historians have read more than a touch of arrogance into the conference proceedings: 'It exuded confidence and aggression to the point of triumphalism.'[2] There is evidence to support this view. The presiding genius of the conference was the great American missionary John R. Mott. In his closing address to the conference, Mott did not hesitate to say, 'The end of the conference is the beginning of the conquest.' God was summoning the missionary movement to a 'larger comprehension' of the peoples of the world, and '[o]ur best days are ahead of us'. Evidence of Mott's belief in the evangelical future was even stronger in the volume *The Decisive Hour of Christian Mission* that he prepared in advance of the conference. Of Africa, for example, he could write, 'the larger part of a vast continent [is] in the beginnings of transformation from ignorance, barbarism, and superstition, into the light of modern civilisation'.[3]

But it would be wrong to suppose that this was the only strain to be heard at the conference, or indeed that it was evidence of a one-dimensional appreciation of the benefits of Western civilization and imperialism on the part of Mott himself. Mott was capable of a much more nuanced assessment of the prospects of Western Christianity. If anything, at Edinburgh in 1910 he strove to stir up the enthusiasm of the delegates with an evangelist's pardonable hyperbole. Quite different emphases emerged from the eight reports commissioned before the conference on various aspects of the missionary movement, and they contained remarkably prescient observations on world affairs. Temple Gairdner claimed the Japanese victories over Russia in the war of 1905 signalled that the tide of 'western advance and domination' was about to be rolled back.[4] In fact the emergent leadership of a rapidly industrializing Japan, along with reform in China, preoccupied the conference as a whole. The report on *Carrying the Gospel to all the Non-Christian World* spoke of the 'Asiatic peoples' awakening from their 'long sleep' under Japanese influence.[5] The rapid spread of Christianity in Korea was noted, where conversions were so extensive that missionaries feared that proper Christian education could not keep pace. Above all, counter-movements to Christian mission were noted in the resurgence of other faiths, particularly Islam. Already, near the beginning of the twentieth century, warnings were sounding about the growth of Islam, and of religious conflict between Muslims and Christians, that were almost identical to those heard at the end of the century. Islam was advancing in Malaysia, parts of India and Russia, and above all in North and Central Africa. One speaker even urged the necessity of tripling the numbers of Christian missionaries in Africa, in order 'to throw a strong missionary force right across the centre of Africa to bar the advance of the Moslem'.

Moreover, if an external threat to Western Christian mission was present, with a resulting sense of insecurity, there was also deep unease about the health of Christianity 'at home', in Europe and North America. The sixth commission's report, on the *Home Base of Missions*, was written in full awareness of the advance of secularism in Europe and America. Though it did not offer a systematic reflection on the problems of Christianity in the West, speaker after speaker followed the lead of the report and acknowledged the depth of the problem. As one put it, 'men are not coming forward as ministers, nor coming forward as missionaries, because they are not coming forward into the membership of the Christian Church at all'. There was much underlying unease about this. The conference urged renewed efforts to galvanize home contributions to mission. Missionary advance throughout the world would depend on the home churches themselves becoming missionary churches in their own societies. But it was impossible to be sanguine about the prospects of that.

The Christianity of the Protestant West, then, if the Edinburgh Conference is anything to go by, was ambivalent about its future prospects on the eve of war. Empire and technological progress gave Christians an unnerving sense of expectation. Even where the grip of European political influence seemed to be waning – as in China and Japan in particular – this was only because Western values, institutions and practices were being copied so effectively. Yet there was little complacency about the condition of Protestantism in the West. Years of controversy over science, biblical and historical criticism, and the rise of new leisure styles had convinced the churches that organized religion was on the defensive even in their own cities.

Much the same was true of Roman Catholicism, too. Like Western Protestantism, Catholics everywhere could be forgiven for assuming the intrinsic durability of their Church. Catholicism was far and away the dominant religious tradition in Latin America, in Southern Europe and in parts of Eastern Europe. It had achieved spectacular growth in North America in the late nineteenth century, partly because of migration from Catholic Europe, and had also grown substantially in Africa, Asia and Australasia, in places surpassing Protestantism. Looking out from the Vatican, the centre of the Catholic world, it could be said of Catholicism as of no other single Christian church that it was a truly worldwide communion. There was scarcely a corner of the globe in which Catholic congregations were not to be found.

Moreover Catholics could look back on their recent history with some satisfaction. The nineteenth century had been a period of extreme instability and change for the papacy. It had opened with the pope practically a prisoner in Rome, as the Napoleonic armies trampled through Italy. Restoration of the papal states in 1815 had proved controversial and unstable, as the papacy was drawn into conflict with the *Risorgimento* and cast as an opponent of constitutional reform and Italian nationalism. The humiliating exile of Pius IX from Rome in 1848–50 had been followed by the eventual loss of the papal states in 1870. Yet territorial loss had been accompanied, paradoxically, by the moral and religious regeneration of Catholicism across Europe. The trauma of the suppression of Catholicism under the revolutionary regime in France had been followed by widespread Catholic revival in the middle decades of the century. Vigorous assertion of papal control over episcopal appointments had centralized the hierarchy and enhanced the pope's ecclesiastical authority. The First Vatican Council in 1870 had defined the doctrine of papal infallibility, symbolically compensating the papacy for its loss of territory with a corresponding affirmation of its spiritual authority. The person of the pope had become much more significant in Catholic culture. There had even been efforts to raise a voluntary tax throughout the Catholic world – 'Peter's pence', as it was nicknamed – to help cover the hole in Vatican revenues left by loss of its territories.

Even so, not all was well. Catholics were not isolated from the secularizing social pressures facing Protestantism. Even in the proud 'heartlands' of Catholic Europe – such as southern Ireland, Belgium, Spain and Italy – church leaders were concerned about the 'leakage' of children of believers away from the Church. This was perhaps sometimes rather a question of perception than reality. When were the churches ever completely full? When was society ever fully 'Christian'? The mere fact of non-attendance, however marginal, could raise anxieties about imminent decline even when the churches remained powerful, all-pervasive institutions in the modern city. It is too much to claim, as has one historian, that the Roman Church 'was ill placed to resist alliances of politicians and secularists'. 'It did not seem able to exploit new techniques and devices such as the mass-circulation newspapers', because exploiting these techniques and devices was precisely what it had done so successfully in the nineteenth century.[6] It had clung on and weathered the hostile environment of the modern city. Even so, it had given way, and semi-unchurched urban populations were a significant feature of Catholic countries.

As if to underline the embattled context of Roman Catholicism, Catholics in parts of Europe were also still, in 1914, undergoing the effects of a century-long conflict between church and state. Under the pressure of war, revolution and nationalism, European states had been forced to adopt increasingly centralized, bureaucratic methods. The philosophy of constitutionalism – even if adopted as not much more than a pose in some countries – clashed directly with aspects of Catholic culture, particularly in relation to education. In France the conflict between Republicanism and the Church had left a legacy of popular anti-clericalism, which finally resulted in the dissolution of the Napoleonic Concordat in 1905. In Spain the anti-clerical legacy was, if anything, even more bitter, and it was to lead to the slaughter of thousands of Catholic clergy during the Civil War in the 1930s. The Catholic Church had declared a religious war on constitutionalism, as well as on liberalism, socialism and almost all aspects of 'progressive' thought. The *Syllabus Errarum* of 1864, under which propositions favourable to a host of 'modern' beliefs were condemned, proved a defining document in this respect. Its final sentence, a *carte blanche* denial that 'the Roman Pontiff can, and ought to, reconcile himself to, and agree with, progress, liberalism, and modern civilization', said it all. As Owen Chadwick has written, 'No sentence ever did more to dig a chasm between the pope and modern European society.'[7] This clash of Catholic Church and modern society was re-confirmed by the condemnation of Catholic Modernism, a movement of intellectual reform and renewal in the Church. One of its major protagonists, Alfred Loisy, was still active in 1914 as an excommunicant, teaching and writing at the Collège de France. It is easy to exaggerate the significance of Modernism. It scarcely reached the awareness of the masses of the Catholic faithful. Few clergy were drawn to it, so far as we can tell. It was a phenomenon of European Catholic intellectuals at best and says little about the actual beliefs of Catholic clergy and people alike across the world.

Nevertheless the impression of conflict and resistance cannot be gainsaid. Catholic ubiquity went hand in hand with a certain fragility, an awareness that the Church remained peculiarly vulnerable to political change and criticism. The same was true of that other great block of Christian opinion, the 'Greek' or Eastern Orthodox churches. Here too, despite the continued depth of popular support for Christianity, the Church was often compromised by its relationship with established governments. This was particularly true in Russia, where, since the time of Peter the Great, a strong tradition of government interference in the affairs of the Church had developed. The replacement of the role of the patriarch of Moscow by the Holy Synod, under Peter's reforms, had been underlined by the power of the Procurator-General, a lay representative appointed by the government who had come to exercise extensive administrative authority within the Russian Church. Church and state in imperial Russia had become closely intertwined. Nowhere was this clearer than in the liturgical calendar, where public holidays, apart from the major feasts, included celebration of tsar's days, such as the anniversaries of coronations and birthdays. Yet this exceptionally close association of church and state had unhappy implications. Popular dissatisfaction with government spilled over into suspicion of the clergy. A culture of passivity infected many of the clergy. Moreover divisions of poverty and mutual suspicion flowed through the hierarchy of Russian Orthodoxy, with the resentment of parish clergy at the wealth, prestige and negligence of their ecclesiastical superiors encapsulated lastingly by the publication of I.S. Belliustin's *Description of the Clergy in Rural Russia* (1858): 'bishops not only do not wish to see these priests as [Christ's] Servitors – they do not want even to see them as people, and regard them as filthy dogs!!'[8] Belliustin's immensely controversial work, though prompting some efforts at reform, showed nevertheless the existence of social as well as ecclesiastical conflict in Orthodoxy that persisted right up until the revolution itself.

Not only in Europe, but across the world, Christianity seemed at once triumphant and uncertain. Divided by centuries of argument and internal conflict, the Christian churches had faced escalating criticism from the educated elites of the West, just at the same time as immense effort had been expended in extending Christianity throughout the world. Expansion generated expectation. The dawn of the century would bring, so many thought, spectacular gains for Christianity in the lands of other faiths and in the newly mapped lands of Africa. It might also encourage renewal in Christianity's European heartlands. But that hope did not suppress more sober reflection. Beneath the swagger and bluster of Christian confidence a different, more self-critical tone could also be heard. For all its success, Christianity was also on the defensive. Was it contracting in Europe just as it was expanding elsewhere?

Numbers and members

Assessing the numerical size of the Christian Church in 1914 is a difficult task for the historian. No reliable worldwide religious statistics were available. Population estimates often remained just that – especially outside Europe and North America. Moreover assessing the 'Christian' nature of a population was not easy. What figures it is possible to collate from different sources are often incompatible and can only be regarded as approximate. But it is important to make the effort in order to reach some assessment of the relative strengths of the various Christian communities, however tentative.

Possibly the most convenient starting point for a statistical analysis of Christianity is the division of the worldwide Church into three main groups – Protestant, Roman Catholic and Eastern Orthodox. I will present various sets of figures throughout this book. Mostly they are derived from the *World Christian Encyclopedia* (2001), which has collated membership and attendance series for the very beginning and end of the twentieth century. The global population in 1900 was 1,619,626,000.[9] Of these, some 34.6 per cent, or 558,132,000, were Christians. Independents and Marginal Christians represented no more than around 0.6 per cent of the world's population. There were 266,548,000 Roman Catholics, 133,594,000 Protestants and 115,844,000 Orthodox. Accepting the accuracy of these figures at face value, the predominance of Catholicism in world Christianity at the very beginning of the century is evident.

But there were enormous regional variations. In 1900, in Africa, of a total Christian population of 8,369,000, some 1,910,000 were Roman Catholic, some 4,600,000 were Orthodox and some 2,206,000 were Protestant. The strength of Orthodoxy was due to the Coptic and Ethiopian churches. Yet in Africa the existence of this large block of Orthodox was virtually ignored by Catholic and Protestant missionaries alike, who regarded it as a primitive religion. Latin America, on the other hand, presented a picture of almost complete Catholic domination. Of a total Christian population of 60,026,000, some 58,689,000 were Catholic. North America presented another contrast. The Christian population in 1900 was 59,570,000, with some 13,011,000 Roman Catholic, 415,000 Orthodox and 39,472,000 Protestant – a clear Protestant preponderance by a large margin. But Catholicism in America was growing with extraordinary rapidity.

What are we to make of these kinds of figures? In the end it is difficult to do anything other than draw the most general of conclusions, on a continent by continent basis. In all parts of the world except Russia and Asia, Roman Catholicism was strongly represented. It was certainly dominant in Latin America. It was already significant in North America, at possibly around 20 per cent or so of the total population, and growing fast. It achieved almost 20 per cent of the total population in Australasia and the Pacific Rim, and around 5 per cent in Africa. Here too it was growing. In Asia it registered probably around 1.5 per cent of the total population in 1910, and that figure was not to change substantially for years. Orthodoxy was confined largely to Eastern and South-Eastern Europe, to Russia and to North-East Africa. There was also a small but growing Orthodox population in North America. Protestantism was strong in North America above all, and in Europe, but it was also represented by significant colonial churches in Australasia, in Africa and in Asia, as well as by mission congregations in virtually all the lands of European empire (except French North Africa). It was in Europe that the complexity of Christian diversity was particularly in evidence. Here, if we include European Russia, somewhere around 50 per cent of the population overall was Catholic, around a third were Orthodox and the remainder Protestant. Since European expansionism was so much in evidence still in the early twentieth century, this relatively diverse, contested religious pattern was obviously not without implications for the nature of Christian mission. Triangular religious rivalries of Catholics, Protestants and Orthodox were in evidence in a few parts of the world, such as China, but elsewhere competition was usually between Catholics and Protestants, and of course among the Protestant churches themselves.

These basic facts about the relative strength of the main divisions of Christianity were often conveniently forgotten by the adherents of particular churches. It was not surprising that Roman Catholicism, by far the largest single 'block' in world Christianity, with congregations in every continent, and an organization ever more centrally coordinated from Rome, should so often see itself as the real powerhouse of world Christianity. Its ecclesiological understanding underlined this, seeing communion with the See of Rome (involving submission to the authority of the pope, and full acceptance of Catholic teaching) as the main criterion by which one could identify the true extent of the Christian Church – a position that was not to undergo modification officially until the Second Vatican Council in the 1960s. But a similar short-sightedness could be found in Protestantism, too, even though Protestants had mostly abandoned the anti-Catholic stridency of earlier ages. The representatives of the Anglo-American Protestant missionary societies at Edinburgh in 1910 did not see themselves as partners in mission with Catholics and Orthodox. They were not overly concerned to make converts from Catholicism: it did not make much sense practically to try to do so. But nor were they willing, generally, to cede designated areas of territory to the Catholic Church. Was there a residual element of anti-Catholicism in this? Almost certainly there was, but this was perhaps by this time as much a product of ignorance and separate development as it was of positive hostility.

Two further observations about religious statistics on the eve of the First World War are pertinent. The first is that the impression they tend to give of compact 'blocks' of religious affiliation is remarkably deceptive. Press below the continental level to the national level, and lower still to the local level, and situations of great complexity come to light. The diversity of European Christianity was immense. Even in solidly Catholic countries such as Spain and Italy there were small minority Protestant churches, which had been harried and persecuted for years. Correspondingly, in the Protestant north, Catholic minorities clung on. In the European colonies and the British dominions religious pluralism was often a fact of life and it had forced a reassessment and revision of the close alliance of church and state originally exported from Europe. If South America was almost entirely Catholic, it was not exclusively so. Round the turn of the century there were probably almost a million Protestants scattered throughout the continent. North America was already exhibiting a situation of remarkable Christian diversity. And all this is to say nothing of the relations between Christians and those of other faiths.

The second observation, which further undermines the apparent solidity of the statistics, is that comparisons between denominations – even assuming the figures themselves are basically accurate – are difficult to sustain, simply because what was actually being counted varied enormously from denomination to denomination, and from tradition to tradition. Dominant Protestant and Catholic churches in Europe, and Orthodox in Eastern Europe and Russia, were 'territorial' churches, in which (especially in the countryside) virtually all the local community might in some sense be counted as 'members'. But this did not necessarily imply that all went to church, or that all indeed had any explicit or recognizable form of Christian belief (though most surely did). In America, however, and also in many Protestant dissenting denominations in Britain and the British colonies, churches often had very clear and explicit conditions of full church membership, and accurately recorded rolls of members. To compare Methodist membership in Britain, for example, with the Catholic faithful in Italy is not to compare like with like.

The figures for church affiliation in the early twentieth century are thus far from the accurate, comparative data statisticians would have us believe, and all of the statistics quoted in this book have to be treated with some scepticism. National methods of collecting statistics varied enormously. Much of the data on which these statistics are based was approximate at best. But they do at least give some indication of the relative strength of Christian traditions within the worldwide Church on the eve of war.

Christian authority and culture

But what kind of world was it in 1914? It was above all a European world. By the beginning of the twentieth century, the wars of European colonial expansion were almost at an end. Much of the world was ruled by European governments, either directly as colonies or indirectly through the influence of migration and trade. The 'scramble for Africa', intensified in the 1880s by the eagerness of the new German Empire to acquire overseas territory, had led to the division of almost the whole of Africa into zones of European influence. Only Ethiopia, or Abyssinia, remained (in theory) independent. Much of Asia was in European hands – India ruled by the British, Indochina and Indonesia by the French and Dutch. China was undergoing gradual modernization, but was evidently weak and susceptible to the military and economic influence of the imperial powers. Alone of the Asian powers, Japan alone was truly independent and had modernized rapidly; it looked set to become a significant power in the region. In the Middle East the Turkish Empire was evidently in decay, with the Russians, British and French all eager to carve up its territories should the opportunity arise. Australasia was mostly settled by the British, though now Australia and New Zealand were dominion territories and therefore self-governing. South America alone of all the continents had achieved independence for most of its constituent nations much earlier, in the nineteenth century. Yet even here European and American influence was paramount, through trade.

Today in the West a certain proper embarrassment at the legacy of colonialism is evident in the eagerness to counterbalance imperialist triumphalism from this period with an acknowledgement of the sufferings and oppression of the subject peoples. Moreover the stark fact of European conflict in two world wars appears to underline the insecurity of imperialism. And yet, all this should not blind us to the dominance of European culture and values before 1914. Historians have been prone to describe the late nineteenth and early twentieth centuries as a time of economic globalization, anticipating the much more extensive globalization of the world economy in the late twentieth century. The invention of the telegraph and wireless, the steamship and railway, the cutting of the Suez and Panama canals, the establishment of networks of trade across the globe, had all helped to shrink travel and communication times and to facilitate the imposition of Western values on the colonies. Later some Britons were to look back nostalgically on this as a time when a quarter of the world's map was red, that is, British; but they forgot that much of it was Russian, French, American, Belgian, Dutch and German. Explanations of Western success, when they did not rest on the crudest racial assumptions about innate intelligence or national character, lighted on Western economic power as the single greatest factor determining this first global economy. Lenin accounted for European imperialism by the need for capitalists to export surplus capital. But it was a commonplace of the age that the flag followed trade.

So did the Bible. The expansion of the European empires had led, inexorably, to the export of European confessional identities. The Anglican Communion was a characteristic by-product of British colonialism. Even when the colonial authorities regarded it with suspicion – as was often the case – Christian missionary work flourished under the umbrella of European rule. This is not to propose a form of economic reductionism. Though trade and the market had a logic of their own, their flux was shaped by policy and politics, and in turn Christianity influenced the view Western rulers took of international relations. Thus it was possible to cast what is now seen as the brutality of imperialism as a crusade for Christian civilization against heathenism and barbarism. The word 'mission' itself had a strangely ambiguous application, for it was applied not only to Christian evangelism but to business and even to diplomatic and military initiatives. The myth of European or Western benevolence was a remarkably persuasive one. And, for the most part, the voiceless remained precisely that. When they did not, they were crushed. In China the 1900 Boxer Rebellion had led to the slaughter of Christian missionaries and converts, but its equally savage suppression, with the sack of Beijing, had left a legacy of suspicion and resentment. China was an exception, however, as was India. Elsewhere, in 1914 there was little sign of open hostility to the religion of the colonial powers.

If, give or take variations in language and military uniform, imperialism looked much the same, whether it was British or American or French or German, Western ascendancy nevertheless was fragile. It was, for one thing, contested internally, in religion as well as in politics. For the previous two centuries Europe and North America had witnessed the growth of secularism as a challenge to Christian faith. Even in the late nineteenth century, the flight of the intelligentsia away from active religious belief was probably nowhere near as great as contemporaries often assumed. Secularists, inheriting the mantle of religious scepticism from the *philosophes* of the Enlightenment, were a noisy, pushy minority. Organized secularism was small beer in most European countries and in America. A more inchoate form of secularism, religious indifference (or at least indifference to churchgoing) was much more common and indeed typical of many of the rapidly urbanizing cities of industrial Europe. Barriers of language concealed common anxieties across confessional divisions. When pastors in Lutheran Hanover complained about a falling away of communions, as the city's working-class quarters expanded towards the end of the nineteenth century, they were articulating an experience comparable to that of Anglican and Free Church clergy in Manchester or Liverpool. By 1914 there was a widespread belief on the part of clergy across Europe that the working class were abandoning the churches. The belief was premature and exaggerated. One of the effects of the early nineteenth-century revivals of religion was to convince clergy that the only adequate mode of social life was an ordered, respectable one marked by churchgoing. This simply did not reflect the complexity of popular religious belief. Nevertheless secularism existed. Churchgoing was declining in most of Western Europe, relative to population. Christianity was on the defensive.

There were other ideological challenges, too. Along with the growth of secularism went the rise of secular political ideologies. Elements of the early nineteenth-century traditions of republicanism and liberalism, themselves inheritors of the spirit of the French Revolution, remained powerful in bourgeois political circles well into the twentieth century. Their influence had been confirmed through the growth of representative government in many European countries and embedded in certain specific political traditions, such as that of French Republicanism, with its strong element of anti-clericalism. They had been eclipsed in notoriety, however, by socialism and by international Marxism. Not all socialists were anti-religious, but many were, and the followers of Marx were atheist almost without exception. Before 1914, with the brief exception of the failed Russian Revolution of 1905, Marxism appeared not to pose a serious threat to the stability of Europe's governments. But ruling elites were nervous and easily threatened. The political left posed as the champion of technological and scientific modernity. Marx, after all, had been a great admirer of Darwin. Whatever the real relation between science and religion, it was popularly supposed that science was usurping the explanatory power of religion in the West. This perception had been reinforced by the history of biblical criticism and doctrinal revision in the nineteenth century, with Christian theologians and church leaders arguing among themselves about the implications of the critical study of history and biblical texts for the traditional beliefs of the Christian Church. The cultural power of long-established churches was still immense in the West, but their intellectual credibility was threatened.

Much of this was still hidden from view in the mission stations of Africa and Asia. But indigenous peoples themselves could not but notice further weaknesses in the Christianity of their colonial masters. Christians were divided among themselves. A myriad of rival missionary societies operated in the field. Protestant competed with Protestant, and Protestant with Catholic. On the ground, missionaries started to cooperate, often fired up by a vision of Christian unity informed by progressive nineteenth-century theologians such as the Anglican F.D. Maurice. But early ecumenism was restricted to cooperation between Protestant churches. Cooperation with Roman Catholics would have to wait for another 60 years. The association of Christianity with colonial rule naturally also could not escape the notice of indigenous peoples. This was the reason for the Boxer hostility to Christianity in China. It also was a theme of the young movement for Indian independence. Bishop Azariah, the Indian Anglican Bishop of Dornakal, was subsequently to be called Gandhi's 'Enemy Number One', though the two did not meet until 1916. Already, however, the main point at issue between them was evident: Azariah pressed for conversion to Christianity from within Hinduism, but Gandhi wished to reform Hinduism and saw Azariah's Christianity as a form of capitulation to the West.

Nationalist movements such as those in India and China were as yet piecemeal and ineffective. But they pointed to a further difficulty for Western Christianity as a missionary religion: the existence of indigenous religious traditions. In some places, these were themselves Christian. The Indian Christians of St Thomas, for example, were ancient communities of Christians that had been established in the south and west of the sub-continent probably as early as the fifth or sixth centuries and had maintained an independent existence despite attempts to absorb them into Roman Catholicism in the sixteenth and seventeenth centuries. In North-East Africa several ancient independent churches also survived – most notably the Ethiopian

Church and the Coptic Orthodox Church in Egypt. But there were new indigenous forms of Christianity springing up, too. Full of significance for the future were the emergent black churches of North America, and particularly the Pentecostal churches, which today trace their origins largely to a congregation meeting in Azusa Street, Los Angeles, in 1906.

Nor was Christianity alone in the world. However much the mass of European and American Christians at this time might look down on the other great religions of the world, there was no gainsaying the fact that, in world terms, Christianity was a minority religion. As we have seen, Christians represented around a third of the world's population of 1.6 billion in 1900. Admittedly Christianity was the world's single largest religion. Islam and Hinduism had around 200 million adherents each, or some 12 per cent of the world's population. Next came Buddhism, with 127 million, or 7.8 per cent, and then the traditional, indigenous, animist religions of the developing world, with 117 million, or some 7.3 per cent of the world's population. This last figure must surely be a particularly uncertain one. The largest single non-Christian category of all was represented by Chinese 'folk-religion', which had some 380 million followers, or 23 per cent of the world's population.

We should be careful to avoid stereotyping interfaith relations on the eve of the First World War. It is almost certainly true that for the broad mass of Christian believers non-Christian religions were distinctly inferior, if not altogether untrue. But there were other voices beginning to be heard, urging a more positive appreciation of the insights of other faiths. Partly because of the rise of historical and anthropological studies in the universities of the West, and partly because of the realization on the part of many missionaries themselves that what they were encountering were actually sophisticated belief-systems, non-Christian religions were now beginning to be seen in a fresh light. Their sacred texts were being translated with more scholarly care than ever before. The rise of Japan as an economic power disabled the common Western assumption that only Christianity could promote the benefits of modern technology and social progress. All this left Christians feeling much less confident of their place in the world.

It is indeed difficult to look at the Christian world in 1914 without the benefit of hindsight. So much of the history of the twentieth century has overthrown the assumptions and expectations of the churches then, that it is tempting to magnify the fault-lines running through the Christian Church to the point at which contemporaries themselves would not recognize our account of their Christian experience. Christians were edgy, alert to difficulties and conflicts the world over. But those who came from the churches of the West had recently seen the extraordinary expansion of their horizon. They had no compelling reasons to doubt that their churches would continue to grow. Recently scholars have adopted the notion of Christianity's 'centre of gravity' to demonstrate the changing location of the bulk of Christians worldwide.[10] Assuming a point on the map at which numbers of Christians are identical east, west, north and south of the point, the 'centre of gravity' can be seen moving westwards and northwards from Jerusalem in the history of the Church, until, in 1900, it reached Madrid, thereafter only to shift southwards and eastwards, with the expansion of Christian churches in Africa and Asia. But this is a statistical and illustrative conceit. It relies on numbers alone as an index of significance. The real axis of power and influence in world Christianity before 1914 lay on the line from New York to London, where it forked towards Berlin and Rome.

PART I
1914 TO 1945: THE CRISIS OF IMPERIALISM

CHAPTER I

From Imperial Wars to Wars of Ideology

The outbreak of the First World War

The First World War was the greatest of the wars of European imperialism. Turkey's alliance with Germany and Austria-Hungary drew it into conflict with the 'Entente Cordiale' powers of Britain, France and Russia in the Middle East. There was fighting in Africa because Germany had four African colonies. There was little fighting in Asia, although Japan seized the opportunity to invade a clutch of small German colonies. Naval warfare carried fighting around the globe, and the entry of the United States into the war in 1917 widened the conflict even further. The nature of the 'Great War' as a war between imperialisms was confirmed by the presence of colonial troops on the Western Front. Nearly half a million French colonial soldiers fought alongside French troops. Few troops from British territories in Africa, with the exception of South Africa, fought in Europe, partly because they were engaged in prolonged fighting against German colonial forces. Britain's great source of overseas manpower was India, which supplied almost a third of the troops fighting in France by the end of 1914. Over a million Indian troops fought for Britain outside the sub-continent during the war. Even more troops came from Australia, New Zealand, South Africa and Canada.

It was also the greatest of the wars of imperialist Christianity. Churches lined up solidly behind their governments. In Russia, Orthodox clergy blessed icons carried by regiments departing for the front, said prayers for the protection of Holy Mother Russia and spurred on their congregations in support for the war. An American reporter on the Eastern Front in 1914 was mesmerized by the impressive figure of an Orthodox priest blessing an assembled regiment of Russian soldiers:

> With golden hair hanging down to his shoulders, and a head transfigured with the light of one lifted above earthly matters, he stood in all his gorgeous

robes before six stacked rifles, the bayonets of which served to support the Holy Bible and the golden cross that symbolizes the Christian faith. With eyes turned in rapture to the cold leaden heavens above him, the priest seemed a figure utterly detached from the earth.

In their systematic persecution of Christianity, the Bolsheviks later were to make much of the Russian Orthodox Church's unquestioning support for the Tsarist regime and its entry into the war. The shifty, obsequious, bearded Orthodox priest was to be a staple caricature of Soviet anti-religious propaganda, from the crudest broadsheet to the films of Sergei Eisenstein. But much the same point could be made against the clergy in Germany, in Austria-Hungary, in France and in Britain. If church leaders had any doubts about the wisdom of the conflict, mostly they were silent. The fervently militaristic Bishop of London, Winnington-Ingram, preached in military uniform to departing troops and notoriously called on them to kill the Germans, good and bad. All the French bishops, declares one historian, were united in their conviction that the war was holy. The Bishop of Arras told troops in December 1917, 'You are modern crusaders. ... You fight with God'.[1]

One of the most disturbing aspects of the war to later generations was that it was fought mostly by religious people. Both sides used the language of crusade, the French and British in defence of innocent Belgium against the barbaric 'Hun' invaders, the Germans and Austrians in defence of Christian civilization against the barbaric hordes of Russia and the mixed race barbarism of the British Empire. These sentiments were not restricted to Europe. They were shared throughout the church elites of overseas colonial possessions, though these elites were mostly white and European themselves. In Australia, for example, the leadership of the Anglican Church (which called itself the 'Church of England in Australia' until 1962) wholly accepted the common British view of imperial destiny. As one Tasmanian bishop put it in 1923, 'If there is a feature in the British character upon the possession of which we pride ourselves, it is our instinctive love of freedom and truthfulness.' A manifesto in support of Kaiser Wilhelm II and the German war aims was signed by 93 German intellectuals, including many leading Protestant theologians, on the day war broke out. The appalled Karl Barth, noting the names of many of his theology teachers among the signatories, was later famously to comment that 'they seemed to have been hopelessly compromised by what I regarded as their failure in the face of the ideology of war'.[2]

It was only as the war ground to a halt on the Western Front late in 1914, and the casualties mounted relentlessly through 1915 and 1916, that public perceptions of the war began to change. Horror at the impact of the technology of modern war – the use of mustard gas from early 1915, for example, aerial bombardment, long-range artillery, the tank – gradually replaced a naive pride in technological progress. The staggering scale of losses sustained in trench warfare, when the machine gun ruled the battlefield, inevitably strained arguments about sacrifice, duty and honour. This was to engender cynicism about the motives of Christian leaders of all persuasions in due course, even though the common soldier often voiced his horror and fear in explicitly religious terms. One British soldier, facing the prospect of action on the Western Front in 1917, prayed and 'gathered strength and a little calmness from the thought that in greater Hands than man's lay the decision of life and death'. That was a common enough sentiment. But it did not include respect for the Church as an institution. Mounting criticism of church leaders was offset by admiration for the work of military chaplains and priests at the front, but only partially so. In the armies of secular France, for example, priests were obliged to serve as regular soldiers (if mostly in the non-combatant role of nurse, stretcher-bearer or chaplain), an arrangement that in principle was at odds with their canonical standing, but which enormously enhanced their standing with their fellow soldiers.

Yet for all that the war was defended and justified by church leaders on both sides, one of the most salient facts about it was that it was not a war *about* religion. On the Entente side, an officially secular France with a predominantly Catholic population was allied to Orthodox Russia and to religiously pluralist (if mainly Protestant) Britain. On the other side the predominantly Catholic Austro-Hungarian Empire, which included substantial Orthodox and other minorities, was allied to the religiously mixed German Empire and to the Islamic Ottoman Empire. The war arose from international rivalries and mutual suspicions that had little or nothing to do with religion and everything to do with national security. Its origins lay above all in Austrian fears about Russian intervention in the deeply unstable countries of the Balkans, and in the growing German conviction that its only sure defence against encirclement in Europe was to initiate a 'two front' conflict and knock out France before the cumbersome Russian armies could mobilize fully against the German Empire. In these circumstances, nothing church leaders could say or do would have had much effect on events. Even the Vatican was divided over the war, with a strong pro-German and Austrian faction counterbalanced by Italian nationalist suspicions of Austria.

Even so the religious effects of the war were considerable. The catastrophe of defeat and social disintegration in Russia led to the collapse of the Tsarist regime in early 1917 and then the Bolshevik Revolution in October of that year. This was to pitch the Russian Orthodox Church into a situation of prolonged and savage persecution. It also prompted an Orthodox diaspora throughout the non-communist world. In Central Europe, if the collapse of the Habsburg and Hohenzollern empires did not fundamentally challenge the existence of the churches, still it marked in Germany itself the ending of vestiges of state Lutheranism (but not the church tax), and more importantly it created an acute resentment of defeat that was to simmer into radical, right-wing nationalism. So entrenched was the resentment of defeat, and the accompanying conviction (which had some merit) that the Versailles settlement of 1919 was unjust to Germany, that the churches were to find it extraordinarily difficult to recognize Nazism for the cult of hatred and murder it was until it was too late to do much about it. Even Dietrich Bonhoeffer, later to die at the Nazis' hands and thereby to earn a reputation as a modern martyr, shared the almost universal German dismay at defeat and the injustice of the settlement. As Friedrich Siegmund-Schultze, a theologian exiled from Germany during the Nazi years, was to say of the Great War: '[It] educated our German people to peace, [but] this peace educated it to war.'[3] In Italy, if military honour was partially salvaged after the disastrous Battle of Caporetto in 1917 by territorial gains as the war ended, the losses of the Caporetto campaign helped to create the mood of disillusionment on which Mussolini's *fascisti* would draw. In Britain and France the terrible losses on the Western Front may have engendered among soldiers themselves a deepening scepticism about the competence and motives of their superior officers. But back home, after the war, they were folded into a national cult of heroic sacrifice that drew much on Christian culture and iconography. Many thinking Christians were appalled, retrospectively, by the way the war seemed to have spiralled out of control, and lent their support to movements of pacifism and internationalism – laudable in themselves, but hardly the material out of which serious resistance to fascism might have been moulded. In Britain the Peace Pledge Union, launched by the former army chaplain Dick Sheppard in 1934 – the year after Hitler came to power – achieved over 100,000 members by 1937 and undertook 'to renounce war and never again support another'. Were the lessons of history ever misread so disastrously?

We should not neglect the wider political and economic consequences of the war. Four empires of the old Europe fell – the German, the Austro-Hungarian, the Russian and the Ottoman. In their place new national states came into being. But many of these were inherently unstable, containing minority groups rapidly disillusioned with government by the dominant ethnic and linguistic communities of their lands. The British and French empires appeared, on the contrary, not simply victorious but augmented by acquisitions in Africa and the Middle East. But this was illusory. The real story of the First World War was the beginning of the emergence of two superpowers, the United States and the Soviet Union. The economic indices pointed relentlessly that way. The war exhausted the financial reserves of Europe, but it was a major benefactor to America. In 1914 the American economy was already the largest in the world. The four economies which had led the world in economic growth in the early years of the twentieth century – Belgium, Britain, France and Germany – suffered ruinous losses. War thus handed America a huge business opportunity. Its surplus in international trade soared from $56 million to $352 million during the war years, and it became a net exporter of capital for the first time in 1919. This change in the balance of economic power was fraught with implications for the future. So too was the emergence of the Soviet Union, with its huge reserves of manpower and raw materials. But the significance of these developments was concealed by the withdrawal of the United States from European affairs after the war, and by the exclusion of Germany and the Soviet Union from the new League of Nations. Nevertheless the end was in sight for European imperialism. That much was evident too in the colonies themselves, where independence movements began to gain momentum in the years after the war. The Christianity of old Europe, rooted by missionary endeavour in the soils of overseas empire, faced a bleak future there.

The postwar settlement

The 'Versailles' settlement of 1919 was a series of treaties and agreements that varied greatly in scope and in durability. Its prospects were undermined almost from the very beginning by the one-sided burden of reparations imposed on Germany, by the (self-willed) exclusion of the Soviet Union from negotiations and by the failure of Woodrow Wilson to convince the United States to join the new League of Nations as guarantor of international peace and stability. At the centre of the settlement in Europe was the principle of national autonomy. It is difficult to see the years 1918 to 1939 as anything other than a troubled interlude in one long period of worldwide conflict. But in the early years after the Great War it looked as if a new era of internationalism was in prospect. Soviet aggression, after the ending of the civil war in Russia, was halted by Marshal Pilsudski's Polish armies in Eastern Europe in 1920. The 'Miracle on the Vistula' for the time being protected the newly created nation states there from Bolshevik interference. In Ireland civil war led to partition and the creation of the Irish Free State in 1922. Everywhere in Europe it looked as if the principle of national autonomy and democracy, combined with the new internationalism of the League, could create the conditions for stability and prosperity.

If European politicians were often slow to make the connection between national autonomy in Europe and the possession of overseas empire, their subject peoples were not. One of the war's more sobering lessons was that the European peoples had no intrinsic moral superiority. The emergent nationalist leaders of Asia and Africa were appalled at the use to which European states put their overseas troops on the Western Front. For all the evident fervour of colonial elites in 1914, by 1918 it was difficult for them to portray the war as anything other than a costly, futile conflict of no immediate concern to the peoples they ruled. The effect was clearest in India. Mahatma Gandhi returned there in 1915, after 20 years of fighting British imperialism in South Africa, where he developed his principle of passive resistance, *satyagraha*. Initially written off even by Indian politicians as an eccentric phoney, Gandhi's genius was to turn specific acts of peaceful resistance into a widening circle of protest. British attempts to suppress rising nationalism in India faltered after the massacre of nearly 400 protesters at Amritsar in April 1919, an event disastrous for British standing in India. China was another instance. There, nationalist resentment at the European powers had already sparked the Boxer Rebellion of 1900. Japan's aggression against China during the First World War only heightened tension, and whereas European influence in China waned after 1918, Japanese influence grew in strength. Japan's invasion of Manchuria in 1931 echoed an earlier age of European imperialism and was a striking sign of the changing balance of power in Asia. French territories in Indochina were also increasingly under threat from nationalist sentiment. The formation of the Vietnamese National Party in 1927 owed much to the influence and example of Chinese nationalism. The influence of communism was particularly strong on Asian nationalists, especially with the example of the Bolshevik Revolution before them. Ironically all these colonial nationalist movements thrived on European influence and education: their leaders were usually educated in Europe and their model of political and social revolution owed much to European revolutionary history.

It is not difficult to imagine what all this implied for the churches. Colonial nationalists were often wary of Christianity for the very obvious reason that they had experienced it in a European form. The immense missionary activity of the European churches did not collapse overnight but the churches found themselves having to work in ever more volatile and unsympathetic contexts. This was more evident in Asia in the 1920s and 1930s than it was in Africa, where the grip of colonialism was more vigorous. But it was enough to shake the presumption of European religious supremacy even there. An early sign was the short-lived revolt led by John Chilembwe in Nyasaland in 1915. Chilembwe was a Baptist minister, who objected to the savage treatment meted out by plantation owners on their employees;

his rebellion was crushed after it had killed several of the owners. This seemed an isolated incident. Ironically it was above all in Africa, later in the twentieth century, that a generation of African nationalist leaders was to emerge whose members were influenced by what they saw as the true spirit of Christianity to cast off the European cloak with which it had been clothed. But in the period between the two world wars, in Africa the work of the missions and the consolidation of church life went on much as before, under the scrutiny of the European colonizers. This is not to say that Africans simply accepted European colonization willingly; the growth of African independent churches from early in the century was an expression of a desire to find an authentic Christianity separate from the Christianity of the colonizers. It was an independence movement, but a religious one, without specific national aspirations.

In Western Europe and in America, the First World War did not mark as much of a catastrophe in church life as is sometimes thought. In a way that may strike us as odd today, given the horror of the war through which they had just passed. Church people across Europe simply returned to the old ways, attending church, running schools and Sunday schools and campaigning on any number of moral issues that long predated the war, such as teetotalism and opposition to prostitution. It was as if the horror could only be managed by being pushed back into the familiar rhythms of local life. In villages and towns across Europe memorials to the dead appeared, lovingly tended by local people and blessed by priests or pastors. The iconography of these memorials was resonant with the theme of sacrifice, and time and again they concentrated on the suffering of the common soldier. They might speak of the glorious dead, but there was little triumphalism in that. They expressed an implicit *theologia crucis*, identifying the suffering of the soldier with the suffering of Christ, and not a *theologia gloriae*. This was a theme fit for mass democracy, but the rituals of remembrance that sprang up in the interwar years were sober, disciplined and mostly accepting of social realities. For all the continued anxiety over church decline, in fact the social geography of European religion had changed little. In North America, by contrast, the long period of church growth continued unabated.

But it was in America, paradoxically, that the apparent stability of the interwar years began to unravel. The United States was not uniformly prosperous in these years. Its agriculture in particular languished and farm incomes fell as European consumers were able once more to rely on their own produce. American industrial production soared, however, and surplus capital poured into the stock market. Yet the world economy had become too dependent on American capital, and the Wall Street Crash of 1929 triggered collapse in the world's money markets. The democracies of America,

Britain and France and their overseas dominions were robust enough to withstand the ensuing social unrest, but the same was not true of Germany and of many of the newly established states of Eastern Europe.

The rise of ideology

Social discontent in the interwar years played into the hands of two distinct forms of revolutionary, totalitarian ideology. Marxist-Leninism had a long revolutionary pedigree, dating back to the utopian socialist movements of the early nineteenth century. What little religious sympathy some of these early movements – such as Saint-Simonianism – had preserved had been purged by the rigorous philosophical atheism of Marx and Engels. How far Bolshevism truly represented Marx's intellectual programme is questionable, but in Lenin it had found an astute but doctrinaire champion. Seeing itself as a harbinger of proletarian revolution the world over, Marxist-Leninism sought to recruit followers across the Western world. The churches offered nothing but an obstacle to its worldview. In Soviet Russia, soon after the October Revolution, a brief period of religious tolerance rapidly gave way to persecution. It was an ominous enough sign that the new Soviet constitution of 1918 permitted both freedom of religion *and* freedom of anti-religious propaganda. 'Freedom of religion' sounded fine in theory, but in practice it was non-existent. The printing of Bibles was banned, the Orthodox Church was stripped of its legal rights and its ability to own property, and thousands of churches were closed to worshippers. Orthodox clergy and monks were murdered in their thousands, and their bishops imprisoned or executed. Perhaps as many as 12,000 Orthodox clergy had been killed within ten years of the revolution. Anti-religious propaganda, on the other hand, was promoted relentlessly by the Soviet state.

Fascism, in contrast to the philosophical system and international ambition of Marxist-Leninism, was reactive and localized, fusing radical nationalism with varying degrees of racism. In Italy Mussolini's coup of 1922 brought to power an authoritarian and militaristic movement that was sentimental in its view of Italian and Roman history but hardly racist in any systematic sense. It was, however, hostile to the Catholic Church, which it saw (with good reason) as a potential opponent of its military ambition. In Spain the name 'fascist' was doubtfully applied to the militarist nationalism of General Franco, who certainly indulged the sympathies of Hitler and Mussolini but who was also supported by traditional wealthy elites and the Catholic Church. His victory in the Spanish Civil War of 1936–39 was widely seen as a sinister prelude to a Europe-wide war, but Spain's refusal to join Germany and Italy after 1939 has left the Spanish 'fascist' experience looking like a curious, rather atypical one. Antonio Salazar's military dictatorship in Portugal in the 1930s had a similar basis of support, but in Germany things were very different. There, Nazism emerged from the lower middle classes and found its mouthpiece and strategic genius in Adolf Hitler, the son of a Catholic Austrian bureaucrat. Hitler's ideological commitments were a suffocating blend of pseudo-science (especially drawing on the racist theories of the exiled Englishman Houston Chamberlain), German romantic nationalism and Nietzschean theories of 'overcoming'. In all this, the single most prominent theme touching on religion was of course Hitler's hostility to Judaism, but Christianity did not exactly emerge unscathed from his scorn either. Hitler posed as a defender of Christianity when it suited him, but shared much of Nietzsche's contempt for its 'slave morality' and spoke darkly of crushing the influence of the churches in his *Reich*.

This brief survey of fascism may give a misleading impression of its strength, because it has concentrated on those countries where, notoriously, it gained power. It was not an internationalist movement. Its roots in nationalism necessarily limited its cross-border connections. Fascism was, if anything, an ideology of fragmentation and control. But it stirred up radical nationalist movements across Europe and was to achieve further brief successes in Eastern Europe under the impact of war.

Thus, under worldwide economic recession, Christian churches found themselves alternately challenged and courted by ideological movements hostile to the Gospel. The churches drew on long-established practices of welfare and social commitment to try to combat the worst effects of poverty and unemployment. In Catholic Europe and America, a host of organizations under the umbrella of Catholic Action sought to galvanize the faithful into ever more effort to support the faith and relieve the needy. Protestant churches promoted charity and dabbled with collective theories of social welfare. In America the legacy of Walter Rauschenbusch's 'Social Gospel' had not quite run its course. The young Dietrich Bonhoeffer, studying in New York in 1930–31, as the effects of depression were deepening, attached himself to the Abyssinian Baptist Church in Harlem, working in its Sunday school and its various social agencies. He studied intensively the problems of racial discrimination in America and almost certainly learnt much there that was to alert him to the implications of Hitler's policies. In Britain this was the period of Archbishop William Temple's Social Anglicanism, a moderate version of Christian Socialism that commanded a surprisingly wide basis of support in the late 1930s and was to influence the 1942 Beveridge Report under which Britain's postwar welfare state was organized.

But the real impact of Christian welfarism before 1939 was limited. The churches could do little more than alleviate some of the worst effects of mass unemployment. Their work was overshadowed by rising extremism. The impatience of the revolutionary cliques who blamed capitalism for their predicament was matched by the resentment of the dispossessed or threatened, who blamed the Jews, the foreigners, the Great War and even the churches themselves for all their ills. Could the churches have done more to resist totalitarianism? They were not without influence. Mussolini and Hitler noted that, and were cautious and duplicitous in their dealings with them. Nazi attempts to subvert Catholic and Protestant youth organizations by scheduling Hitler Youth rallies on Sundays at the same time as church services often backfired, for example, and in other respects Nazi campaigns against elements of Catholic culture – such as the presence of crucifixes in schools – merely provoked stubborn resistance. Church life under the dictators often showed an amazing resilience. In Germany, latterly, this has been called 'self-defence' (*Selbstbehauptung*). The 'Church struggle' in Germany in the 1930s has necessarily attracted a certain romanticized historiography. Bonhoeffer's courageous stand against Nazism, leading eventually to his imprisonment and death, underscores the heroic account. So the churches were short neither of popular support nor of prophetic voices. Why were they so ineffectual in the era of totalitarianism?

It is hard to avoid the conclusion that, in Europe at least, one part of the answer to that question lies in the tangled history of church and state. By various ways and means, churches had found ways of protecting their interests within governmental systems which adopted policies they opposed. For Catholics this was through the medium of concordats, specific agreements between the Catholic Church and national authorities. A concordat with Hitler was concluded hard on the heels of Hitler's accession to power, for example. Protestant and free churches had no means by which they could negotiate an equivalent settlement, but they often achieved a similar security through legal toleration and the protection of property rights. Often they had significant representation among the political elites of Europe. But this was also a moral question, or rather a question of moral discernment. In Western Europe many church leaders were transfixed by the fear of Bolshevism, not fascism. Some supported strong, authoritarian government as a counter to communism. Others simply failed to see the true nature of Nazism in particular. Thus the mounting aggression of the fascist powers – Mussolini's invasion of Abyssinia in 1935, the Japanese presence in China from 1931 onwards, and the successive aggressions of Hitler – were variously excused away or left to the ineffectual devices of the League of Nations.

The Second World War and its effects

When war came the Christian churches were not well prepared for it. The more astute had recognized the dangers back in the mid-1930s. But the desire for peace, memories of the horror of the Great War, the international contacts between Protestant churches rebuilt carefully after the Great War by the fledgling ecumenical movement, and above all the experienced fact of Soviet persecution of religion, all persuaded Christians that the German regime would perhaps not turn out as badly as everyone feared. That sentiment, along with the very widespread anti-Semitism in Europe at this time, is the only explanation for the churches' failure to denounce as clearly as they might have done Nazi racial policies. The racial laws passed by the Hitler government in 1935 (the 'Nuremberg Laws') were clear enough in intent, but German Christians could console themselves with the thought that the Nazi Party had brought to an end the 'degenerate' bohemian culture of the Weimar era, and enacted numerous other laws that seemed to affirm Christian values – censorship of sexual content in the media, prohibition of adultery and blasphemy, animal rights, defence of motherhood and the family, to name but a few. Pius XI's searing criticism of Nazism in his 1937 encyclical *Mit Brennender Sorge* ('With Burning Heart') was neutered in Germany by poor reporting of it in the state-controlled media, even though by then frequent Nazi actions in defiance of the 1933 Concordat had stirred up domestic Catholic resentment too. There was plenty to distract church people across Europe. Stalin's policy forced agricultural collectivization and the war on the landholding peasantry, and the purges and 'show trials' of 1935–38 suggested convincingly that communism was the real threat to the Christian Church. In the Far East the growing power of Japan was also a worry; it stirred up Chinese nationalism and helped to revive the troubled Chinese Communist Party. All of this was a poor omen for Christian mission in large parts of the Far East.

It can be no great surprise, then, that even the viciousness with which the Nazi occupation forces treated the Polish Catholic Church after its invasion of western Poland in 1939 failed to awaken universal condemnation in Western Europe. In the early years of the war there were still strong pro-German sympathies in the Vatican, and much suspicion of the British in particular – even after the shock of the Nazi–Soviet pact. In 1940 many French and British church leaders, just like their politicians, were still inclined to peace. Had the war ended in 1940, after the German conquest of France, much of the truly sinister nature of the Nazi regime would have remained hidden. It was the pressure of war that brought it to the surface. The systematic discrimination against Jews, with outbursts of murderous violence connived at by Nazi officials, turned into the systematic slaughter of them. After the German invasion of the Soviet Union in June 1941, a taskforce ('Einsatzgruppen') of executioners followed in the wake of the regular army. By late 1942 the chaotic slaughter and rounding-up of Jews into urban ghettos had given way to the systematic murder of them in the death camps. By then the few acts of Christian defiance that one could record – the admittedly small numbers of German resisters, various members of the Confessing Church, some Catholic clergy and laity – had convinced Hitler that his hitherto half-hearted efforts to purge or crush the Christian churches should also be pursued more systematically once the war had ended. As he was heard to say, 'The evil that is gnawing at our vitals is our priests of both denominations. ... The time will come when I shall settle my accounts with them and I shall go straight to the point.' In Soviet Russia, by contrast, the war persuaded Stalin that he needed to seek a rapprochement with the Orthodox Church. As historians have convincingly argued, Stalin was above all a pragmatist: Marxist-Leninist doctrine was jettisoned when necessary in the interests of protecting his absolute authority.

Churches across Europe suffered under Nazi occupation. But they were never strong enough to mount more than occasional acts of resistance. And often their record in retrospect was ambiguous. Of no one is this truer than the pope himself. A tedious yet vicious controversy has raged over Pius XII's apparent failure to act decisively enough in condemnation of the Holocaust. He certainly encouraged numerous acts of private compassion and protection for Jews, particularly in Italy after the collapse of Mussolini's government in 1944 and Rome's occupation by the Germans. He often made his views known privately. But Vatican policy was disastrously compromised by the tenacity of its conviction that Nazism was a lesser threat to the Catholic Church than communism, and that the Allies' policy of seeking unconditional surrender was unnecessarily exacting. Furthermore Pius was perhaps realistic in assuming that condemnation would only intensify persecution. If his unwillingness to speak out suggests a certain misplaced naivety or lack of steel, at the same time it is not at all clear that his doing so would have made much difference materially.

When the war drew to an end in 1945, the moral certainty with which it had been conducted by opponents of the Axis powers was massively underlined by discovery of the full extent of the Holocaust. But there was little time for rueful reflection on what might have been had politicians and church leaders been more forceful in their criticism of Nazism before the war. Political crisis continued almost unabated in East Europe and in Asia. It was to be almost a generation before there was any serious, extensive discussion on the implications of Nazi savagery. It was then to be a case of 'delayed shock', as if the trauma of the Holocaust – at least as it was experienced collectively in Europe, since the trauma for the survivors themselves of course was immediate and life-long – was all the greater for being postponed. By the late 1960s and 1970s it had come to represent the greatest crime of the century and the greatest challenge to Christian explanations of guilt and evil.

CHAPTER 2

The Catholic Church: Triumphant and Resistant 1914–45

The popes and war

From the outbreak of war in 1914 to the end of the Second World War in 1945 war and totalitarianism overshadowed all four papacies of the period. Pius X died just after hostilities began in 1914, heartbroken, some said, by the failure of his peace efforts. Some wrongly blamed him for encouraging Austria to think its will in the Balkans would prevail after the assassination of the Archduke Franz Ferdinand. Vatican loyalties were indeed to be tested, especially by Italy's entry into the war in 1915 on the side of the Entente powers against the pro-Austrian sympathies of many in the papal court. Pius's legacy was mixed. Elected in 1903, Giuseppe Sarto's reign typified the dilemma of the modern papacy, caught between principled resistance to the culture and values of the modern world and the pastoral need for flexibility and adaptability. He had proved himself a reformer in liturgy and papal government. He had promoted church music and catechesis. He had reformed the papal diplomatic service, establishing the Secretariat of State as the principal administrative authority for external affairs. But all this was forgotten in the aftermath of his condemnation of Modernism, a movement which sought to reconcile Catholic teaching to modern critical thought. His two encyclicals of 1907, *Lamentabili* and *Pascendi*, began an anti-Modernist witch-hunt. Teachers, bishops, theologians and seminarians were bound by an anti-Modernist oath. Some lost their positions or were forbidden to teach or write. Excessive zeal in the prosecution of this campaign caused enormous damage to the intellectual credibility of the Catholic Church.

It was the anti-Modernist campaign, rather than papal policy in war, that polarized opinion among the cardinals in the conclave of 1914. Yet Giacomo della Chiesa, Cardinal Archbishop of Bologna, was elected as Benedict XV almost certainly because his mixture of administrative, pastoral and diplomatic experience best seemed to fit the Church's wartime needs. A diminutive Italian aristocrat for whom all the available papal robes on his election were too large, Benedict was self-assured. His first encyclical, *Ad Beatissima* (1914), repeated the condemnation of Modernism, yet urged moderation in the treatment of Modernist writers. Benedict's papacy was marked above all by his diplomatic efforts for peace. This was the main theme of *Ad Beatissima*. Papal policy since the end of the nineteenth century had been predicated on a strong relationship with the Catholic dual monarchy of Austria-Hungary as a counterbalance to the mainly Protestant German Reich. Yet, in spring 1915, after secret negotiations in London, Italy entered the war against Austria-Hungary. The official Vatican policy of neutrality was endangered. Not only the Pope himself, but also the curial staff were nearly all Italian. The surge of Italian patriotism against Austria, the old enemy of the *Risorgimento*, could not but affect Italian Catholics. In turn, their support for the Italian war effort helped to blur memories of the Church's hostility to the secular Italian state. How in these circumstances could Benedict act as a disinterested advocate of peace?

It is immensely to his credit that, despite everything, a peacemaker is how he came to be seen. His reputation rests on his peace note of August 1917, a six-clause proposal for an armistice, restoration of all pre-war boundaries and negotiation of outstanding territorial claims. But the proposals were so neutral that they attracted no one's support. The French did not even bother to respond. The Americans, recent entrants into the war on the Entente side, claimed there was no basis on which to trust Germany's present rulers. Ironically President Wilson's 'Fourteen Points' of January 1918 were close in substance to Benedict's peace note. So the Pope was not far from the heart of the matter. But he had no power to deliver peace and represented no interest worth appeasing, since Catholics were to be found in large numbers on both sides. His practical influence in the end was confined to humanitarian work, which financially strained the Vatican, including schemes to repatriate prisoners of war. In his encyclical *De Pacis*, issued in 1920, Benedict returned to the theme of peace, appealing for worldwide disarmament and lamenting the injustices of the peacetime settlement. No one could accuse the papacy of standing idly by.

Unfortunately, the dilemma Benedict had faced in war – how to be neutral and yet also promote the interests of Catholics – had to be faced in peace too. In Italy itself the formation of the Partito Popolare Italiano, a broad-based, loosely 'Catholic' political party, raised tensions between church and state. Its leader was a cleric. Elsewhere in Europe the formation of Catholic centre parties posed the same problem for the Vatican, particularly when they were led by priests, as in Austria and Germany. Catholics were also among the opponents of the centre parties. The difficulty of a non-partisan approach to politics was all too obvious. Like his predecessor, Benedict was no opponent of reform. Under him, Cardinal Gasparri and Eugenio Pacelli, later Pope Pius XII, oversaw reform of the Canon Law. This was the natural legal, institutional development of the centralized hierarchy symbolized theologically by the declaration of infallibility in 1870. Benedict died in January 1922.

The election of Achille Ratti as pope surprised everyone. A librarian for most of his ministry, he had little experience of Vatican diplomacy and of church administration. He took the name Pius XI to conciliate disgruntled former supporters of Pius X, for Ratti was very much the protégé of his predecessor and of Cardinal Gasparri, and he continued many of Benedict's policies. His experiences as nuncio in Poland in 1919 scarred him for life, leaving him with a deep hostility to communism. In trying to understand the ambiguities of Pius's attitude to fascism in Italy, and the slowness with which Catholics generally in Europe reacted to the rise of Nazism, it is vital not to be blinded by hindsight. Scarcely anyone in Europe in the 1920s and 1930s could foresee the horrors of the Holocaust. Radical, anti-Semitic nationalism, the well from which fascism across Europe drew, was hardly benign, but it did not, for all that, look genocidal. Christians across Europe were much more likely to be convinced of the dangers of Bolshevism. Stalin may have abandoned Lenin's policy of world revolution in 1924, when he adopted the slogan of 'socialism in one country', but neither the Soviet Union nor its opponents ever forgot that communist parties across the world looked to Moscow for leadership. The Bolsheviks had proclaimed a crusade against religion and had persecuted and massacred Christians. All this had happened well before most people had even heard of fascism.

Constant awareness of this threat explains much of the otherwise ambiguous policy of Pius XI. On the one hand, he did not retreat into the mindset of the anti-Modernist campaign. He continued Benedict's rehabilitation of some of those scholars and teachers most hurt by Pius X's policy. A true scholar and historian, he had real breadth of intellectual interest. He re-founded the Pontifical Academy of the Sciences in 1936 to encourage research in the sciences. He had a strong commitment to Catholic engagement with the problems of contemporary society, exemplified in his encouragement of Catholic Action, the movement for social Catholicism through much of Catholic Europe and the Americas. On the other hand, his was a pontificate characterized by the concentration of authority in his own hands. He was a born autocrat. He delegated with difficulty and could brook no slackness in his officials. As one papal historian has it, 'Even visiting diplomats noted that the key word in the Vatican had become obedience.'[1] And he had strong leanings to the right. His opponents could point to his apparent softness towards Italian fascism, his readiness to conclude concordats with Mussolini and with Hitler, and his hostility to anything that touched on communism, sealed in his 1937 encyclical *Divini Redemptoris*, the tone of which was certainly even more hostile than was his encyclical against Nazism of the same year, *Mit Brennender Sorge*.

Yet this last criticism is too harsh. The policy on concordats was hardly of Pius's making. Concordats were an ancient way of regulating the relationship between the Church and civil powers, usually in order to protect the corporate and sacramental life of the Church in times of conflict. The first concordat of the modern age was that with the Napoleonic regime in 1801. Concordats were defensive: their goal might be to prevent a situation already unpromising for the Church from deteriorating into something far worse. The two controversial concordats of Pius's reign have to be seen in this light. The first resolved the anomalous position of the Vatican in Italy whereby it did not recognize the Italian state. Like his predecessor, Pius was determined to regularize the situation. A treaty could not be concluded until early 1929, issuing in a concordat that effectively acknowledged a tiny sovereign state for the pope, the Vatican City, in the heart of Rome, maintained certain Catholic rights, allocated to the pope the means to maintain a diplomatic mission and to communicate with the outside world, and gave him a one-off payment of almost 2 billion lire as compensation for the loss of the papal states over half a century earlier. The settlement came at a price: Mussolini demanded in return the suppression of the Catholic Popular Party. Unwittingly Pius had aided the consolidation of the one-party state. Moreover the Lateran treaty did not end tensions between church and state in fascist Italy. Mussolini's efforts to dismantle Catholic organizations brought renewed conflict with the Church throughout the 1930s.

A similar experience blighted the concordat concluded with Hitler in 1933. Negotiated by Eugenio Pacelli, the future Pius XII, as Secretary of State, this offered Hitler the dubious fiction of legitimacy in the eyes of Germany's Catholic population. It appeared to guarantee the autonomy of the Catholic Church within the law, freedom of worship and the protection of Catholic teaching and Catholic schools. But just as in Italy, there were losses as well as gains. Under a poorly defined clause in the concordat, Hitler banned the Catholic Centre Party and again sought to eliminate Catholic schools, youth organizations and other groups, even though Catholic Action was supposed to have been protected explicitly.

How valid is the common criticism that Pius was naive or even complicit in his dealings with Mussolini and Hitler (and, further, with Franco in Spain)? The answer must surely be 'valid only up to a certain point'. It is true that Pius was no democrat, and that he wept few tears over the disappearance of Catholic political parties. It is also true that he was perhaps misled by the readiness of these authoritarian regimes to resist communism, for, as we have seen, from the Catholic standpoint in the 1930s communism represented a proven, systematic and vicious threat of a kind that far surpassed anything even the Nazis were capable of until the outbreak of war. But the Church had no armies at its disposal, after all, and the question Catholic leaders had to face in the early 1930s was what they could do to protect the life of the Church. This was a legitimate goal. It is, admittedly, a more serious point that Catholic (and Protestant) defence of the Jews was muted, and that their criticism of the anti-Jewish and inhumane policies of Hitler was too little and too late. But Pius himself cannot really be included in that final comment, for his experience of the cynicism with which both regimes treated the Church produced outspoken criticism in his last years.

This criticism was to have been taken even further, in a draft encyclical against Nazi racial policies. Unfortunately this was never published, for Pius died in February 1939 before it could be completed, and his successor quietly shelved it. Eugenio Pacelli, Pius XI's Secretary of State, was elected at a short conclave and took the name of Pius XII as a sign of his willingness to continue his predecessor's policies. He was a smooth, experienced diplomat, perfectly suited, it seemed, to the role he had to take on himself. No sooner was he elected than war was upon Europe again. Pius's failure to condemn the evils of Nazism as loudly as many wished has already been pointed out. There were some extenuating circumstances. His freedom of action was not as great as some supposed – he was, after all, cooped up in a tiny enclave within a militarized fascist state. But the Vatican was already receiving evidence of German atrocities by 1941. Pius attempted to uphold an even-handed policy similar to that of Benedict XV in the First World War, with knowledge of the anti-Christian and inhumane policies of the Germans balanced by suspicion of the motives of the Allies, and especially Britain, as they fought alongside the old enemy, Bolshevism. The papacy took a neutral line. Diplomatic lines of communication were kept open to Berlin as well as to London and Washington. Openings for peace were sought, along with guarantees about protection for the Church – all of these without success, of course. What could be done privately to aid refugees and Italian Jews was done, including opening the religious houses of Rome for sanctuary. Public criticism of the Nazis was muted, though not altogether absent. Not just Pius himself, but many other Vatican diplomats were caught up in this, as it proved, lamentably short-sighted view of the moral realities

of the conflict. Angello Roncalli, the future John XXIII, for all his amia-
bility, demonstrated a complete inability to understand the political motives
of the German government and had a correspondingly favourable view of
Mussolini. The Under Secretary of State, Domenico Tardini, was appalled
at Roncalli's gullibility over conversations with Franz von Papen, Hitler's
ambassador to Turkey, and exclaimed, 'This fellow has understood nothing.'
A papal policy that was right, perhaps, in the First World War was disastrously misplaced in the Second. By the time the Germans occupied Rome,
after the collapse of Mussolini's government in 1943, it was probably too late
to speak out plainly. The moment had passed.

The Catholic world

For all the travails of the papacy itself, this was a period in which the Catholic Church made major strides worldwide, not least in Africa, Asia and
the Americas. It faced significant difficulties, but proved itself capable of
overcoming them even in the most unpromising circumstances. Here was
confirmation that the twentieth century was to become an age in which
the centre of world Christianity would begin to shift away from Europe.
Catholicism was both sponsor and beneficiary of that change. Both Benedict
XV and Pius XI were committed to supporting and expanding the overseas missions of the Church. Benedict's apostolic letter of 1919, *Maximum
Illud*, had called for a native priesthood and episcopate in the mission field.
In 1925 Pius celebrated a missionary exhibition in Rome which attracted
nearly three-quarters of a million visitors. The following year his encyclical
on missions, *Rerum Ecclesiae*, repeated Benedict's appeal for a native clergy.
The proposal faced formidable obstacles, including the inflexibility of the
largely Latinate culture of the Catholic Church and hostility among some
(especially African) cultures to the practice of celibacy.

It was in Africa, nevertheless, that some of the most dramatic growth
in Catholic missions took place in these years. Estimates have to be treated
with some caution, but it seems likely that the total number of Catholics in
Africa increased in the 40 years from 1910 to 1950 threefold, reaching over 18
million.[2] The key instruments of this growth were the religious orders, and
especially those orders founded explicitly to evangelize Africa. The 'White
Fathers', or Missionaries of Our Lady of Africa, for example, were begun by
Cardinal Lavigerie in Algiers in 1868, with a commitment to follow the ways
and means of African society as closely as was compatible with their Christian calling. By the 1920s they were one of the principal means of Catholic
mission in Central and West Africa. Elsewhere the Holy Ghost Fathers, or
'Spiritans', founded in the early eighteenth century, were especially active
on the west coast, and in East Africa. But there were many other orders at

work. A canonical injunction against nuns working as midwives impeded women's medical work until it was lifted in 1936, but women nevertheless composed over a half of Catholic missionaries by 1910. After the First World War, numbers were swelled particularly by Irish clergy, monks and nuns, and later by Americans. In the French colonies, despite the anti-clericalism of officialdom and the separation of church and state, colonial administrators tended to favour Catholic missions, which were mostly French. In the British territories, the policy of 'indirect rule' favoured by British governments between the wars also implied a more pluralist approach to religious policy, and Catholic educational institutions often received subsidies alongside their Anglican rivals. Catholicism often flourished under British rule, even when British colonial administrators disapproved of it. In Buganda and West Uganda, for example, the great Catholic missionary bishop Henri Streicher saw his congregation swell from some 30,000 to over 300,000 between 1897 and his retirement in 1933. Thus, with the exception of North Africa, where Islam proved an altogether more intractable rival, in these years Catholicism spread consistently throughout the continent and began to supplant the Protestant societies.

In a few parts of Asia it was a similar story. Bald numbers suggest again a substantial increase in numbers of Catholics in the region as a whole, reaching some 28 million by 1950, though the increase as a proportion of population was marginal. But there were significant variations within this. China was the most startling example of failure to make many inroads. Though Christian missionaries of all denominations received some support from the Nationalists, for all of this period they laboured under the common Chinese hostility to foreigners. Often in extraordinarily adverse circumstances, Catholic missions tried to develop educational and catechetical systems. But this was a formidable task, given the difficulties of learning Chinese, even without taking into account serious political interference. One example will suffice. The American Passionists first sent a group of missionaries to China in 1921, in order to carry out the mandate of *Maximum Illud*. They were sent to Hunan in central China, a poor, mountainous area which was politically unstable for most of the 1920s. It took them four years to put together an independent organization, but even in the first five years of their operation their impact was minimal. Their report for 1930 sombrely noted the minimal effect of their work: 'Pagans – 4,500,000. Native Catholics – 2,504. Lay persons at work in the territory – 34 men, 28 women.' Money to support the mission was cabled from America, but even that began to dry up after the Great Crash in 1929. China never yielded the great mission harvest all had hoped for; the communist threat and then Japanese occupation and persecution put an end to serious hopes of mass conversions. For different reasons India was also an area of, at best, modest Catholic growth, though significant steps were taken eventually towards the formation of an indigenous clergy. There the independence movement inevitably tarnished all Christian missionary effort. Elsewhere in Asia there were centres of more substantial growth, including the Philippines, but throughout the whole region Japanese territorial ambitions were a threat to the Christian churches (especially where they had European or American leadership), and the brief but traumatic period of Japanese military ascendancy from 1941 to 1945 brought with it much local suffering.

In South and Central America the dominance of Catholicism continued almost unabated. This was a time of reconstruction in ecclesiastical organization, with determined efforts to found new dioceses and to recover ground lost in the nineteenth century when social and political conflict, following the great period of independence, had led to protracted tensions between the Church and governments in some countries. There were again, however, some local variations, especially where the Church faced revolutionary movements. In Mexico the revolution entered a much more militant, anticlerical phase in the 1920s. The 1917 constitution had subjected the Church to severe control. Church defiance produced further extreme measures, including the closure of monasteries and schools and the deportation of foreign clergy, as well as tacit support for the burning of churches by government agents. Wholesale rebellion by Catholic peasantry broke out in 1926 in what came to be called the *Cristiada*. It had petered out by 1929, but tensions remained acute throughout the 1930s. Partly because of crises like this, partly perhaps because of temporary gains made by some (albeit small) Protestant churches, the proportion of Catholic adherents to the population of Latin America overall slightly dipped in mid-century. Still, the continent remained almost solidly Catholic.

North American Catholicism, by contrast, was experiencing sustained growth. Freed from the jurisdiction of the Sacred Congregation of Propaganda (the Vatican office that administered missionary affairs) in 1908, America was no longer a mission field but a settled church. Catholicism in America was mostly an urban and immigrant phenomenon. It benefited enormously from the massive industrial and economic growth of America in the years up to and after the First World War. Just as this was to be the 'American century', American Catholicism increasingly was a net contributor to the financial and organizational operations of the Catholic Church worldwide. Even so, its national profile took time to be established. This was still a time of Protestant ascendancy. The era of Prohibition, when the sale of alcohol was banned throughout America, reflected the aspirations of the Protestant temperance movement. Some anti-Catholic sentiment may even have lain behind the curtailment of immigration in the mid-1920s. American Catholicism was distinctively multi-ethnic or multi-national, and yet it was also ethnically segmented (with Italian priests serving Italian migrant churches, for example) – something the hierarchy fought hard to restrain.

Similar processes were at work in Australasia, where permanent Catholic hierarchies had been installed by 1920. Here again growth in the Catholic community, though not spectacular, was significant and sustained, and it was to become, by mid-century, the largest single Christian tradition there. In Australia in particular the Catholic Church was essentially a community of Irish migrants; it was therefore sceptical of British political culture and proud of its ethnic descent. The Catholic Archbishop of Melbourne from 1917 to 1963, when he died at the age of 99, was an Irish nationalist, Daniel Mannix, who criticized Australian participation in the First World War, fought against conscription and was loathed by the Anglo-Australian establishment. The Irish character of Catholicism in Australia began to change only in the 1950s and 1960s, with further waves of migration from Catholic Europe.

Catholic culture: devotion, classes and thought

The 'cultured despisers' of Catholicism in nineteenth-century Europe surely would not have foreseen the spectacular international growth of the Church in the following century. What were the secrets of the Catholic Church's success? It is easy to enumerate various factors. The bureaucratic centralization of the Church undoubtedly eased the coordination of its activities worldwide, and was aided by modern transport and communications technology. Education of the Church's elite was also centralized: many of the most able candidates for the priesthood – future leaders of the Church – studied in Rome, where they developed a sense of loyalty and identity that stayed with them when they returned home or went abroad to the mission field. Careful protection and extension of the papacy's right to appoint and consecrate bishops in the course of the nineteenth century had paid off by the early twentieth century, so that Rome exercised a more effective control over Catholic clerical hierarchies the world over than at any time in the preceding centuries. The religious orders in particular were vital agents in Catholic mission. They were a kind of missionary vanguard for the Church: bound together by oaths of obedience, their complementary vows of poverty and chastity meant that they travelled light and willingly undertook the most challenging tasks in the most dangerous of contexts. They were not necessarily more zealous than their Protestant rivals, but they had immense corporate support behind them. Moreover the comprehensiveness and clarity of Catholic teaching on any number of particular issues was matched by an instrument of absolute authority in the Church – the papacy itself. Roman Catholicism was a 'command' system, it seemed.

Yet here there is a paradox. To concentrate on these hierarchical and organizational factors in Catholic growth is to miss much of the point. It is true that the culture of devotion in the Catholic world in this period remained strikingly consistent. It was what historians, broadly speaking, have rightly called 'ultramontane': it emphasized the authority of the pope throughout the Church, but also humanized it and universalized it in the cult of 'Il Papa'. It was deeply Marian and rigorously Latinate. Yet it was not a monolith. It was remarkably adaptable to local cultures and traditions. The Marian *cultus* was a case in point. One Lady there might be, but she adopted many different contexts – Our Lady of Lourdes, the Virgin of Guadeloupe, Our Lady of Fatima, among many others. Sociologists and cynics might sneer at the appropriation of Mary this way. But Mary blessed those to whom she appeared. The apparitions near Fatima in Portugal in 1917 rapidly attracted huge popular interest, which was not merely inquisitive. It is estimated that some 70,000 people were present in a rainstorm at the last apparition in October 1917, hundreds of whom claimed to have witnessed the plunging of the sun to the earth and its return to the sky after drying their clothes.

Fatima is full of ambiguity. There are all the usual questions surrounding apparitions and miracles. Why did others not see these things? How are they compatible with a modern scientific understanding of the universe? But there are political questions too. The cult that sprang up there was adopted by the nationalists as a useful sign of Portugal's divine favour, in the nationalist 'trinity' of 'Fado, football and Fatima'. Catholicism thus went hand in hand with right-wing nationalism in Portugal, as elsewhere. Later Fatima was drawn into the political rivalries of the Cold War, 'her message', as one historian has memorably put it, 'a fear-laden denunciation of Communism, laced with calls for Rosary Crusades'.[3] But was Mary merely a political instrument? Surely not. For all that the apparitions at Fatima lent themselves to exploitation, they also reflected deep, traditional religious loyalties among the poor. Catholicism was a populist religious culture. The cult of the saints, and of Mary, enabled believers to express local identities through what one anthropologist who studied Marian cults in northern Spain called 'territories of grace', and to sanction and bless elements of local life in a way that often transcended the confected identities of nation or political party.[4] If it tended in this period to sponsor right-wing politics and looked askance at left-wing anti-clericalism, even so eventually Catholicism proved flexible enough to embrace centre parties and democracy at the local level. It would be misleading, then, to suggest that it was purely, or only, a hierarchical religious system. It was a powerful combination of centralized authority and deeply localized religious sentiment, with 'top–down' authority in tension with the 'bottom–up' authority derived from local congregations and laity. It was by no means the case, then, that the Catholic faithful jumped when the pope said so.

One of the clearest illustrations of this was the changing status of women in Catholicism in this period. For most of the first half of the twentieth century, papal teaching on the role and status of women was consistent. It did not necessarily emphasize the inferiority of women, but it did stress the principles of distinctiveness and complementarity in gender roles, and women's subordinate status in marriage. Women's vocation was above all to the home and to motherhood, a position underlined by Leo XIII in his social encyclical *Rerum Novarum* in 1891. Pius X, Benedict XV and Pius XI broadly followed this line, but gradually began to accept the changing role of women in Western society. Pius X grudgingly approved the entry of women into higher education and the professions. Benedict approved the idea of women's suffrage and political involvement. There were even some (albeit small) Catholic women's suffrage societies in the early twentieth century, such as Action Sociale de la Femme, founded in France in 1900, which received official papal disapproval. It was the First World War almost certainly that proved decisive in arguments over suffrage, as the inclusion of women in wartime into a host of roles formerly dominated by men demonstrated the fallibility of assumptions about women's fragility and incompetence. The Ligue Patriotique des Françaises, a solidly conservative French Catholic women's movement before the war, openly supported women's suffrage after the war. It has even been suggested that in secular and anti-clerical France the extent of Catholic women's support for female suffrage was one very strong reason why its implementation was delayed until after the Second World War. Women, both in Catholicism as well as in Protestantism, evidently dominated the churchgoing public.

The position of women is just a snapshot of the mixed history of Catholicism in this period. Catholic theology might serve as another instance. Officially this was a time of close central supervision of Catholic teaching and research. The revival of Thomism – 'neo-scholasticism', or 'neo-Thomism' as it was also called, based on the work of the medieval theologian Thomas Aquinas – was a product of the late nineteenth century, promoted above all by Leo XIII in his encyclical on the 'revival of a Christian philosophy', *Aeterni Patris* (1879). Neo-scholasticism sought a *philosophia perennis* ('eternal philosophy'), a systematized synthesis of theology and philosophy, following a Thomistic system purged of what were now regarded as false

or valueless elements. Its arguments were set out in tight logical propositions and could be taught through official textbooks imposed throughout
the Catholic world in the wake of the condemnation of Modernism. It had
great merits and formidable defenders, such as the French Dominican Reginald Garrigou-Lagrange, whose teaching on Aquinas at the Dominican
college in Rome, the Angelicum, influenced a generation of church leaders,
including the future John Paul II. Garrigou-Lagrange was nicknamed 'The
Rigid' by some of his students, and this captured nicely the difficulties other
Catholic theologians were beginning to encounter with the neo-scholastic
synthesis. In these years Catholic philosophers such at Étienne Gilson and
Jacques Maritain were attempting to pioneer a more creative interpretation of Aquinas, taking into account existentialism and other movements
in contemporary philosophy and theology. They laboured under the shadow
of the anti-Modernist measures, which remained officially in place. But the
early development was under way of the *Nouvelle Theologie*, the movement
loosely associated with a cluster of stellar names in twentieth-century Catholic theology, including Marie-Dominique Chenu, Henri de Lubac, Yves
Congar and Hans Urs von Balthasar, which set itself the task of extricating
Catholic theology from the ahistorical, over-systematized and deductive
character of neo-scholasticism, placing it once more in the great tradition
of Western metaphysics and historical interpretation. Direct confrontation
with the official theology was yet to come, but it is a sign of the complexity
and richness of Catholic thought in this period that such contrasting moods
could emerge.

Catholic culture and thought exhibited the same double character as
Catholic high politics more generally in this period. A later generation was
to see this as an age of stagnation, dominated by a backward-looking papacy
afraid of change. This was never a satisfactory or fair analysis. It neglected
the salient fact that even in the highly centralized, not to say authoritarian,
papacy of Pius XI, Catholicism was undergoing an extraordinary transformation in the mission field. The popes certainly misunderstood the nature
of right-wing and fascist totalitarianism, as they did not underestimate the
threat of communism, and the Church's record of opposition was a mixed
and far from progressive one. But Catholicism was never reducible to papal
policy alone. It remained a dynamic, complex and above all immensely
popular portion of world Christianity and in this period easily maintained
its position as the single largest church of Christendom.

CHAPTER 3

The Orthodox Churches

The Orthodox dilemma

At the beginning of the twentieth century, there were well over 100 million followers of Orthodox Christianity scattered across Eastern Europe, the Russian Empire, the Middle East and, including Oriental Orthodoxy, down into the horn of Africa. A few small Orthodox communities – mainly Greek and Russian – were in existence already in North America and Australasia, and, through the Russian connection, in China. Orthodoxy was thus on the way to becoming a global phenomenon. By far the largest number of Orthodox were concentrated in the Russian Empire. But Orthodoxy was in fact composed of many different churches, perhaps united only in the negative sense that they were distinguished historically from Western Christianity.

Most of this account will be obliged to concentrate on the larger churches of 'Eastern Orthodoxy', and especially the Russian Orthodox Church, but it should always be remembered – and reference will be made to them from time to time – that there were also a number of ancient churches which can be clustered loosely under the umbrella of 'Oriental Orthodox', namely the Coptic, Syrian, Armenian, Ethiopian, Eritrean and Indian (Malankara) churches. These were relatively small, with the exception of the Ethiopian Church, but they were distinctive ethnic expressions of Christianity. They were descended from churches which had refused to accept the Council of Chalcedon of 451. These churches have often been called 'Monophysite', that is rejecting the Chalcedonian doctrine of two natures in one person, but this is not strictly accurate for some of them, since they regard monophysitism as implying the obliteration of Christ's human nature, whereas they affirm a divine–human nature in Christ. 'Non-Chalcedonian' is thus a better description of them. Here I shall generally use the equally common 'Oriental Orthodox'.

To return to Eastern Orthodoxy for the present, the four ancient patriarchates of Constantinople, Alexandria, Antioch and Jerusalem had long laboured under the difficulty of being formally part of the Ottoman Empire. Constantinople, as the 'ecumenical patriarchate', in a sense held a primacy of honour. But Jerusalem inevitably attracted most attention from ordinary believers, including those outside the jurisdiction of the ancient patriarchates. Over 10,000 Russian Orthodox pilgrims a year made their way to Jerusalem before the First World War for the Easter celebrations. Most of them were not affluent, but peasants. They made the journey largely on foot, taking ship from the Crimea. Jerusalem was a multi-denominational Christian site, but the Russians were by far the largest contingent of visitors until the First World War. In Eastern Europe and the Balkans, Orthodoxy was mainly organized under 'national churches' descended from the Byzantine conversion of the Slavs in the Middle Ages. The greatest and most powerful of these by far was the Russian Church.

The twentieth century was to prove one of exceptional turbulence for Orthodox believers. There were signs of that even before the First World War. In Russia, since the mid-nineteenth century, powerful internal tensions within Orthodoxy had arisen over proposals to reform the Church's administration. Partly this was prompted by the reforms of Tsar Alexander II's reign (1855–81), including the emancipation of the serfs, but it was intensified by the legislative changes in the brief period of liberalization that followed the failed revolution of 1905. Though the Russian Church was not technically subordinate to the state, in the reign of Peter the Great in the early eighteenth century its patriarchate had been abolished and the Holy Synod of the church subjected to the supervision of a state functionary, the Procurator-General. Orthodoxy had become much more than an 'official' religion. Its history and culture were inextricably entwined with those of the monarchy. In 1905–6 the creation of religious toleration and the protection of property of non-Orthodox churches in Russia pitched the Church into a situation of legal pluralism (numerically it was still paramount) for which it was ill prepared. Divisions opened up between those who wished to resist church reform and to defend the traditional relationship of church and state, and those who wished to uncouple it from the monarchy and free it from the oversight of the state. Influenced in part by the theological vision of various Orthodox thinkers such as Alexei Khomiakov (1804–60), with his concept of *Sobornost* – an understanding of the Church as a community in which laity as well as clergy were integral witnesses to the catholicity of the Church – reformers looked to the restoration of the patriarchate and the reform of the parish system and of the education and status of the clergy. Such was the disillusion of many people with the Tsarist regime, however, that even before 1914 Orthodox clergy were reporting growing abandonment of the Church by the rural as well as urban population. The era of repression that set in again in the years immediately before the war merely intensified this trend. The reputation of Orthodoxy particularly suffered from the disastrous influence of the peasant faith healer Grigori Rasputin over the royal family. Apart from a circle of infatuated St Petersburg ladies, almost everyone deplored it – the army, most of the nobility, the radicals and even the Holy Synod itself. The power of the 'Mad Monk' (he was never actually a monk) was probably much exaggerated, but the damage he did to the Church and the royal family was not. There was, however, substantial disaffection with the Church among the intelligentsia long before then.

Elsewhere in Eastern Europe, there were other signs of fragility. The recently restored Orthodox churches of Bulgaria, Romania and Serbia were also closely identified with nationalist sentiment, but as a result vulnerable to the political rivalries between the Russian Empire and the German and Austro-Hungarian empires. War could not but affect them. They were, moreover, faced with greater religious diversity than was the case mostly in Russia. Of all the religious rivalries in Eastern Europe, none was as acute as that of the Orthodox churches with the Roman Catholic Church, and there were substantial Catholic minorities in many Orthodox-dominated parts of Eastern Europe and the Balkans. A further complication was the existence of various 'Uniate' churches, churches that were Orthodox in liturgy but in communion with the See of Rome. The 'Eastern rite' or Greek Catholic Church of Romania, to give one example, had been aligned to the papacy since the late seventeenth century, but its relationship to its Orthodox neighbours had always been tense and marred by mutual suspicion. Strictly speaking the history of the 'Uniate' churches is part of the history of Roman Catholicism, but their very existence alongside Orthodox churches in Eastern Europe was to prove an important factor in the turbulent history of Orthodoxy itself in the region.

Greece by contrast was solidly Orthodox, and the Church, autocephalous since the mid-nineteenth century, had aligned itself wholeheartedly to the project of building a 'Greater Greece', a vision fired by past Byzantine glories. But this rested on international tension. As late as 1912 new territories had been acquired for Greece in Macedonia and Crete from the Ottoman Empire and added to the Greek Church. Ottoman weakness might well present further opportunities for expansion, though this did not attract the support of the ecumenical patriarch, who would not willingly exchange the direct jurisdiction he enjoyed under the Ottomans for the very indirect and insubstantial honour he was given under the Greek arrangements.

Thus whereas in Russia and Eastern Europe it was the threat of social revolution, in the Mediterranean and Middle Eastern worlds it was the prospect of the death-throes of the Ottoman regime that provided an

exceptionally volatile context for Orthodox belief. The sufferings of Orthodoxy in the twentieth century were, nevertheless, to have an unforeseen
consequence. In encouraging, albeit unintentionally, the emigration of
Orthodox believers overseas, the persecutors of Orthodox Christianity
were to promote the growth of worldwide Orthodoxy.

Russia: revolution and persecution

The history of Russian Orthodoxy, given the size and political prominence
of the Russian Empire, inevitably must dominate the narrative presented
here. The coming of revolution in 1917 hardly caught the Orthodox Church
unawares. Ever since 1905 the urgent need for the Church to adapt to wider
social and political reform had been on everyone's mind, though there was
no consensus on how to achieve this. Gradually, however, in the upper levels
of the hierarchy the feeling had grown that first and foremost the Church
needed to restore the patriarchate of Moscow and, by implication, loosen
(but not cut altogether) its links with the state. This was the first instinct of
the new All-Russia Church Council finally convened in August 1917 after
the fall of the monarchy but, crucially, before the Bolshevik Revolution.
The Council itself was an innovation, and a first practical step towards the
implementation of the principle of *Sobornost*, since it included a majority of
laymen. The Council never completed its work, however. Having elected a
patriarch, Tikhon, the presiding Bishop of Moscow, its work was overtaken
by the impact of the October Revolution.

Persecution of Orthodox church life, and certainly of Orthodox clergy,
followed almost immediately. Whatever the theoretical freedoms of the 1918
constitution, in practice severe and mounting restrictions began. This was
to be a recurrent pattern of Soviet treatment of religion, however much it
varied in intensity: the profession of freedom of opinion masked the actual
repression of religion. Ultimately Marxist-Leninism envisaged no future
for religion in the socialist state: without denying freedom of worship in
principle, the Soviet state positively denied that Christianity could ever be
regarded as an authentic expression of popular opinion. The entire appa-
ratus of state power was at the disposal of those who were convinced that
religion was a thing of the past. The separation of church and state, decreed
in January 1918, was thus the prelude to a serious *subjugation* of religion.
The new patriarch, Tikhon, condemned the Bolsheviks' seizure of church
property and suppression of schools and other agencies, and excommunicated the Bolsheviks; this naturally made matters worse. During the Civil
War the political vulnerability of Orthodoxy increased, since the 'Whites',
opponents of the 'Reds', often included prominent Orthodox supporters.
The eventual triumph of the Red armies sealed the Church's fate, and a

prolonged period of repression began, rising steadily throughout the 1920s and 1930s. Central to this was the virtual decapitation of effective Orthodox leadership. Between 1918 and 1926 nearly 100 bishops were executed and others thrown into prison. Tikhon himself was interned from May 1922 to June 1923.

How should Christians react in such a time of trial? Many churches were closed, and clergy executed, imprisoned or exiled. One response – probably the response of a majority of Orthodox clergy – was stubborn, silent resistance. The centralization of Soviet power and the brutality with which the new regime's rule was enforced emasculated any effective opposition within the new Soviet Union. A constant barrage of atheist propaganda was mounted against religion. The Church was, in effect, driven underground, where, to the frustration of the Soviet authorities, it survived in the reluctance of ordinary believers to let go of whatever semblance of church life, ritual and reassurance was available to them. The secularization of Soviet society certainly could not be achieved in a generation alone. Another response – short-lived, as it turned out – was accommodation to the new regime. A League of Democratic Clergy and Laymen had been formed early in 1917, adopting a strong reform agenda with its roots in the nationalist, democratic Slavophile movement of the nineteenth century. Many of the members of the League formed the nucleus of the 'Living Church' movement, a left-wing Orthodox movement briefly patronized (and exploited) by the Bolsheviks in an attempt to draw away popular support from the Orthodox hierarchy. Some 'Living Church' clergy, in a thoroughly unpleasant instance of intra-Christian hostility, were even used by the regime to denounce Orthodox leaders who had resisted the seizure of church property. For a time it looked as if the 'Living Church' might actually supplant official Orthodoxy, not least when it was recognized as the sole legitimate authority in Russia in 1924 by the ecumenical patriarch of Constantinople. But it proved impossible to persuade ordinary Orthodox believers to support the 'Living Church', and the regime quickly lost faith in it. When Tikhon seemingly underwent a change of heart in prison and adopted a more conciliatory approach, its rationale, from the regime's point of view, disappeared. By 1926 the 'Living Church' was irrelevant.

Tikhon died in April 1925. His attempts to create a viable leadership for the Orthodox Church after his death came to nothing, as his successors were intimidated, imprisoned or executed. In the late 1920s and 1930s, the years of Stalin's rise to power, a 'Catacombs Church' came into existence in Russia – Orthodox believers led by clergy who were invisible as clergy, taking up ordinary occupations to mask their religious activity and to support themselves. With the closure of almost all churches (some 500 only were still open by 1939, out of the 54,000 in existence in 1914), the Orthodox Church had, at least on the surface, apparently ceased to exist. The attitude of the Soviet writer Maxim Gorky, writing to Stalin, is typical of the official policy:

> It is furthermore imperative to put the propaganda of atheism on solid ground. You won't achieve much with the weapons of Marx and materialism, as we have seen. Materialism and religion are two different planes and they don't coincide. If a fool speaks from the heavens and the sage from a factory – they won't understand one another. The sage needs to hit the fool with his stick, with his weapon.

Had the level of hostility and repression achieved by 1939 continued for another generation or two, who knows how well the Orthodox Church would have survived. As it was, however, a dramatic change in its fortunes was on the horizon. It came improbably at the hands of Hitler, with the German invasion of the Soviet Empire in 1941. Perhaps influenced by the readiness of Orthodox clergy to proclaim a national crusade against the invaders, but more likely by a simple but pragmatic desire to shore up popular support, Stalin eventually (in 1943) approved a reversal in the policy of repression. Churches that had not been demolished or turned over to other uses were permitted to open again. In the Kiev diocese, one authority suggests, within a year the number of churches open for worship had risen from just two to over 700. The official Russian Orthodox Church, led by Sergius, *locum tenens* (that is, acting office-holder) of the patriarchate from 1925, and a controversial figure in Russian religious life because of his former membership of the 'Living Church' movement, now resumed a more open, public life. The patriarchate, vacant since Tikhon's death, was officially filled by Sergius in September 1943, and on his death in 1944 by Alexius Simansky. Restrictions remained in place, nevertheless – atheist propaganda continued, there were no church schools and the numbers of clergy and churches could not return to anything like their pre-1917 level. It was a concession to the tenacity of popular Orthodoxy and not a change in the nature of the Soviet state.

The diaspora

Even before the First World War, Orthodoxy had spread around the world. In North America, for example, there was a fully constituted Orthodox diocese, derived from migration to the United States from the mid-nineteenth century, with five bishops, 700 parishes, and some 400 clergy. The church was a somewhat unstable mixture of nationalities under the umbrella of the Russian Church and began to splinter into distinct ethnic groups almost as soon as the Bolshevik Revolution destroyed the ability of the Russian Church to communicate with its daughter churches across the world. In Australia, Orthodoxy was dependent mostly on Greek emigration to the cities of Sydney and Melbourne. There, the relative disorganization of Orthodoxy overseas, and in particular its inability to put in place any effective hierarchical organization, had allowed a novel development in the form of virtual congregationalism: *koinotites*, locally elected bodies of lay officials, had come into being to oversee the establishment and running of parish institutions. These were to prove resistant to attempts by the ecumenical patriarch later in the century to establish full hierarchical control of the Australian Greek Church. Everywhere, Orthodoxy was especially susceptible to ethnic divisions. By the 1930s there were, for example, no fewer than three different Ukrainian Orthodox churches in America alone – the Ukrainian Orthodox Church, the Ukrainian Orthodox Church in the United States and the Holy Ukrainian Autocephalic Orthodox Church in Exile. Such fissiparousness was arguably encouraged by Orthodox ecclesiology, according to which the unity of the Church was secured through a binding common faith and not through ecclesiastical structures.

But it was also encouraged by the way in which particular Orthodox churches could function as expressions of ethnic or national identities. In Soviet Russia, and elsewhere in Eastern and Southern Europe, this was to prove an extraordinarily powerful survival mechanism for Christianity in the face of persecution. But transposed to the emigrant communities of America, Western Europe and Australia, it was bound to cause significant internal tension. Orthodoxy might present a united, concentrated witness in Greece, in Russia and in Romania, for example, when differences between national Orthodox churches were irrelevant, but put Greek, Russian and Romanian emigrant communities together in one city and the differences become all too apparent. A further problem arose from long-standing patterns of church–state relations. The very ability of Orthodoxy – based perhaps ultimately on its Byzantine inheritance, in which the emperor's authority was almost sacralized – to function as national churches made it particularly useful to traditional governing elites. In a way all that Stalin did in Russia in 1943 was to revive something of the old pattern of church–state relations. But in the early years of the Bolshevik Revolution, the attempt to eradicate Orthodoxy in the Soviet Union effectively politicized Orthodox life and worship outside the communist sphere of influence. Bishops and clergy expelled after 1917 sought to reconstitute a Russian Orthodox Church in exile. The first meeting of the bishops in exile, driven out of South Russia after the collapse of the Whites there in 1921, took place on the boat to Constantinople. Later that year a *sobor*, or council, was held at Sremski Karlovci in Yugoslavia, where the administrative offices of the exiled church were to remain until 1944. This Provisional Sacred Synod of the Russian Orthodox Church Abroad (ROCA), as it was called, committed itself to the restoration of the monarchy. But this put Patriarch Tikhon, back in Russia, in an impossible position; he was obliged to cut his links with the Synod.

Over the following years, parallel jurisdictions came into being outside Russia, as ROCA refused to accept the authority of Tikhon's *de facto* successor, Sergius, and in turn found its authority refused by the metropolitans of Western Europe and America, and the Moscow patriarchate also in turn tried to extend its authority over the churches in exile. Into this fundamental split, the brief influence of the 'Living Church' was a further complication. In America, for example, in a legal struggle over ownership of church property, the cathedral of St Nicholas in New York even passed temporarily into the control of representatives of the 'Living Church'. By 1926 there were three Russian church jurisdictions in America: ROCA, the Orthodox Church of America (composed especially of those churches that owed their foundation to the first waves of Russian migration in the nineteenth century and were now under their own metropolitan, Platon), and the 'Paris jurisdiction', that is emigrant community churches under the jurisdiction of the church in exile in Paris, but ultimately under the ecumenical patriarch. And that was the Russians alone. Thus successive waves of exiles from the Soviet Union were faced with bewildering choices about church membership, in which national rivalries were overlain with deep, competing convictions about how to react to the catastrophic events of the Bolshevik Revolution and its aftermath.

Put all this in a global context, nevertheless, and we can see that the events in Russia and Eastern Europe had a quite unexpected consequence. Soviet attempts to eradicate Christianity in the area of communist influence merely dispersed and promoted Orthodoxy throughout the world. For centuries Orthodox clergy had worried about the influence of Western culture on Orthodoxy. In the twentieth century the Russian diaspora had a reverse effect, producing an Orthodox influence on Western thought. New institutes of theological education were founded to educate an émigré clergy. The St Sergius Orthodox Theological Institute was founded by émigré clergy in Paris in 1925 under the 'Paris jurisdiction' of Metropolitan Evlogim. Its goal was to continue the work of Orthodox institutes suppressed in the Soviet Union. It attracted some of the best minds of Russian Orthodoxy, including Sergei Bulgakov, George Florovsky, Nicholas Afanasieff and, later, Alexander Schmemann. Vladimir Lossky, later dean of the St Dionysius Institute, also in Paris, was another strong supporter. An institution of comparable significance to St Sergius was St Vladimir's Orthodox Theological Seminary, founded in New York in 1938. Florovsky was also to work there, as was Schmemann and John Meyendorff. The works of many of these theologians were published in Russian at first, but gradually translations into English, French and other languages appeared. By this means, a vital tradition within the Christian Church that had not been well understood before 1917 began to become known much more widely in the 1920s and 1930s, and then in the period after 1945. Themes and insights from Orthodox theology began to arouse interest in Catholic and Protestant circles. Through the work of the émigré Orthodox community, the Orthodox Church also began to play an active role in the ecumenical movement. Western theology – especially Catholic theology – found material for its own renewal in this new source of reflection. A work like Yves Congar's *Divided Christendom* (1937), one of the first (and most significant) sympathetic Catholic studies of the ecumenical movement, drew heavily on contemporary Orthodox theology and is probably inconceivable without the post-1917 diaspora.

The complex interweaving of politics, Russian history, philosophy and theology in the theologians of the diaspora is probably best seen in particular lives. Sergei Bulgakov, for example, was born in Livny in Russia in 1871 of a priest's family. He rebelled against the faith in his youth and turned to the study of economics and philosophy, becoming, by the 1890s, a convinced Marxist. His major work, *Capitalism and Agriculture*, was published in 1900, but he was already showing signs of divergence from orthodox Marxism. Gradually he was moving back to Christianity. One of the essayists in the notorious *Vekhi* volume, published in 1909 and articulating a programme of moderate reformism, and influenced in part by writers such as Dostoyevsky, he attacked the Russian intelligentsia for its superficial materialism and moral irresponsibility. His ordination followed hard on the heels of the October Revolution. Moving south to the Crimea to teach, he was eventually dismissed by the Bolsheviks and expelled from Russia. In 1925 he moved from Prague, where he had settled briefly, to Paris, and took up a position as professor of dogmatics and dean at the St Sergius Institute, where he remained until his death in 1944. Bulgakov's theological odyssey was not, however, a simple matter of returning to his roots. He never repudiated altogether the critique of autocracy and capitalism he had developed in his years as a Marxist. His position in some ways was akin to that of Western Christian Socialists, though he rejected the term and concept of 'socialism'. His revolt against the Orthodoxy of the late nineteenth century was morally right, he was to say, 'in so far as it was inspired by love of freedom and disgust at the servility which then reigned in the clerical world'.[1] His later theological position was a subtle, complex and almost mystical one, in which the principle of *Sophia* – the divine wisdom inhabiting and illuminating the world – was central. Moving away, as he did, from the rather narrow and fossilized Orthodox dogmatics typical of the theological world of the Russian clergy before the revolution, Bulgakov, along with many others, found a new freedom in exile to re-animate Orthodox theology, in dialogue with the West.

Greece, the Balkans and the Middle East

It was not only in Russia that catastrophe fell upon Orthodox believers at the end of the First World War. The collapse of the Ottoman Empire and the associated creation of the modern state of Turkey brought in its wake intense local conflict in various parts of the Middle East. Most of the Orthodox communities within the Empire suffered terribly as a result, both during and after the war. The Syrian Orthodox Church saw around a third of its members – some 90,000 people – massacred by the Turks in 1915. During the Kurdish rebellion against the Turkish state in 1925–26 they suffered again. The Armenian Orthodox suffered on an even greater scale, with some 1.5 million dying in the wave of persecution and murder encouraged by the Turkish government in 1915, again in 1918 when the Turks extended their campaign into Russian Armenia, and then again in 1920 when there was a concerted effort to wipe out Turkish Armenia altogether. In 1922 war between Turkey and Greece provoked the murder and deportation of another 1.5 million Greek Orthodox from Turkey. This sad tale of murder was only indirectly the product of inter-religious rivalry. It was above all the consequence of the twin policy of national consolidation and secularization carried out originally under the aegis of the 'Young Turk' movement, which ran the Ottoman Empire after the overthrow of Sultan Abdul Hamid II in 1909, and later under Kemal Atatürk. Its primary cause was therefore in essence a cultural conflict between a 'modernizing' nationalist movement and distinct local, ethnic cultures which resisted absorption into the newly emergent Turkish nation.

Though it suffered a humiliating defeat in 1922, Greece was itself by now a nation state with a virtually monolithic religious culture. One of Greece's most prominent modern writers, George Theotokas, was later to describe Orthodoxy in Greece as a 'national religion, indissolubly woven with the customs and character of these people, the climate and fragrance of the country'.[2] This romantic vision of an Orthodoxy in the Greek bloodstream had strong historical justification. Orthodoxy, in its liturgical language as well as its pastoral ministry, had carried the distinct cultural and national identities of Greek-speaking peoples in the Ottoman Empire for centuries before independence was achieved in the nineteenth century. It was to remain an 'official' or state religion in Greece in a way almost without comparison elsewhere in Europe into the twenty-first century. And yet the position of the hierarchy was never as secure as Theotokas's description might have implied. Under the surface of constitutional privilege and protection, a policy of separation of church and state had been followed by successive governments, with the suppression of hundreds of monasteries in the mid-nineteenth century, the removal of church influence from education and the subjection of the Church to a form of civil control comparable to that of pre-revolutionary Russia, with the Holy Synod of the autocephalous Greek Church overseen by a state-appointed procurator. Unlike the situation in Russia, however, the Greek Church had no automatic sympathy with the Coburg monarchy foisted on Greece by the Continental powers in the nineteenth century. Nor did it with the dictatorship established by Ioannis Metaxas in 1936. This gave it a certain distance from the complexity and bitterness of Greek politics and enabled Archbishop Damaskinos to act as a focus of national opposition to the Nazis during the German occupation of Greece. He was a stubborn but courageous leader. Even Churchill was later to call him 'a pestilent priest'. When the occupation came to an end, Damaskinos was appointed regent until the return of the king – a situation inconceivable in almost every other European state in the mid-twentieth century.

One element of the Greek Church's pan-Orthodox significance was its connection with the monasteries on Mount Athos in Macedonia. Seized from the Ottomans in 1912, a formal settlement of the jurisdiction of Mount Athos was delayed until after the First World War. It gave self-government to the peninsula, under the sovereignty of Greece. For much of the twentieth century, the monastic life on Athos was in decline. Some 7,500 monks at the beginning of the century had dwindled to just over one and a half thousand by 1959. But the loss was due above all to politics and not to a decline in the spiritual life alone. Well over a half of the monks in 1900 had come from outside Greece, from Orthodox countries later to fall under communist rule. By the 1950s the vast majority were Greek, though even their numbers had fallen. But Athos remained, as it still is, a unique concentration of monasteries representing different national branches of Orthodoxy – Serbian, Russian, Romanian, as well as Greek – preserving vital elements of Orthodox spirituality and learning.

The other major Orthodox Church in the Balkans, the Serbian Church, underwent a great revival in the interwar period, only to face the decimation of its clergy, churches and people during the Second World War. It was the major beneficiary of the creation of the Kingdom of Yugoslavia in 1918. It had carried the national aspirations of the Serbs for decades, but its ecclesiastical organization had been fragmented into different constitutional arrangements in no fewer than four different states before then. The new kingdom represented a significant victory for Serb hegemony over Croats, Bosnians and Slovenes, and the Serbian Orthodox Church moved into a position of *de facto* establishment, with financial aid to the Church under-girded by the constitutional settlement in 1920 which united the Church throughout the realm under a revived patriarchate. But the interests of state security and stability were not identical with those of the Orthodox Church, and a protracted struggle began between church and state over the precise nature of the state's powers. It took nine years for this to be resolved in the Church's favour, only for a further conflict to break out in the 1930s over the state's attempt to conclude a concordat with the Croatian Catholic Church. The state lost this battle too in 1937, when a draft concordat of 1935 was finally abandoned by the state under concerted pressure from the Orthodox hierarchy and opposition Serb parties. Unfortunately this only served to intensify Croat hostility to Serbian Orthodoxy. During the German occupation from 1941, with the creation of a Croatian fascist state, Serbian Orthodox nationalism was viciously suppressed, and in Croatia in particular the fascist militia, or *Ustaše*, carried out a campaign of system-atic slaughter and expulsion of Orthodox clergy and believers. Within a few months Croatia was cleared of all Orthodox clergy, with 217 murdered and the remaining 350-odd deported. By the end of the war thousands of Serbian Orthodox churches in the Balkans had been damaged or destroyed, and a legacy of inter-church hatred created.

This was a period of relative stability for the Coptic Church, the Orien-tal Orthodox Church of Egypt, though Islamic revivalism in the late 1920s and 1930s under the Muslim Brotherhood stimulated a revival of Coptic consciousness through the development of separate Coptic associations. But the rather larger Ethiopian Orthodox Church, which had many millions of members, and possibly as many as 15 million in the 1930s, was perse-cuted during the six-year occupation by Italian troops after the invasion of Abyssinia in 1935. Lasting suspicion between the Catholic Church and the Ethiopian Church resulted from the Vatican's less than wholehearted condemnation of Mussolini's venture and from the bringing of Italian Catholic missionaries into Ethiopia during the occupation. At this period the Church was still under the jurisdiction of an archbishop appointed from the Coptic Church.

Orthodoxy in Africa was largely confined to the Coptic and Ethio-pian churches. But it was flourishing in its own distinct communities, and represented a tenacious branch of Christianity that intermittent persecution throughout the century was not to break.

CHAPTER 4

Worldwide Protestantism

Varieties of Protestantism

In his groundbreaking work of religious sociology, *The Social Teaching of the Christian Churches* (1912), the German theologian Ernst Troeltsch called Protestantism 'a new sociological type', in contradistinction to the medieval Church and to the radical sects that had split from the Church.[1] Protestantism represented a new understanding of the theology of grace, which was no longer a mystical substance communicated through the sacraments but 'a Divine temper of faith, conviction, spirit, knowledge and trust' imparted to the believer as an 'inner miracle' of faith.[2] Descriptions like this gave a misleading impression of coherence and unity to worldwide Protestantism. By the beginning of the twentieth century it had diversified into an astonishing range of different churches and traditions, many of which had a merely derivative relationship to the European Reformation. A threefold typology derived from history provides a useful way of summarizing its major sub-groups.

First, there were the churches of the Reformation – 'classical' Protestantism. By 1914 there were three major clusters. The Lutheran churches of Northern Europe were national or state churches that followed the theological inspiration of Martin Luther and had preserved elements of medieval ecclesiastical organization to a greater or lesser degree. Some (particularly in Germany) had dispensed with bishops. But all claimed the Augsburg Confession, or *Confessio Augustana*, as interpreted by the formula of the *Book of Concord* of 1580 as their theological basis. Second, in Switzerland, parts of Southern and Central Europe, in a few areas of Germany and in Scotland, the 'Reformed' churches had followed the way of Calvin. Their doctrinal basis rested on Calvin's additions to the original theological insights of Luther, especially in the doctrines of predestination and soteriology. Many but not all Reformed churches had adopted the system of elders and church courts labelled 'Presbyterianism'. In parts of Germany by 1914 the 'union' movement of the early and mid-nineteenth century had

produced hybrid state churches in which both Lutheran and Reformed
elements were present. The third sub-group was an offshoot of the Reformed
tradition. The Church of England and Wales had fallen under the influence
of a theology akin to Calvinism in its early years after the death of Henry
VIII but had retained as a matter of accident (as much as anything else)
more of the ecclesiastical paraphernalia of the late medieval Church than
any other form of Protestantism. This had allowed the Church of England
in time to develop a more traditional and sacramental movement than many
of the Anglican Reformers would themselves have countenanced.

These three groups of churches of the European Reformation –
Lutheran, Reformed, and Anglican – were the dominant strands of Protestantism in Europe in 1914. But they had all been influenced by successive
renewal movements from the late seventeenth century on. Pietism as it was
called in Germany and Scandinavia, or Evangelicalism as it was called in
Britain, had developed a highly personalistic understanding of conversion
and faith. In most churches it was a distinct movement or tradition. There
were Pietistic Lutherans and Evangelical Anglicans, for example. But it
had also prompted the emergence of new churches, usually separating from
the older churches after years of internal conflict. The pattern of mutual
influence was complex. Thus the Moravian church communities that had
emerged in Germany under the leadership of Count Nicholas von Zinzen-
dorf had influenced what became Methodism in Britain and America, and
Methodists in turn had founded churches across the Continent, including Germany. Methodism itself in the nineteenth century had undergone
a bewildering series of schisms. But so had other churches. In the Church
of Sweden, a Lutheran national church, a movement of Pietistic revivalism in the mid-nineteenth century had produced a breakaway church, the
Mission Covenant Church of Sweden, which called itself Lutheran and
kept the sacraments of baptism and Eucharist, but dispensed with bishops
and infant baptism. It was always a small church, but with a strong evangelistic culture, insisting, for example, that not being baptized was no bar to
communion. Other examples included the Scottish Free Churches and the
Salvation Army.

A third cluster of churches was more amorphous. These were 'independent' or 'dissenting' churches. They often originated in movements of radical
rejection of ecclesiastical establishments, though they were later influenced
by Pietism and Evangelicalism. They included the Baptist churches, which
traced their descent ultimately from Continental Anabaptism and from the
Englishman John Smyth's separatist movement in the early seventeenth
century. They also included the Society of Friends, or Quakers, which
emerged out of the radical sects of the English Civil War. Arguably – but

controversially – they also included Unitarian churches, or 'Free Christians', which had separated from established churches at various times, mainly over the doctrine of the Trinity, which some of them rejected. Congregationalists, on the other hand, were a branch of Reformed Christianity that had split from the Church of England after the English Civil War, and so as 'Independents' pre-dated Evangelicalism, but were later profoundly affected by it.

This threefold typology is hardly satisfactory as a comprehensive analysis of European Protestantism, for the three 'types' crossed and criss-crossed. But it helps to characterize the way in which, in Europe, the national or state churches which had come into separate existence out of the medieval Church at the Reformation had spawned various movements of schism or renewal which had developed in turn into distinctive elements of world Christianity. But Protestantism, too, by 1914 had ceased to be merely European. To the perhaps 80 million believers who fell into one of these three groups in Europe in 1914 must be added the many millions of Protestants in America, Australasia, the Far East and the colonies. Here – and especially in America – the typology ceases to be of much value at all. In the United States the proliferation of Protestant denominations had been assisted by the constitutional separation of church and state, by successive waves of migration from Europe and by the seemingly limitless expansion of the American frontier. This last point is probably the most significant of all. It was an internal frontier, an ever-expanding frontier of the heart as well as a geographical one, for even in the conditions of settlement, the sheer size and expansiveness of American society provided the possibility of a spiritual home for anyone breaking away from an existing church to start another one. By 1900 there were over 40 million Protestant Americans – well over two-thirds of the population – in a seemingly endless procession of denominational permutations. Episcopalians – descendants of Anglican settlers – were now a small, if rich, church of some 2 million. Lutherans were also small, at just over 2 million. The Methodist, Baptist and Presbyterian churches were the Protestant mainstream. European patterns of Protestant belonging had been exported to Africa, India and the Far East by the missionary movement. In the 'white' dominions of the British Empire, Anglicanism still held a precarious dominance, but it was rapidly ceding strength in numbers to other Protestant churches, and above all to Roman Catholicism. A straw in the wind was the Pentecostal movement in America, as yet small in number but set to become the most dynamic force in twentieth-century Christianity. Its nature and development are so different from that of the older Protestant traditions that it is best handled in a separate chapter later in this book.

With all this diversity, the reader might wonder what, if anything, held Protestants together? The short answer is, not much. Anti-Catholicism had been a unifying ideology for Protestants in the past, but its power was on the wane in Europe, with the exception of a few pockets of hostility such as Northern Ireland. In America it also remained powerful in some parts of the union, especially in the southern states where it helped to foment what became the white Protestant 'supremacist' Ku Klux Klan movement. The 1910 Edinburgh Missionary Conference was a symptom of a growing awareness of the need for organized Protestant collaboration in mission. Anglo-American and German societies in particular were exploring that, reinforced by theological and educational links between Britain, America and Germany. That came to a bitter, if temporary, end in the First World War. Most of the German missions were in British imperial territory. German missionaries were interned or deported if they were not able to flee. The attempts of British church leaders such as J.H. Oldham, Secretary of the Edinburgh Conference, to protect the German missions came to nothing. If there was one thing the war above all demonstrated, it was that a common Protestantism had no impact whatsoever in restraining the belligerence of the opposing powers. There were other forms of cooperation, but these were usually more limited in scope. The Evangelical Alliance, for example, had been founded back in 1846 in Britain in an attempt to unite Evangelical Christians across different denominations. But it was dominated by the British churches, and strongly Evangelical, and as a voluntary association had no official standing with any of the mainstream Protestant churches. The YMCA was another British Evangelical product that had an international existence, but again a limited constituency. In Britain, and in parts of the British Empire, non-Anglican Protestant churches had increasingly formed local 'free church' councils since the 1890s, but these voluntary representative bodies had little power, if some symbolic influence.

Church and state between the wars

By the early twentieth century, large areas of global Protestantism had ceased to be defined closely by their roots in the European Reformation. Protestantism was not a community of churches. It was an amorphous, expanding cluster of churches, many of which had little more in common than a basic loyalty to the supreme authority of Scripture (however diversely they interpreted it) and a refusal to accept the authority of the papacy. Protestantism's great strength was its capacity for endless self-generation. It could embed itself in a dazzling variety of different contexts, because it was permeable to the influence of particular cultures. For almost every imaginable human community, there could be some form of Protestantism. It was in America, and in the very different contexts of Africa and Asia, that the true diversity of Protestantism was to become evident in the course of the century. Here in particular Pentecostalism was free to flourish. What made Europe, by contrast, different from the rest of the world was its historic pattern of church–state relations.

Until the nineteenth century most European rulers had assumed that a common religion was essential to social harmony. The wars of religion in the sixteenth and seventeenth centuries had demonstrated the intractability of religious conflict. Most states had, thereafter, made minor concessions to religious minorities, while seeking to uphold a dominant church tradition, sometimes by active persecution of dissenters, but more often by legal privilege, by discrimination and by restrictions on freedom of worship. These settlements had begun to falter in the course of the nineteenth century, when they came under pressure from growing populations and from political and social criticism in the wake of the French Revolution. By the early twentieth century, Protestant religious establishments were in retreat. Where they survived, as they did in Britain, Scandinavia and Germany, they had been forced to concede much to rival religious traditions. Numerically they were often still preponderant. They were also intimately connected with the educational and social institutions of their countries. They remained influential expressions of national identity. This made it difficult for dissenting churches, however well supported, to develop as they had in America. In Germany, where the constitutionally privileged position of the Protestant churches in most states was brought to an end in 1918, and in Scandinavia, the collection of church tax favoured the established churches. The Scandinavian churches were 'folk churches': their overwhelming numerical dominance underpinned a concept of service to the whole community and made little allowance for any alternative. In Finland, for example, the introduction of full religious freedom in 1923 produced a negligible number of seceders from the (Lutheran) Church of Finland – some 0.5 per cent. The proportion of the population who were at least nominally members of the Church of Finland did not fall below 90 per cent until the 1980s. In Britain church tax arrangements did not apply. The Church of England (Anglican) and the Church of Scotland (Presbyterian) were financially independent and faced far stronger competition from rival religious traditions than was true in Scandinavia and parts of Germany. The Church of Wales, formerly part of the Church of England, was finally disestablished in 1920 – a recognition of the immense growth of Nonconformist (dissenting) Protestantism in Wales since the early nineteenth century. But this was not the prelude to the disestablishment of the Church of England itself, which retained its connection with the monarchy and its representation in parliament.

Privilege came at a price. Where legal establishment remained, there was always a danger of government interference. Having gained some legislative autonomy immediately after the First World War, English Anglicans were shocked to find they had no redress when parliament prevented them from reforming their liturgy in 1928. But the drawbacks of the historic position of these churches went beyond that. In the course of history their religious identity had become closely tied up with national culture. Anglicans thought of Anglicanism as quintessentially English, and German Lutherans saw Lutheranism as the German national religion. Whatever the unfortunate implications for other Christian churches, the result was all too often a certain complacency or hesitancy when it came to challenging the actions of government. Not that that was true only of established churches. In Holland, for example, where a formal separation of church and state had existed since the end of the eighteenth century, Catholics and Protestants (particularly the Dutch Reformed Church) had formed rival networks of ecclesiastical, political, social, educational and even economic institutions. So too had Social Democrats. This practice of 'pillarization', as it is called, on the one hand enabled a remarkable degree of religious toleration to thrive in pre-war Holland. But on the other hand it fragmented society and made the organization of effective resistance to government difficult.

Resistance was always possible in theory. The growing separation of church and state in Europe, accompanied by the expansion of state responsibility into areas formerly the preserve of the churches (such as education), provoked criticism, resistance and renewal. There were, accordingly, complex patterns of resistance and acquiescence running through the relationship of the historic Protestant churches to the state between the wars. Notoriously these are best seen in the conflict between the Nazi state and the German churches. A later generation has been captivated by the aura of heroism surrounding Karl Barth, Martin Niemöller and Dietrich Bonhoeffer. The truth is more mundane, though perhaps not less dramatic. Hitler's accession to power in 1933 did not meet with universal condemnation from Germany's Protestant believers. On the contrary, many prominent church leaders spoke out in favour of him. Niemöller, a former U-boat commander, initially welcomed Hitler, hoping he would lead Germany out of the failure of the Weimar Republic. Niemöller was also anti-Semitic, at least in the early years of Hitler's rule. Bonhoeffer was much more sceptical. But he was a young man, scarcely known, and out of line with the mainstream of German Protestant opinion. It later became a matter of historical controversy how far Germany's Lutheran population in particular assisted the rise of Nazi power, given the tradition – derived somewhat loosely from Luther himself – that, according to the 'two kingdoms' view of Luther, the church should not seek to question or to challenge the authority of the state, but rather existed to serve Christianly the interests of the state. There were those who took this view to an extreme conclusion. The 'German Christians', as they were called, supported a programme of Nazification of the Church, with its symbol a swastika superimposed on a cross. Coralled into the united 'Reich Church' formed by diktat in 1933, all of the German state churches were obliged in theory to accept the leadership of Ludwig Müller, head of the German Christian movement.

It was the German Christian movement that proved the undoing of Hitler's ecclesiastical policy, however. In 1933–34 its proposals for a 'positive' Christianity, purged of its Judaic elements and subservient to the state, provoked a movement of Protestant opposition, the 'Confessing Church', led by an increasingly disillusioned Niemöller among others. At its first synod in Barmen in 1934 the Confessing Church adopted the 'Barmen Declaration' drafted by Karl Barth, a statement of confidence in the uniqueness of the Christian revelation and a corresponding rejection of the Nazi attempt to absolutize the state – a characteristically 'confessional' position. As the declaration famously asserted, 'We reject [as] false [the] doctrine [that] the Church could and would have to acknowledge as a source of its proclamation, apart from and besides this one Word of God, still other events and powers, figures and truths, as God's revelation.' Barth was forced out of Germany, and persecution of the Confessing Church began in earnest. Bonhoeffer's role in leading the Confessing Church's secret seminary at Finkenwald from 1935, and his later association with the circle of German conspirators against Hitler, is well known, as is his criticism of the Nazis' racial laws and anti-Jewish policies. Yet the Confessing Church was a minority within Protestant Germany, and Bonhoeffer a minority voice within the Confessing Church. The tradition of loyalty to the state was enormously compelling, even in the face of manifest tyranny.

This was even true of Germany's dissenting churches, which one might have expected to criticize Nazism more openly. It was not to be, however. The relatively small German Baptist and Methodist churches had always had to struggle against the suspicion that, as inheritors of traditions re-implanted in Germany by British missionaries, they were not truly German. They were eager to prove their national loyalty. Some leaders, such as Dr F.H. Otto Melle, director of the Methodist Seminary in Frankfurt-am-Main, were out-and-out Nazi sympathizers, naively suggesting that God might 'use this [Nazi] movement to preach the Gospel of the cross of Christ to our people'. Others were more muted and apolitical, fearing Nazi reprisals if they spoke out.

Germany under Hitler is but the most extreme example of a common pattern by which some Protestant churches acquiesced in, or positively encouraged, the emergence of racist or totalitarian ideologies. The Dutch Reformed Church in South Africa is another instance. Here again the close relationship of ethnic identity and religion drove forward an extreme form of nationalism. Increasingly the programme of the nationalist Afrikaner Broederbond, designed to defend the interests of poor Afrikaners, became wedded to white supremacist ideas. The creation of the apartheid state did not take place fully until after the Second World War, when the Afrikaner Nationalist Party seized power in 1948, but the growing influence of Afrikaner racism was inseparable from the Dutch Reformed Church. In the southern states of America, too, white supremacist ideas also found fertile ground in the ranks of white Protestantism. They were fuelled by fears of the growth of Roman Catholicism and of the black-led churches, and by Jewish immigration. The revival of the Ku Klux Klan fed on a sense that white Protestant America was under threat. The years of the Great Depression ate away at the confidence of southern whites and helped to perpetuate the association of a narrow Protestantism with racism, anti-communism and anti-Catholicism.

Elsewhere there were ambiguities aplenty. The transposition of British and American Protestantism into the colonies of the British Empire produced other permutations of the link between religion and national identity. Establishment – state religion – was not by itself an issue in most of the Empire. In theory all Protestant denominations operated on something of a level playing field. They were equally free to pursue converts and to create schools and welfare agencies. But their leadership was mostly drawn from Britain and they were reluctant to criticize imperial policy. Until well into the era of decolonization, the episcopate of the Anglican Communion was mostly born, bred and educated in Britain. The same was true of the top levels of leadership of Methodism, Presbyterianism and Congregationalism throughout the Empire. Efforts to develop indigenous church leadership were sincere but piecemeal. They were prompted by a shortage of missionaries in many parts of the Empire, especially Africa. Yet the reluctance of church leaders to modify long-established mission policies (particularly in regard to the level of education required of missionaries) meant that, practically speaking, indigenous ministers and lay assistants were confined to subordinate positions. White missionaries were not all, by any means, uncritical admirers of empire. But they were acutely conscious of loyalties to the 'mother' country and all that it stood for. Actually the words of the Moderator-General of the Presbyterian Church of Australia in 1931 *were* uncritical: 'Presbyterians should be outspoken as to their loyalty to King and Country and their respect for patriots and statesmen who have made under God's grace our flag a symbol of the highest civilization yet reached by the human race.' Sentiments such as this were far from uncommon. It was ironic, then, that it was the system of education brought to parts of Africa by the missionary societies that was to prove a seed-bed for the emergence of African nationalism. But this had little directly to do with missionary policy.

Protestantism, however, has a double character that can cut in very different directions. Its roots in the European Reformation's revolt against a centralized ecclesiastical jurisdiction have arguably encouraged the adaptation of Protestant Christianity to certain dominant ideas, including nationalism, racism, militarism and imperialism, as well as a tendency to sub-divide. And yet its implicit doctrine of Christian internationalism – arising out of its perception that the one Christian Church exists in different contexts in a diversity of forms of church order through a common faith – has also encouraged practical expressions of political internationalism. As we shall see in the next chapter, it was above all in the Protestant churches that the ecumenical movement initially found its most ardent supporters. But Protestant church leaders were also, between the wars, often at the forefront of popular pacifism, and of the call for the establishment of international standards of arbitration and human rights. When war came in 1939 there was no surge of Christian militarism, unlike 1914. Instead – and this was true particularly of the American churches – increasingly through the war Protestant church leaders were influential in discussions about the postwar international order. Through the Commission on Human Rights established under the aegis of the new United Nations, a defence of religious freedom as a key element of a more general understanding of basic human rights found its way into the UN Declaration of Human Rights.

Theology and culture

As the century opened, it looked as if the Liberal Protestantism of the nineteenth-century German and Anglo-American schools had finally triumphed. The great battles over evolutionary biology and historical criticism of the Bible were over. The theology of Adolf von Harnack (1851–1930) and Ernst Troeltsch (1865–1923), grounding Christian doctrine in historical study, was read and admired across the world. In Anglo-American circles, only the most dedicated studied these authors closely. But their influence was part of the theological atmosphere that Protestant church leaders breathed. It was the basis of what one historian has called the 'new theological establishment' of the seminaries and universities of America, for example.[3] And there were home-grown equivalents, such as the 'New Theology' of the British Congregationalist R.J. Campbell (1867–1956), which married conventional criticism of traditional Evangelical doctrines of the atonement to vague assertions about the results of historical study. Campbell was no more than a popularizer, who later recanted, but his work struck a chord with many clergy and laity and was read in clerical circles throughout the British Empire. It had its equivalents in America, especially with out-and-out Modernist thinkers like Shailer Matthews (1863–1941), whose *The Faith of Modernism* (1924) was a bestselling text. There were more progressive and more cautious (or orthodox) voices on either side of the Liberal Protestantism of a Harnack or a Campbell or a Matthews. But few disputed that Christian theology, if it was to have anything relevant to say to the modern world, had to be a *critical* theology, alert to the historical study of the biblical texts and to the historical experience of the Church.

This thread of 'Liberal Protestantism' remained enormously influential all the way through the twentieth century. That this was so was obscured by oversimplified accounts of twentieth-century Protestantism, which cast the emergence of 'neo-orthodoxy' after the First World War in the hands of Karl Barth and Emil Brunner (1889–1966) as a straightforward rejection of all that liberalism represented in religion. Barth in particular denied that history and philosophy could presume to judge the truth of revelation. Neo-orthodoxy, or 'dialectical theology' to give it its other common designation, was conservative doctrinally and re-emphasized the theological breadth and insight of the magisterial Reformers. But much of the working method of Liberal Protestantism was simply assumed into neo-orthodoxy's theological approach. Barth certainly saw a place for critical enquiry. His work was philosophically astute and open to biblical criticism. This was even more evident in the work of Barth's one-time associate, Rudolf Bultmann (1884–1976), and in the parallel American movement sponsored by Reinhold Niebuhr (1892–1971).

Neo-orthodoxy represented a vigorous reassertion of Christian particularity over and against the bland, universal category of 'religion' within which Liberal Protestant theologians at their least convincing had located Christian faith. For this reason it looked like a fellow-traveller with conservative Evangelicalism. Yet willingness to accept critical enquiry has constituted a basic fault-line in modern Protestant theology. For all their hostility to theological liberalism, the neo-orthodox stood on the same side of that line as the liberals, along with many Evangelicals and High Church Anglicans. Resistance to critical enquiry came from two directions and highlighted the way in which the fault-line divided not only theologians, academics and clergy, but believers themselves. One direction was simply the ordinary piety of many Protestant church members. Critical methodology was a demanding intellectual exercise and its results did not translate easily into new practices of piety, or into readily grasped formulae that could nurture a living faith. The intense personalism of Evangelical and Pietistic Protestantism – the sense of Jesus as a close and dear friend – sat uneasily beside the cerebral approach of theologians. A gap began to open up between what many believers still thought their churches should be proclaiming and what they actually heard from the pulpit. And yet of course congregations were themselves divided, with many members also frankly puzzled as to how Christianity could be reconciled with the results of modern science.

The gap created space for the resuscitation of theories of verbal inerrancy, the second direction. Notoriously this happened in America in the movement that came to be labelled 'fundamentalism'. With deep roots in nineteenth-century conservative Evangelicalism, fundamentalism was not an invention of the twentieth century. But it was ironically a 'modern' phenomenon: its inspiration was a desire to counter the corrosive effects of critical enquiry and to propagate a view of the simplicity or 'plain sense' of faith which had never needed articulation and defence in the ancient Church. A series of booklets published by various American and British theologians between 1910 and 1915 under the title *The Fundamentals: A Testimony to the Truth* sought to re-focus contemporary Christian piety on the basic articles of the Christian creeds. The group was rather eclectic and by no means agreed on how to evaluate modern science and history. One of the leading theorists of the group, the American Presbyterian Benjamin Warfield, for example, actually accepted the theory of evolution. But their appeal to the 'fundamentals' of the faith rapidly got linked with strongly conservative views of the inerrancy of Scripture as the inspired Word of God. By the 1920s the movement was also becoming associated in the public mind with resistance to evolution. Its symbolic moment came in the notorious 'Scopes Trial' in Dayton, Tennessee, in 1925, when a local teacher, John T. Scopes, sought to overturn a state ruling preventing teaching of any theory that called into question the biblical account of creation. The defence was mounted by the Presbyterian lawyer and critic of evolution, William Jennings Bryan. Though inconclusive, the trial generated enormous publicity and helped to discredit fundamentalism as a political force. It remained, however, extremely influential and a vital force in shaping elements of popular Protestantism in America.

Yet even the extreme conservatism associated with American fundamentalism could not altogether hold back the tide of social change and its impact on Protestantism. In America the failure of Prohibition underlined the failure of a whole moral and social programme associated with the attempt to create a Protestant nation. If the temperance movement – a pet project of Evangelical Protestantism in the English-speaking world at the beginning of the twentieth century – had its greatest but short-lived triumph in America, elsewhere it was by now in retreat. Along with it went Sabbatarianism, gradually ebbing away as new forms of leisure and entertainment drew people away from the strict observance of Sunday as a day of worship and rest. Gradually, too, most denominations began the long (and slow) movement towards recognizing women as potential candidates for church leadership. There had been lay women preachers in various branches of Methodism before. Now, as women gradually forced their way into the learned professions, received the vote and even began here and there to serve as political representatives, a small tide of opinion began to rise in favour of their inclusion in the ordained ministries of the churches. Here and there, too, were women who pushed directly at the ceiling of opportunity – women such as Maude Royden, an Anglican who felt a call to a preaching ministry so strongly that she temporarily crossed denominational boundaries in 1917 to become a preacher at the Congregationalist City Temple in London, eventually helping to found the Society for the Ministry of Women in 1929.

Decline and renewal

Gradual changes of this kind in the Protestant churches, and the confrontation between critical enquiry and theories of inerrancy, took place against a background of declining confidence in the ability of the Protestant denominations to create a Godly society. Protestant churches were not necessarily more vulnerable to social change than their Catholic and Orthodox counterparts. In Europe in particular the impact of rapid population growth, industrialization and urbanization from the mid-nineteenth century on stretched the ability of churches (especially established churches) to respond creatively to the challenges of the city, whether they were Anglican, Lutheran, Reformed, Catholic or Orthodox. By the 1920s several successive generations of church leaders in Western Europe had spoken of the failures of the Church in the city and of a situation of crisis. They were convinced that the working class in particular stayed away from church. Modern social analysis of the available historical data about the composition of church membership in fact suggests a more mixed conclusion: as a class, on the whole workers and their families were less inclined to attend church regularly than were the middle class, but the working class still constituted a significant proportion of the congregations of inner-city churches. Somehow this latter fact never struck church leaders as forcefully as did the first. Fears about the incidence of popular atheism were exaggerated, and there was a tendency to reach for the nearest apocalyptic judgement forecasting the end of Christian civilization as everyone knew it.

This perception of crisis was the product of several converging trends. One was the fashionableness of agnosticism and atheism among the intellectual elite of Europe and America. Intellectuals may have been a small and largely unrepresentative minority in most countries, but they were vociferous and influential and usually good self-publicists. Another trend was a definite tailing-off of church attendance in many Western European cities from the late nineteenth century on. Mostly this was gradual and by itself certainly did not justify the language of crisis. A third trend was the increasing 'professionalism' (for want of a better term) of the churches and in particular their growing preoccupation with measuring performance through financial and attendance statistics. Counting churchgoers was never conceived as a valid index of religiosity much before the nineteenth century. By the early twentieth century all of the main Christian denominations had centralized bureaucracies and bureaucratic methods, and counting the faithful (and agonizing over what to do about their loss) was universal.

The language of crisis bandied about at Edinburgh in 1910 already had a long and honoured history behind it, even if it was actually (at least from the perspective of the end of the century) much too premature. But it showed how the confidence of Protestant church leaders was failing and, above all, how they were unable to grasp adequately the complexity of popular belief. Their preoccupation with statistics clouded their judgement about the breadth of human religious experience. It was a sign that the churches had too narrow a view of religiosity, and frequently discounted things that – on a long view – were actually a reflection of the pervasive influence of Christianity. Clergy now often dismissed certain popular religious beliefs and practices as a relic of superstition. The 'churching' (as it was called in Britain) of women after childbirth was a good example of a ritual practice that implied the impurity of the woman who had just given birth – a view considered unnecessary and inhumane by many clergy – and yet which remained resolutely popular with working-class women. Another example was churchgoing 'by deputy', when a whole family might count itself as churchgoing through the occasional attendance of just one member of the family.

More often than not, that 'deputy' was a woman. The sheer dominance of women in most congregations was a commonly noted but rarely discussed fact. The statistics are constantly striking. Women were almost always a clear majority. Gender analysis of church membership in a variety of churches in Glasgow and Aberdeen at the beginning of the twentieth century, for example, demonstrated a consistent pattern: around 60 per cent were women. This could be matched by data for England, for the European churches and for America. But it was not a feature only of Western religion. Even when transplanted into the missionary context, Christianity drew the active participation and interest of women much more readily than that of men. So dominant were women, that time and again they provided practically all of the volunteers who ran the various societies and charities locally. Methodists surveying their church membership in southern Africa in 1945, for example, found that 57 per cent of the congregations were made up of women, with men at only 7 per cent and children the remainder. Yet this was still a period in which the men held practically all the cards when it came to making decisions. Clerical elites were almost entirely male. So pervasive were the assumptions about women's domestic role that even female missionaries – who themselves expressed concern at their male colleagues' failure to give them sufficient responsibility – tried to perpetuate the same model of gender differentiation and practical subordination of women when it came to dealing with indigenous cultures. The Methodist revival in Rhodesia in 1918 led to the formation of a spontaneous women's prayer union, Ruwadzano (from the Shona word for 'fellowship'), which grew so rapidly that it soon posed a threat to the male ministers and missionaries and led to half-hearted attempts to bring it under official control.

Women were thus key to the continued existence of all of these denominations, and yet their real contribution to the life of the churches was barely registered and certainly not reflected in the official decision-making structures of the churches. Yet there was a second area of blindness in the attitudes of the leadership of many of the main Protestant traditions, with the exception arguably of America. This concerned the culture and values associated with revivalism, the highly experiential and emotive but systematic form of evangelism that American and British Evangelicals had developed in the nineteenth century out of the spontaneity of earlier revival movements. Revivalism, with its orchestrated public prayer and preaching, with its use of rehearsed choruses and with its deliberate promotion of tension in the hearts of the audience as a prelude to triggering a decision for conversion, was still a powerful tool of evangelism. But it was now rarely used in the mainstream denominations, as its intellectual credibility was called into question by an educated and critical clerical elite. Increasingly it was the preserve of smaller, more marginal denominations or of new movements of the Spirit. Protestant worship had become ordered and rational and cerebral, even when – as had happened in some denominations, especially Anglicanism and some of the Lutheran churches – it had also become more ritualistic. America remained a source of revivalist preachers, even from some of the mainstream denominations, but even there the Protestant churches increasingly tended to avoid the histrionics of revivalism. But this was surely a strategic mistake, whatever defence might be made of critics' view of revivalism, for in the long run it was precisely the kind of worship associated with revivalism, deepened and transformed into the charismatic gifts of Pentecostalism, that was to prove such a powerful source of evangelism in the non-Western world.

CHAPTER 5

Christian Internationalism: Mission and Ecumenism

The legacy of the nineteenth-century missionary movement

'I go back to Africa to try to make an open path for commerce and Christianity; do you carry out the work which I have begun.' David Livingstone's famous speech in the Senate House of Cambridge University in 1857 lit the enthusiasm of generations of undergraduates eager to Christianize the new worlds opening up to European trade. His sentiments were at odds with British imperial policy; after the Indian Mutiny the British authorities were wary of explicit evangelism. Post-revolutionary tensions between church and state in France also made French colonial administrators sceptical of mission, though they favoured Catholic missions nevertheless.

Despite these difficulties, and the hardships of tropical life, by the beginning of the twentieth century Western missionaries had massively extended their activity in Africa and Asia. In 1910 there were some 19,000 foreign Protestant missionaries in the field, supplemented by nearly 100,000 native workers. If this sounds a lot of people, it should be kept in perspective. Of these 19,000 missionaries, for example, just five and a half thousand were ordained. At this time, the Church of England alone had around 24,000 ordained clergy in England. The missionary movement may have attracted huge interest and drained the sending churches of human and financial resources, but it was a minor activity for the mainstream Protestant churches. In 1910 at Edinburgh they spoke of the mission 'fruitage', meaning the numbers of converts from non-Christian peoples to Christianity, counting some 12 million Protestants and 5.5 million Catholics and Orthodox. This probably underestimated Catholic numbers. But the figures already indicated strain on the numbers of missionaries. There were nearly 3,500 main mission stations and 32,000 sub-stations. Given that the large mission stations would have many mission workers, the sheer number of sub-stations stretched the remainder of available personnel to the limit.

Missionaries and their co-workers were thin on the ground, particularly in Africa.

The range of societies involved was immense. There were hundreds of them. Every denomination and state church in Britain, America and the continent of Europe had not only at least one principal missionary society, but a bewildering number of additional agencies. Many of these were highly specialized. The Oriental Society for Promoting the Education of Deaf Mutes (American, founded 1887), which worked in China and Korea, aimed 'to prove to the Chinese that the deaf can be educated and become useful members of society'.[1] Alongside the great missionary societies that had long been sending men and women into the field primarily for evangelism were a host of medical and other agencies. There were even campaigning societies, controversial with colonial governments, such as the Society for the Suppression of the Opium Trade (English, Quaker, founded 1874), which had been sidelined in the late nineteenth century by the government in India's resistance to this policy. There were now also German societies in the field, such as the Deutsche Hilfebund für Christliches Liebeswerk im Orient, or the German Aid Society for Christian Charity in the East (founded in 1891), which actually worked mostly in Turkey. Only when the numbers of organizations and the numbers of missionaries and their workers are held together with the huge geographical spread of missionary endeavour is it clear how the Protestant movement was stretched to its limits. Essentially, the societies' operations were scattered across India, China, Korea and Japan, southern Africa and the coastal and inland river areas of West and East Africa. Catholic missions were present in these areas too, though they were also concentrated in areas of French, Belgian and Portuguese colonization, including North and Central Africa, South-East Asia and, of course, in Latin America.

With all these organizations, is it any wonder that by the beginning of the twentieth century Protestant missionaries were realizing that their best hope of successfully achieving the 'evangelization of the world in this generation', the 1910 Edinburgh watchword, lay in mutual cooperation? Under 'comity' agreements in many areas mission societies pledged not to interfere with each other's work, and there were mission stations shared between two or more denominations. But increasingly missionaries were reporting back the bewilderment with which the varieties of European Christianity were met by would-be converts. It was this feeling above all that was to lead the mainstream Protestant churches to make positive efforts towards Christian unity. But Edinburgh also reflected a new appreciation of non-Christian faiths. The dominant perspective among church leaders in the West assumed not only that the Christian revelation was unique and absolute, but that other faiths were primitive and would fade with the growth of Christian civilization. But some missionaries in the field took a different view. Many of the written questionnaires returned in advance of the Edinburgh conference reflected a new-found respect for other faiths. William Harris of the Presbyterian Church of the USA, based in Chang-mai, Thailand, for example, said that the missionary should be 'at all times thoughtful of the feelings and prejudices of the people among whom he labours. He should frankly appreciate the good and true element in the religion of the people.'[2] T. Grahame Bailey of the Church of Scotland, based in Wazirabad in the Punjab, commended 'an attitude of thorough comprehension and knowledge, an attitude of sympathy, admitting all the good in non-Christian religions'.[3]

Where did such views, new as they were, come from? They were not a sign of failing energy. Up until the Second World War, the Protestant missionary movement, like its Catholic counterpart, went from strength to strength. Despite the disruption of the First World War, the numbers of foreign missionaries increased on average by around 50 per cent between 1910 and 1925 alone. Increases among native mission workers in Africa and Asia were even more dramatic, as were numbers of recorded communicants, which almost doubled. The interwar years in many ways were the peak of the movement, with an unparalleled amount of effort poured into mission. An increasing proportion of it came from the United States of America, which in mission, as in so many other areas, was now beginning to flex its muscles. Nor did these years see a significant change in the strategy of mission. That had to wait for decolonization.

Rather, the change was intellectual and theological. By the beginning of the century missionaries were being trained according to the liberalism of the Western churches, including the critical study of Scripture and the new discipline of comparative religion. There was also a growing scepticism about imperialism, reinforced by the First World War. These views were stated with even more force at the Second World Missionary Conference, held in Jerusalem in 1928. Disillusionment with the Christian West deepened in the 1930s and in the Second World War, and made an assumption of Western superiority difficult to sustain. But liberalism did not hold sway for long. There was a counter-reaction among theologians of mission, under the influence of Barth and neo-orthodoxy. The Dutch Reformed missionary Hendrik Kraemer rejected the compromise he discerned in liberalism and reasserted the message of Christian distinctness. Kraemer's *The Christian Message in a Non-Christian World* (1938), with its criticism of cooperation with other religions, superficially looked like a return to the older perspective on mission. But it was not in the old tone, and not without awareness of the difficulties missionaries faced in the field. It was not fighting against the tide of change.

Ecumenical origins

The Protestant contribution to the ecumenical movement had its mainspring in the missionary movement – in particular the perception that Christian disunity seriously damaged the task of evangelism. But we should be cautious about drawing too close a connection. Through the International Missionary Council, established after the First World War, the missionary societies made a vital contribution to the emergence of ecumenical institutions in the 1920s and 1930s. Many missionaries such as John Mott and Joseph Oldham were closely involved in these new ecumenical organs and played a decisive role in shaping their agenda. But the ecumenical movement had a distinct goal and evolved quite quickly its own specialized body of officers and administrators.

We should also be cautious about confining the ecumenical movement to the Protestant churches for much of the century. Catholics and Orthodox were also committed to church unity. Catholics were officially held to a 'return' model of unity until the Second Vatican Council. There was little official interest in Protestant ecumenism, though there were informal gatherings of theologians and clergy from time to time, such as the conversations between Anglican and Catholic theologians at Malines in Belgium from 1921 to 1926, with the hospitality of Cardinal Mercier. But Catholic interest was made problematic by Pius XI's condemnation of Protestant 'indifferentism' in 1928 in *Mortalium Animos*. Orthodox participation was also problematic, but for other reasons, including the continuing chaos in Russian Orthodox circles during the Soviet persecution. Nevertheless there were significant Orthodox voices among the diaspora churches that supported a new spirit of cooperation with other Christian communions. In 1920 the ecumenical patriarch issued an encyclical letter, 'Unto the Churches of Christ Everywhere', calling for a world council of Christians. From then on there were some Orthodox participants from outside the Soviet world at many of the most important early meetings of the new ecumenical institutions. There were always many Orthodox suspicious of Protestantism, and in particular of its understanding of a really existent 'invisible' unity of the Church. But Orthodox participation probably in turn made eventual Catholic participation inevitable.

All the same, much of the initiative and most of the resources deployed in the movement came from Protestant churches. Most branches of Protestantism, despite important doctrinal and liturgical differences, subscribed more or less to a common doctrine of church unity: the unity of the Church subsisted in Christ in all Christian communities, whatever their actual historic features. Protestants – with the exception of Anglo-Catholics (who mostly disliked the word 'Protestant' anyway) – tended to regard differences of church order as secondary. It was easier to envisage schemes of unity on this basis. Several models of church union or cooperation within Protestantism already existed. There were cases of churches reuniting after years of division, such as happened in British Methodism in 1906 and 1932, when the main strands of British Methodism eventually came together to form the Methodist Church of Great Britain, and in the Church of Scotland in 1929, when the United Free Church finally recombined with the established Church of Scotland. There were also cases of traditions that were close theologically uniting to form a new denomination, as happened in Canada in 1925 when Presbyterian, Congregationalist and also Methodist churches united. The most dramatic instance was the Church of South India, formed in 1947 after nearly three decades of discussions between Presbyterians, Congregationalists, Methodists, Reformed and Anglicans. There were the various Free Church councils that came into existence from the 1890s onwards in Britain and the British dominions. There were again also significant cases of international cooperation or federation within distinct traditions, such as the World Alliance of Reformed Churches, originally formed in 1877, and the Anglican Communion. And there were also international and interdenominational organizations, such as the World Missionary Conferences and the International Missionary Council itself.

In all these ways the Protestant churches had a practical ecumenism that undergirded the emergence of worldwide ecumenical instruments. But the key elements of the movement between the wars were three in number. The first was the missionary movement, through the International Missionary Council. The second was 'Faith and Order', which emerged out of a proposal of the American Bishop Charles Brent after Edinburgh 1910 to call together a conference of world communions to discuss 'questions touching Faith and Order'. This was not finally implemented until 1927 in a conference at Lausanne. The third element was 'Life and Work', a complementary stream based on the pursuit of a vision of Christian cooperation in social justice and welfare – an approach called by the Anglican George Bell 'the method of love'.[4] 'Life and Work' came into being through the leadership of the Swedish Archbishop Nathan Söderblom, and again was organized around the principle of ecumenical conferences, with the first taking place in Stockholm in 1925. Each of these three elements required permanent organizing committees and led inexorably to the proposal that there should be one overarching representative ecumenical body, a 'World Council of Churches' along the lines advocated by the ecumenical patriarch's 1920 encyclical. A serious proposal to create such a body did not finally emerge until just before the Second World War and could not be implemented in practice until 1948, when the World Council of Churches (WCC) held its first world assembly in Amsterdam, drawing together both 'Faith and Order' and 'Life and Work'. The International Missionary Council was finally absorbed into the WCC in 1961.

Depending on your point of view, the creation of the WCC was either a triumph for the bureaucrats or a remarkable act of prophetic ecumenical witness. In favour of the first view is the fact that the tangible achievements of the WCC and its associated ecumenical elements were minimal, if by 'achievement' is meant something like a major realignment or convergence in world Christianity. The vision of a great, reunited Christendom that motivated so many of the early ecumenical enthusiasts proved elusive – as it still does. The WCC soaked up time, energy and money, and yet often seemed to puzzled local churches little more than a grand talking shop. Time and again the churches' leaders were to have great difficulty translating the ecumenical vision they encountered at national and international level into language that was meaningful for the ordinary church member.

What can be said, then, in favour of the WCC? Its creation was a major achievement in itself, not least because it included Orthodox (at first in limited numbers) and Protestant churches in a single conciliar body. It had no legislative authority over its member churches, and controversy obliged it to issue the 'Toronto Statement' of 1950 which clarified its self-perception as an assembly of churches, each of which has its own ecclesiology and its own understanding of what constitutes the unity of the Church of Christ. The WCC is not a 'superchurch', and 'does not prejudge the ecclesiological problem'.[5] It was essentially only a means of moral persuasion. It was not even a negotiating body. Its aim was to put churches in touch with each other and to stimulate and encourage the ecumenical vision. The Catholic Church has never joined formally, though it now participates in some of the activities of the WCC and sends observers to the major assemblies. In effect the WCC was just a beginning. What has become clear, in the course of its as yet short history, is that the achievement of lasting church unity, even on a small or local scale, is often the work of decades of careful negotiation and gradual, organic convergence in church life and witness. Real church unity cannot be imposed 'from above', but nor can it emerge only 'from below' if it is to remain connected to the universal Church. It requires hard theological discussion, a growth in personal trust, the acknowledgement of memories of difference and (often) persecution, and material and organizational change, all of which takes time.

The inevitably slow pace of progress towards church unity was perhaps not fully appreciated in the first flush of ecumenical enthusiasm in 1948. But it was already apparent that the movement was caught by conflicting arguments over strategy. Should it, for example, concentrate on the 'Life and Work' agenda, developing and encouraging common Christian responses to the problems of the world, and trust that organic unity would follow in due course? Should it, on the other hand, concentrate its energy and attention primarily on the 'Faith and Order' agenda, acknowledging that impairment in common Christian witness must surely exist as long as the churches are actually divided? Or should it, perhaps, recognize the threatened situation of Christianity in the world and concentrate on evangelism, putting the missionary agenda to the fore? In an ideal world, all three goals could and should be pursued resolutely and with maximum effort. But that was never likely to happen. In practice the WCC lurched from one goal to the other.

From the missionary movement to world mission

Part of the problem for the WCC, in any event, was that changes in the churches' ecumenical policies that made the formation of the WCC eventually possible occurred against a background of global social and political change, so that the body that eventually came into being in 1948 faced a world already very different from the one the ecumenical leaders inhabited when they proposed the formation of a world council back in 1937. The age of European imperialism was drawing to an end. As Stephen Neill conceded in the 1960s, 'the colonizing powers have been the Christian powers ... and ... in the main Christianity has been carried forward on the wave of western prestige and power'.[6] Now, as the European colonies began to achieve their independence, time and again the missionary movement was compromised by its association with colonialism. Some Protestant societies did not actively recruit indigenous missionaries until the 1960s. Catholic missions were perhaps a little less vulnerable: the worldwide organization of the Catholic Church made it harder to think in terms of 'home' and 'abroad' in quite the same way as was true for Protestant missionaries, although many nationalist leaders were indifferent to the ecclesiastical niceties. For the Protestant societies, the coming of independence to former colonies raised acute questions. One concerned the cultural identity of Christianity and the West. Could Christianity survive when its Western umbrella was removed? A second concerned strategy, and touched on long-standing conflicts even within the 'parent' churches themselves. Was the goal of overseas mission the evangelization of a whole society as a necessary precondition for the creation of an autonomous, indigenous church, or was it to create an autonomous, indigenous church first as a necessary precondition for the successful evangelization of a society? In the nineteenth century the Anglican Church Missionary Society (CMS) had assumed the first position against High Church colonial bishops who supported the second. Now the dilemma was being forced on all the denominations. And this raised a third question. Could an indigenous clergy and lay agencies be created quickly enough to take over the running of the institutional infrastructure of these new churches?

The answers varied dramatically from place to place. In China, for example, the triumph of Mao Tse Tung's communists in 1949 led to the collapse of Western missions almost everywhere. In 1949 there were around 8,000 Catholic and Protestant missionaries in China. By 1953 practically all had gone. Most withdrew voluntarily. Some were shot, imprisoned or forced out at gunpoint. Few Chinese Christians dared defend them. Many, in any case, joined the communist authorities in denouncing foreign missionaries as agents of Western imperialism. Presumably that was the only hope they had of surviving, whatever the truth of the charge. The effect of the expulsion of missionaries was that the Chinese churches, for the short respite they experienced before serious persecution began, were forced to become indigenous churches almost overnight. Much the same was true in Indonesia in 1949, with the creation of the independent republic, and in North Korea. In some countries independence led to a severe curtailing of missionary activity but not complete withdrawal. In Egypt, for example, the disastrous Franco-British intervention in Suez in 1956 led to the expulsion of French and British missionaries but not Americans. In Iran, schools and colleges run by missionary societies were taken over by the state. In India the restraints were not so much legislative as cultural and administrative. Religious freedom was enshrined in India's new constitution, but there was abiding suspicion of Christianity from the Hindu majority, partly because Christianity had made its most dramatic inroads among low-caste Indians. And above and beyond the question of religion *per se*, there was also suspicion of Westerners. Permits for residence were granted to Western missionaries only if they could demonstrate that no Indian was able to do their job. But in most of Africa, despite lingering suspicion of foreign missionaries, the missionary societies were able to remain active beyond the granting of independence. This was true even in Algeria, where independence came only after a long and bloody civil war.

At some point in the 1950s and 1960s, for much of Africa and Asia, then, the concept of the 'missionary movement' ceased to be relevant, and it is more to the point to speak of autonomous churches or provinces of world-wide communions. The united churches of south India and north India may have had overseas (especially British) clergy and workers into the 1970s, but they were a rapidly decreasing proportion. The Anglican archbishop of Uganda, Leslie Brown, an Englishman, assumed that, in the run-up to independence, his responsibility was to ensure the transition to an all-Ugandan church leadership. Once the organization of the new autonomous province was fully in place, three years after independence was granted in 1962, he resigned his see and returned to England. Similar steps were taken in most of the former British colonies. National denominations came into being, keeping constitutional links with 'parent' churches mainly through the various world organizations such as the Lutheran World Federation, the World Alliance of Reformed Churches, the Anglican Communion and, of course, the WCC. The Catholic Church had long anticipated this process, with the formation of formal jurisdictions under a church leadership that, by the 1950s, was increasingly indigenous. By 1962 there were 69 indigenous bishops in Africa and Asia. Under the pontificate of Pius XII, the Italian majority in the College of Cardinals disappeared. Thirty-two new cardinals, many from non-European parts of the Church, were created in 1945 alone.

Thus by the 1980s, just as decolonization was almost complete, the Christianity of the 'Third World' had come of age and cast off its European shackles. This was effectively the end of the transmission of Christianity from Europe to empire envisaged by the nineteenth-century missionary movement. It was not the end of Western involvement altogether. 'Parent' denominations continued to send financial and other material resources to the new churches. Many mission stations remained in place, run now by local churches or sometimes still by their original societies. In the 1970s some former colonies saw arguments about the issue of a proposed 'moratorium' on help from overseas, but in most cases this came to nothing. It could often now be packaged under the more general heading of 'aid'. Quite apart from the innumerable independent churches springing up everywhere (and especially in Africa), however, the withdrawal of Western agencies stimulated the evolution of new forms of Christian belonging and worship even within the shell of the older denominations. And there were profound arguments to be had about the lasting impact of Western theology. What would Christianity look like when embedded fully in local cultures, with church organizations led by local leaders? Arguments ran – and still run – in Africa, for example, about Christianity's relationship to features of traditional African culture on which European missionaries had always frowned, such as polygamy and the role of the 'ancestor' cult. But as time passed, increasingly it became clear that the African churches had themselves achieved precisely the fusion of African culture and Christianity that had for so long eluded the missionaries. And so there were other arguments to be had about mission. Might African and Asian Christianity, for example, be the means of re-evangelizing the West? Such an idea would have seemed preposterous in the early years of the century, but it was not by the 1980s. The growth of substantial minority Asian and African communities in the West from the 1950s and 1960s was one source of renewed or continuing links to the original 'sending' countries. But they were also a useful base for African and Asian evangelists.

Towards a global church

The creation of the WCC meant that the ecumenical movement was not a pet project of Europeans and Americans for long. As autonomous national churches came into being in the years of decolonization, many of them joined the WCC as full members, swelling its numbers. The number of Orthodox members increased, too, so that by the 1960s the WCC could truly claim to be a representative body for worldwide Christianity – but minus the Catholic Church. This was potentially a crippling omission, of course. As the single largest sector of world Christianity, and as the one fully worldwide communion, the absence of the Catholic Church from the ecumenical movement was a severe limitation. All changed with the Second Vatican Council. In the conciliar decree *Unitatis Redintegratio*, issued by Paul VI in 1964, the Catholic Church committed itself to work alongside 'separated brethren' in pursuit of Christian unity: the Council 'moved by a desire for the restoration of unity among all the followers of Christ … wishes to set before all Catholics certain helps, pathways and methods by which they too can respond to this divine summons and grace'. This did not mean abandoning the basic Catholic position that ultimately church unity had to be achieved through communion with Rome, but it did represent a commitment to common action and joint discussion with other Christian communities. Taken with the Council's teaching on the Church (see Chapter 7), it signalled a movement from an ecclesiology of Catholic triumphalism to one of internal humility and openness. From then on it was no longer possible to speak of one 'ecumenical movement' separate from the Catholic Church, but of two distinct foci within the one ecumenical movement, namely the WCC and the Catholic Church.

In practice it was always recognized that the WCC was too large and unwieldy to act itself as a mechanism of ecumenical negotiation. That was to be undertaken in three distinct ways. The first was by stealth, through cooperation on issues of mutual concern in various commissions within the WCC – in effect the 'Life and Work' strand. It was inevitable that issues of social justice, which had been to the fore even in the pre-Second World War conferences, would become a central preoccupation of a WCC that included churches from across the post-colonial world. But this was to lead the WCC into controversial matters. Its Programme to Combat Racism, begun in 1969, for example, led to sharp allegations of left-wing bias from political conservatives. The impression was underlined by a succession of WCC grants made to South African liberation movements in the 1970s, ostensibly for humanitarian aid but – as was immediately pointed out – with the effect of freeing resources for the purchase of guns. Awareness of the social, political and economic needs of the developing world also emerged in the 'Justice, Peace and the Integrity of Creation' initiative in the late 1980s.

A second method of ecumenical progress, also fostered by the WCC itself, was direct negotiation under the aegis of the Faith and Order Commission. This was a 'multilateral' (that is, 'multi-church') process of study and discussion around issues of central ecclesiological concern. To date, the greatest achievement of Faith and Order has been the multilateral report *Baptism, Eucharist and Ministry* (*BEM*, also commonly called the 'Lima' document) in 1982. *BEM* summed up significant elements of theological convergence on questions contested between participating churches. It did not represent full agreement on all these questions and could not serve by itself therefore as the basis of proposals for church unity, but it was a remarkable step forward in agreement, given the extraordinary range of competing theological positions and of church histories within the WCC. A further multilateral document, *The Nature and Purpose of the Church* (*NPC*), was issued provisionally in 1998, and at the time of writing is still under revision. How gradual and tentative multilateral discussion can be is well illustrated by *NPC*'s subtitle, 'A stage on the way to a common statement'.

The third mechanism of ecumenical negotiation has been bilateral (or at least numerically limited) discussion. Here, since the early 1960s, the breadth of ecumenical engagement has been extraordinary. Virtually any conceivable pairing of major world traditions has occurred in this way – Catholics with Anglicans, Catholics with Methodists, Catholics with Lutherans, Anglicans with Orthodox, and so on. Many of these discussions have been inconclusive, producing impressive theological statements on common points of principle that were counterbalanced by remaining areas of strong division and even by new issues that were largely unforeseen when the dialogue began (such as the ordination of women). But this is not to underestimate their importance. They have often dispelled mutual suspicion and formed bonds of personal affection that have encouraged common action in other areas. Perhaps the most notable was the *Joint Declaration on the Doctrine of Justification* agreed by the Roman Catholic Church and the Lutheran World Federation in 1999, which led to the removal of the anathemas pronounced against Lutherans and against Catholics in the Reformation era. The use of such concepts as 'the whole people of God', and *koinonia*, or 'communion', across most of these dialogues has raised hopes that something like a genuine ecumenical convergence theologically is under way – a process that can only, in all honesty, be said to be somewhere near its beginning, given the long and painful history of Christian division.

Theological agreement and convergence have been crucial in a number of instances in which churches have indeed united or have been drawn into closer relations through agreements of intercommunion, or 'full communion'. A number of church union schemes have succeeded within individual countries, such as the United Reformed Church in Britain in 1972 (Presbyterian and Congregationalist) and the Uniting Church in Australia in 1977 (Presbyterian, Congregationalist and Methodist). The Leuenberg agreement of 1973 drew together Reformed and Lutheran churches from across Europe in a common agreement on 'pulpit and table fellowship' – in effect, interchangeability of ministries. A concordat between Episcopalians and Lutherans in the United States established a relationship of full communion in 1999. In 1992 the 'Porvoo' agreement was concluded between the Anglican churches of the British Isles and the Lutheran churches of Scandinavia and the Baltic, again establishing a relationship of full communion. There were significant failures, too, such as the Anglican–Methodist scheme of 1972, and uniting church schemes in Ghana and Nigeria. The record of inter-church agreement is very much a mixed one, then.

But overall the record of the ecumenical movement, as the century drew to a close, was a story of great expectations cruelly dashed. This was only partially offset by a few striking achievements and much patient groundwork. There can be no doubt that the founders of the WCC had exaggerated confidence in the ecumenical future. Apart from strategic uncertainties about how best to pursue the goal of church unity, there have been new occasions of division underestimated at the outset of the movement. That seems an astonishing thing to say, given the extraordinary depth of mutual ignorance and suspicion that existed between many churches at the beginning of the century. But the creation of the ecumenical movement in its first decades was the work of enthusiastic, visionary Christian internationalists buoyed up by confidence that the prospect of common witness and even full church unity would carry people along with them. It was never going to be so simple. Moreover the world church was itself constantly developing. The WCC was an excellent mechanism for churches accustomed to representative practice, with educated leaderships and access to funding. What about the many emergent independent churches in Africa and Asia, and the Pentecostal churches, that were far outstripping many of the older denominations in growth in large parts of the developing world by the 1980s – would they, could they, be included in such a complex body? Would they even be interested? In fact some of them undoubtedly were, and some of the larger and longer-established African independent churches joined the WCC from the mid-1970s, as did some of the larger Pentecostal churches. But this was a sign, not that these newer churches were signing up to the older, Eurocentric vision of ecumenism, but rather that the vision itself was having to change and to expand to embrace insights and experiences well beyond the scope of the early pioneers of the movement.

PART II
1945 TO 1973: THE END OF EMPIRE

CHAPTER 6

Nuclear Powers and Decolonization

The Cold War: a new kind of imperialism

The end of the Second World War brought little immediate relief to Christians, or indeed anyone else. The devastation it had caused was immense, with estimates of around 37 million civilian casualties alone, and a further 25 million military dead. There were millions of displaced people in Europe and Asia. Resettling them took years. Millions more were homeless or jobless or caught in the desperate uncertainty of not knowing whether husbands or sons were alive or not. Hundreds of thousands of prisoners of war on both sides had to be repatriated. German prisoners of war held by the Soviets were still being released back to Germany into the late 1950s, sometimes returning to find wives dead or remarried. Those who had backed the wrong side, or who had been captured when they were commanded to fight to the death, were herded off to Soviet camps or shot. The terrible consequences of German occupation continued to unfold years after the war had ended, with the westward migration of German-speakers from Poland and Czechoslovakia, and the discovery of the true scale and personal tragedy of the Holocaust.

In the Far East the resentment caused by the ruthlessness of the Japanese invasions lingered on, and Japanese treatment of subject peoples – such as the forced recruitment of young women from China, Burma, Korea and elsewhere as prostitutes, or 'comfort women', for the Japanese military – continued to cause controversy 60 years later. More specifically for the Christian Church, in Europe thousands of churches were destroyed or damaged, congregations displaced and church agencies weakened or destroyed, and in Asia mission networks carefully built up over decades were ruined. The effects were deeper psychologically, of course. But trauma was mostly buried, and guilt and complicity were rarely admitted, once the Nuremberg and Tokyo war trials were over. With some exceptions, such as

73

the declaration of war guilt Niemöller and ten other German church leaders issued from Stuttgart in October 1945, churches in all of the areas affected by the war set their faces firmly to the future and to reconstruction. This was to come to seem, to a later generation, a wilful forgetting, a collective amnesia about cowardice, guilt and selfishness. But it was a response conditioned in part at least by the continuing pressure of economic dislocation and suffering and international tension.

The Second World War came to an end not with a comprehensive series of settlements of the kind achieved at Versailles in 1919 but with a stalemate. The unconditional surrender of Germany in May 1945 left two sets of armies facing each other in Europe, the Soviets from the east and the Allies from the west. And there they stayed for the next 45 years. In the Far East, the surrender of Japan in August 1945 after the atomic bombing of Hiroshima and Nagasaki avoided a final conflict on the mainland of Japan itself, but again Allied and Soviet armies surrounded much of the region and occupied parts of it. The history of the next half-century was to be dominated by three resulting 'blocs' – the United States and its allies, the Soviet state and its allies, and China. These were apparently defined by ideology, and so they seemed to anticipate the totalitarian trio of superstates – Oceania, Eurasia and Eastasia – that George Orwell described in his terrifying dystopia, *1984*, published in 1949. But to suppose that the three dominant powers from the late 1940s on were really akin to the utterly centralized and regimented powers of Orwell's novel would be a mistake. The invention of nuclear weaponry massively distorted the balance of military power in favour of the United States until the Soviet Union managed to develop its own in 1949. China did not develop an atomic bomb until 1964. Britain and France meanwhile had done so in 1952 and 1960 respectively. On nuclear power alone, there was never a straightforward, three-cornered 'superpower' balance of force. Moreover all three spheres of influence were to have very different paths of economic development and faced much more serious obstacles to the actual exercise of power over neighbouring states than the Orwellian parallel might suggest.

Thus the Cold War that hung over the international system for over 40 years was an infinitely more complex reality than popular mythology pretended. The United States' claim to global superpower status rested firmly on nuclear power, on technological sophistication and on economic pre-eminence. The Second World War drained America's allies as well as enemies of resources, but boosted the American economy. By 1945 the Gross National Product (GNP) of the United States almost equalled that of the whole of the rest of the world put together. The American economy entered a period of unprecedented stability and growth, which came to an end only in the wake of the oil crisis of 1973–74. American participation in the United Nations contrasted with American isolationism after the First World War. The combination of commitment to liberal economics and the espousal of the principle of freedom seemed to many Americans to capture the 'American way', and it had been proved to work in the extreme test of war. The Truman Doctrine – support for 'free peoples who are resisting attempted subjugation by armed minorities or outside pressure' – encapsulated America's self-perceived mission to the world. It was all summed up in the phrase, 'leader of the free world'. And it was illustrated in armed intervention in Korea in 1950–53 and Vietnam in 1965–73, as well as in readiness to face down the creation of Soviet missile bases in Cuba in 1962. Religion had its part to play in American doctrine, partly through Christian resistance to communism and partly through the public theology of freedom and personal responsibility that many American church leaders (such as the evangelist Billy Graham) espoused throughout this period. But there were many checks and balances to American power. Western Europe, with the help of American money at first, rapidly recovered from the effects of war and also entered a period of prolonged prosperity. European states had their national interests to consider and did not always dance to American tunes. Decolonization immensely complicated the world political system, adding a whole raft of newly independent countries to the UN.

The area of Soviet influence was more easily identified. The 'Iron Curtain' (Churchill's phrase) that fell over Eastern Europe after 1945 matched the limits of the Soviet armies' advance. Aspirations for national independence in Czechoslovakia, Poland, Hungary and elsewhere were soon crushed, and puppet communist regimes installed. The Warsaw Pact of Soviet-aligned countries did not formally come into being until 1955, but it existed in practice long before then. Soviet hegemony in Eastern Europe was reaffirmed in a series of armed interventions, in Poland and Czechoslovakia in 1948, in Hungary in 1956, and in Czechoslovakia again in 1968, to name but the most notorious instances. To these one must add the failed siege of West Berlin in 1948–49 and perhaps Soviet support for the decision to build the Berlin Wall in 1961. But the very frequency of these interventions tells us something about the inherent instability of the Soviet regime. That was underlined by economic stagnation from the early 1960s on and by the inability to catch up with the West technologically – a failure masked by the dazzling successes of the Soviet space programme. Throughout this period, both in the West and in the East, politics thrived on a perception of mutual threat. The readiness of the Soviet Union to supply arms to revolutionary movements throughout the world, and its later intervention in Afghanistan, sustained this myth. But in practice there was little real substance to it, at least in regard to Western Europe. Possibly the nuclear threat was neutralized by both sides' possession of a nuclear arsenal, but the acronym 'MAD' for 'Mutually Assured Destruction', the doctrine of nuclear deterrence, wonderfully captured the absurdity lying behind it. Even without the nuclear threat, it is likely that there would have been little real incentive for the Soviet armies to attack the West. Nevertheless the fiction of Soviet expansionism was potent. It had, furthermore, a clear anti-religious dimension. Fear of communism remained a powerful motive in Vatican policy until the 1960s, not least because of the strength of the Italian Communist Party in this period. As one papal diplomat put it, 'You can say what you like about the divinity of Christ but if, in the remotest village of Sicily, you vote Communist, your excommunication will arrive the next day.'[1] But this fear was surely exaggerated. Communism was not a very powerful force in democratic politics in most European countries. It was tainted by the terror of the Stalinist era, which was famously condemned by Nikita Khrushchev at the 1956 Party Congress, but it was also tainted by the action in Hungary in 1956. Moreover revolutionary movements across the world, and especially newly independent former colonies, were just as adept at exploiting Soviet as American support for their own ends.

About China there is perhaps less to be said in this period, if only because the communist success in 1948–49 led to a period in which internal reform and the consolidation of the power of Chairman Mao produced a certain isolationism. Certainly the new regime was very touchy about its borders, occupied Tibet in 1950 and supported communist movements in North Korea and in Vietnam. But its tense relationship with the Soviet Union, which developed almost into open conflict in the late 1950s and remained problematic until the 1980s, demonstrated that, for all the ideological commonality, at root more atavistic elements of nationalism were at play. The economic policy of Mao was disastrous in the extreme, based as it was on an attempt to dismantle a complex society and drive it back to peasant production. Millions starved as a result. The stability of the regime could be maintained only by the most savage repression, brought to a peak from 1966 in the infamous 'Cultural Revolution', when Mao used the most youthful, extreme elements of the party to purge the older party leadership. Christians suffered terribly throughout this period.

The world was always much less amenable to control than any of the three superpowers liked to think. If there was a common vision linking all three, despite profound differences, it was a repudiation of imperialism. All three states had been born in a rejection of imperial power. And yet all three also acted to all intents and purposes like an imperial power. All three used military force on occasion and certainly sought to build suitable alliances with neighbouring states to protect their interests. In the case of America and the Soviet Union in particular, influence was sustained by the gift of money and arms. So this was a form of imperialism, even if it disavowed the name.

The end of empires

If the Cold War established a new form of imperialism, a hidden but no less real form, it definitely saw the end of the old European empires. There was no one pattern according to which this happened. Even to use the term 'decolonization' is to some extent misleading, since there was never a single movement as such. What can be said with some assurance is that none of the old European colonial powers willingly gave up on empire – not even Britain, which came to pride itself on having presided over a mostly bloodless transition from empire to a commonwealth of independent states. Essentially European empire had been a monumental game of bluff. European states had never had the military muscle to impose their will for long on subject states if those states resolutely resisted them. The colonial ruling elites were small in relation to the populations they governed, and the territories they administered were huge. Imperialism rested on a kind of illusion, namely that the European powers did have the means to impose their will on their subject peoples. In reality it depended on the willingness of colonial peoples finally to accept European rule. All this collapsed in the middle of the twentieth century, not least because the policies of development, education and proselytizing embraced by Europeans in the artificial territories they had created brought into being precisely the kind of independent, national consciousness that could challenge European hegemony. Moreover none of the three new 'superpowers' were willing to defend European imperialism – that was the sobering lesson of the ill-fated French and British intervention in Suez in 1956, which failed for lack of real political will and of American support.

The first sizeable part of empire to go was British India, split up into India, East and West Pakistan and Ceylon (Sri Lanka) in 1948. The French lost Vietnam and Cambodia after a particularly bitter eight-year war in 1953. The Dutch lost Indonesia in 1949, though they had never fully recovered it after the Japanese invasion. Territories in Africa began to become independent a little later, in the 1950s and 1960s, beginning with Egypt in 1954, the Sudan in 1956 and Ghana in 1957. The British prime minister Harold Macmillan's famous 'winds of change' speech, delivered in South Africa in 1960 – 'Whether we like it or not, this growth of national consciousness is a political fact' – was as much a reflection on a process already under way as a sign of political intention. France was engaged in a vicious struggle against Algerian nationalism from 1954 until 1962, but the bitterness and the protracted nature of the conflict there was as much as anything due to the fact that Algeria was no longer strictly a colony, but (in theory) an integral part of France, with a population of over a million French-born civilians, around 10 per cent of the population. Portuguese colonies in Africa did not finally achieve independence until the mid-1970s, after the 'Carnation Revolution' of 1974 finally overthrew the military regime of Antonio Salazar in Portugal. In many cases independence was granted reluctantly and after some violence.

The role of the churches in this process was not above reproach. Though some church leaders welcomed the abandonment of empire, many European Christians frankly shared assumptions about fitness to rule that made it very difficult to let go of dominion. The end of empire divided Christians just as much as anyone else. Decolonization forced change on the churches, and the more far-sighted embraced this willingly, recognizing its pace and direction. Already by 1950, for example, the newly formed Australian Council of Churches was sending its general secretary on a fact-finding mission to Indonesia, deliberately seeking to build relationships with churches which found themselves part of a newly independent (and mainly Muslim) country. The Australian churches increasingly turned their gaze towards their Asian neighbours and away from Britain.

Though it brought freedom to formerly subject peoples, the end of empire created as many problems as it solved. The birth of the independent state of Israel in 1948 solved the problems of the Jewish diaspora and the displacement of European survivors of the Holocaust, but it raised the problem of Palestinian autonomy. In many African states the artificial nature of national boundaries contained long-term instabilities as rival peoples began to compete for political power. The tensions this produced led to appalling suffering when they broke into open conflict, as in Nigeria between 1967 and 1970, when the southeastern province of Biafra tried to declare itself independent. Well over a million people died in that conflict, through starvation or military action. That was just a sign of the troubles ahead for Africa. White imperialism and racism were not altogether obliterated in any case. Both in Rhodesia and in South Africa white minority regimes clung on for almost another generation. The proliferation of independent states across the world multiplied – needless to say – the possibility of new alliances, and therefore complicated international relations. The term 'Third World' came into common currency, against the 'First' and 'Second' worlds of the capitalist West and the communist East. As the superpowers played out their rivalries on a global scale, time and again conflict in seemingly remote parts of the world raised the awful prospect of regional instability and even (dimly) another world war.

There was another hidden dimension to decolonization, too. European empire had contained and controlled religious difference, just as much as it had tacitly encouraged or openly promoted Christianity throughout the colonies. It had certainly not done so out of a benign regard for the traditions of other religions, but simply as one more aspect of rule. The British and French in North and West Africa had had to come to terms with areas of Muslim domination, and restrained Christian missionaries accordingly. Likewise in India and in the Far East colonial administrators had often had to rein in the enthusiasm of missionary societies. Local interfaith relations were delicate, and experienced administrators were usually wary of raising tension. Once empire was gone, not only were the Christian churches forced to try to redefine themselves as authentically national and indigenous, but new associations between other faiths and national sentiment were given much greater scope. In newly independent Burma, for example, the government positively encouraged a resurgence of Buddhism and withdrew from the British Commonwealth of nations. A policy of official toleration of Christianity was put in place, but combined with discouragement to foreign missionaries. In 1961 Buddhism was declared the state religion. Buddhism also underwent a revival in Sri Lanka, sanctioned by the government, which took over most of the former Christian schools. The Arab world was no longer realistically a Christian mission field either. Nor was India or Indonesia. Increasingly the more strident form of 'Wahhabi' Islam began to gain ground in parts of the Middle East, including Saudi Arabia, as Muslim Brotherhoods – first established in Egypt in the 1920s – spread, often in the face of official government disapproval. The partition of India, strongly resisted by Gandhi and accepted only with regret by the British, was accompanied by vicious Muslim–Hindu violence and led to the creation of bitter religious as well as national state rivalry. Decolonization created the conditions for the renewal of distinct ethnic and religious identities, and that was bound to change the context within which Christian churches had to operate.

None of this is to utter a word of regret about the end of empire. The deliberate conquest and exploitation of one people by another is never justifiable on Christian principles, and the European churches had a poor record when it came to condemning the barbarism of much imperial policy. But the alteration in circumstances between the 1930s and the 1960s was astonishing. From a position of seeming supremacy, bolstered by governing systems centred on Europe and America, the churches of the West had almost completely lost their institutional dominance in large parts of the world. They remained hugely influential, partly through their relative financial strength, and a subtle form of colonialism remained in the relations of dependence created by aid to the Third World. But this was a shadow of the influence and the confidence that imperialism had given Western Christianity. The change was mental as well as actual. For, just at the very point when the process of decolonization was reaching its natural terminus, changes in Western society sharply undermined the confidence of the European churches. Suddenly they had to think in terms of a global Church, of formerly dependent Christians as true brothers and sisters in Christ, and of other religions as serious competitors in the world of truth. The consequences of this sea-change in world Christianity were still working themselves out at the beginning of the twenty-first century.

Christianity, liberation and oppression

Looking back at this period from the beginning of the twenty-first century, it is tempting to suppose that decolonization was the outcome above all of a resurgence of nationalism, and quite distinct from the Marxist-Leninist ideology of revolution espoused by many on the left. The collapse of Soviet communism has perhaps distorted our view of the past. Few independence movements were wholly home-grown. Instead they were a kind of hybrid of revolutionary ideology imported ultimately from left-wing circles in Europe and America, local and regional identities, cultural resentment and religion. The role Christianity played varied from country to country. Guerrilla movements of the left – especially those supported by the Soviet system – generally excluded religion altogether. Such were the various movements in Latin America and Africa aided by the charismatic Marxist leader Che Guevara in the early 1960s. When revolutionary left-wing governments were formed in various Latin American and African countries, such as in Guatemala in 1951–54, usually they reluctantly accepted the existence of the Christian Church. But there were certainly revolutionary movements which included some Christian elements. In South Africa, for example, opposition to apartheid increasingly drew on the support of liberal white church people as well as the black-led churches, in the face of the sustained support for apartheid offered by the Dutch Reformed Church. The ecumenical body for South Africa, the South Africa Council of Churches (which, however, did not include the Dutch Reformed Church), from its inauguration in 1968 was drawn openly into the conflict with racism, and indeed arose out of it. As its 'Message to the People of South Africa' proclaimed, 'excluding barriers of ancestry, race, nationality, language and culture have no rightful place in the inclusive brotherhood of Christian disciples'. Christianity here and elsewhere found common cause with social and political radicalism, and it was assisted by the 'opening to the left' encouraged in Catholic circles under John XXIII and Paul VI.

Though not advocating the overthrow of a government system, the civil rights movement in America from 1955 to 1968 was another example of a movement for radical change which drew in Christian activists, particularly the Baptist minister Martin Luther King, Jr. The intellectual background to the civil rights agitation was surely the prominence of language about human rights in the work of bodies such as the United Nations and the World Council of Churches. President John F. Kennedy spoke of the need for a 'New Frontier' in American life, a phrase resonant with hope for Americans. But Christianity – particularly the Christianity of the black-led churches in America, with its emotional intensity and its profound sense of eschatological expectation of the coming of God's kingdom on earth – also played an important part. Like King himself, many of the civil rights leaders were heavily involved in local churches, and the black-led churches provided a means of organization and a medium of communication that facilitated the various forms of direct action adopted by the movement. Even the rhetorical style of the civil rights leaders was often modelled on that of Christian revivalism. King's famous 1963 address, 'I have a dream', drew its peroration, 'Let freedom ring', from a speech delivered by the black pastor Archibald Carey to the Republican Party convention in 1952, which in turn quoted – as did King – the first verse of Samuel Francis Smith's patriotic hymn 'America', written over a century before. The non-violent action espoused by King and others drew on the example of Gandhi, but Gandhi was also inspired by the teaching of Jesus.

The process of decolonization thus went hand in hand with the emergence of a new language of rights, and with it new conceptions of social and political liberation. These were incredibly diverse, since they developed in widely differing contexts. In much of the Third World, attention was inevitably focused first and foremost on independence, and so the general theme of liberation masked significant strategic and tactical differences across the world – especially where there were still wars of liberation to be fought against those colonial regimes holding on stubbornly to power. In the 'First World', the West, however, liberation was itself beginning to acquire a wide range of meanings as Western society underwent a radical internal transformation in the late 1950s and 1960s. On the back of unprecedented consumer affluence, new youth movements began to emerge which seized on the mood for change and cast the mainstream churches not as expressions of a human yearning for freedom and fulfilment but as suffocating elements of the political establishment.

The 1960s was a decade of immense social upheaval, a near-revolution socially in the West. Just to list prominent features of this is to identify a series of things that by the end of the century would seem relatively unproblematic – legalization of abortion, ease of divorce, legalization of homosexual relations, the widespread use of contraception, feminism and women in the workplace, the recreational use of drugs such as cannabis, cocaine and heroin, and anti-racism legislation. It was no accident that these marked a profound change in the way society regarded the nature of personal and social relations, and an increasing distance between traditional Christian morality and the public expectations the state was prepared to uphold. The pace and extent of change varied enormously from one country to another. Homosexuality was legalized in Poland as early as 1932, but not in Ireland until 1993. Religion played its part in all this, but, as the Polish example shows, not a decisive part, since one might have expected the strength of Catholicism there to have had a retarding effect comparable to the situation in Ireland. Abortion was legalized in Protestant Sweden on limited grounds in 1938, with the grounds expanded in 1946 and 1963; it was not legalized in Catholic Italy until 1978. So religion was not insignificant. Its social status in Western Europe was certainly questioned, however, as membership leeched away from the mainstream churches in the 1960s, having held up relatively well since the end of the war. Even in America, while churchgoing remained much more popular than in Europe, the numbers actively involved in the traditional denominations began to contract. For many people in the West this was a time of personal liberation, whatever they thought of political liberation or social revolution. But political revolution was not far behind. As the 1960s drew to a close, there was serious if sporadic upheaval in many Western states, especially among students from the expanding sector of higher education.

Student-led unrest posed little serious threat to Western governments, with the exception perhaps of France. But it captured a mood that had turned decisively against the institutions and people who were associated indelibly in people's minds with the imperial past. Europeans may well have underestimated the seismic importance of their loss of empire. It was not just that a whole host of newly independent nations came into being – some 60 in all in Africa, for example – with all the possibilities for new alliances and new patterns of trade and cultural interchange that went with this. Every achieved act of independence marked a new national possibility, a new historical trajectory for a free people. Decolonization came about because of Europe's internal conflict and facilitated the rise of new superpowers. But in the process the world became infinitely more complex. The loss of empire changed everything, including the former colonial powers' own status and authority in the world, and the national myths and social institutions that had sustained their own societies and governing structures had fallen into disrepute. They were faced with the task of reconstructing their place in the world. They began to do this in a variety of different ways – through new networks of trade, for example, including the European Common Market, or the 'European Union', as it was later called, through common action at the United Nations (though this was often problematic, given the Soviet veto in the UN Security Council), and through what was sometimes a painful process of internal self-examination and reform. For the Western churches, this only served to underline the importance of the new ecumenical instruments, especially the WCC, though it also encouraged the creation of new associations of churches.

CHAPTER 7

The Catholic Church: Inner Transformation

The popes and change

The history of the Catholic Church since 1945 is dominated by the Second Vatican Council, which met from 1962 to 1965 and was a revolution in the culture and ethos of the Church. It is tempting to see all that came before it as a 'pre-history' of stagnation repudiated by the Council. Such a view – all too common – casts Pope Pius XII, who died in 1958, as the 'problem' to which John XXIII, his successor, was the solution. That would hardly be true to the complexity of the case, however, though it has an element of truth. It would neglect the forward-looking elements of Pius's papacy and exaggerate the competence and planning of John XXIII. It would also side-step what looks much the more interesting question than that of papal personality, and that is, simply, 'What *was* in fact the problem to which Vatican II was the solution?' Here we are back with the question of international politics and the end of empire. Just as decolonization gradually forced on the Catholic and Protestant churches the need to disengage European clerical elites from the indigenous churches of the former colonies, so the emergence of a new kind of international politics, based on new regional alliances, on the rivalry between the superpowers, and on the new international agencies such as the UN, also forced the Catholic Church to confront a series of issues that its highly centralized Italian bureaucracy had never previously encountered. What was needed was an abandonment of the habit of thinking of policy as formulated centrally and imposed on an acquiescent Church. Greater flexibility was required and greater awareness of the diverse needs of Catholic churches across the world.

The tragedy of Pius XII's reign, in retrospect, is that he has never been given the credit for the many significant steps he took towards this goal. He presided over the development of an indigenous Catholic clergy across the world and helped to ensure that the transition from a mentality of overseas mission to a commitment to the local church was carried through relatively smoothly. With his two consistories of 1946 and 1953, the cardinalate became truly international. His successor was to be elected by a conclave more representative of the global church than ever before. A number of important encyclicals marked a new openness to liturgical and even theological change. *Divino Afflante Spiritu* (1943) commended the scholarly study of biblical languages and was a cautious endorsement of critical techniques in biblical scholarship. In *Mystici Corporis* (1943) the mystical dimension of the Church was emphasized as a modification of the common Catholic conception of the Church as a perfect society on earth. In *Mediator Dei* (1947) Pius adopted one of the central concerns of the liturgical movement (the movement for renewal of Catholic worship), when he commended the active participation of the people in the Mass, including their reception of communion (since formerly many ordinary Catholics had refrained from actually receiving communion during the Mass). In 1951 he restored the full liturgy of the Vigil of Easter, the highpoint of the Church's liturgical year that had fallen into abeyance in earlier centuries.

These were all significant developments. But they have been overshadowed by Pius's inability to adapt the method by which papal policy was conceived and implemented to suit the changing demands faced by the Church. An imaginative and highly intelligent man, he was also a control freak and supremely conservative. His hostility to communism knew no bounds. These were years of bitter Catholic opposition to the communist regimes of Eastern Europe. Even in the West, Pius discouraged any contact between Catholics and communists, or indeed democratic socialists, and stifled the development of left-leaning Catholic politics. He suppressed the worker-priests' movement in France. Encouraged by Cardinal Suhard, Archbishop of Paris during the war, this arose from the belief – common across the industrialized world – that the working class were alienated from the Church and that priests had to become workers in order to bridge the gap. Only some 100 or so in a French church of 50,000 clergy were worker-priests. It was an original if marginal experiment, which attracted attention way out of proportion to its practical impact. The young Karol Wojtyla, the future Pope John Paul II, travelled to France and Belgium in 1946 to meet worker-priests for himself. But the movement's associations with trade unionism were too much for Pius, and he disbanded it in 1953.

However much he may have encouraged specific new themes in Catholic theology through his encyclicals, Pius feared too much concession to progressive thought. A further encyclical, *Humani Generis* (1950), was subtitled 'Some false opinions which threaten to undermine Catholic doctrine', and condemned a host of contemporary theological trends which he believed

led to doctrinal relativism. Words were backed up by action. A rising generation of Catholic theologians, including such luminaries as Henri de Lubac
and Marie-Dominique Chenu, were stripped of their teaching authority
and driven into silence. It was a throwback to the anti-Modernist campaign.
Faced with the stark choice of obedience or excommunication, most bided
their time. Yves Congar confided in his diary: 'Today I am afraid that the
absoluteness and simplicity of obedience is drawing me into a complicity
with this abhorrent system of secret denunciations which is the essential
condition of the "Holy Office".'[1]

All this suggests, however, that Pius's papal policy is best seen not so
much as a form of ecclesiastical tyranny – which is how some dissident
theologians saw it – but as a natural development of the ultramontane
Catholic culture of the nineteenth century. It was committed to mission
and to liturgical renewal. But it was also based on the premise that the
Catholic Church's attitude to the modern world should be one of suspicion
and of separate development. The Church was a perfect realm of its own,
presided over by an infallible autocrat. No concessions were to be made to
cooperation with Protestant Christians or with political and social movements that shared some limited aims with the Catholic Church. Pius toyed
with the idea of calling an ecumenical council, but then issued *Humani
Generis* without one, and declared on his own infallible authority in 1950
(the first and so far only exercise of this power since it was defined at the
First Vatican Council in 1870) that the Virgin Mary's body had not suffered
decay after death but had been assumed with her soul into heaven. *Munifi-
centissimus Deus* made belief in the doctrine of the Assumption *de fide* – 'of
the faith' – that is, obligatory for Catholics. This was troubling for many
Catholic theologians, since there was no biblical evidence for the doctrine,
and the tradition of the Church was divided on it. The centenary of the
definition of the dogma of the Immaculate Conception of Mary by Pope
Pius IX – 1954 – was declared a Marian year, a year of special liturgical
celebration dedicated to Mary.

In the last years of his life, Pius was a sick man, attended by a fraudulent
physician. He died in October 1958. His reputation was later to be overshadowed by two events. One was the summoning of the Second Vatican
Council by his successor. The other was the furore which burst upon the
Catholic Church in 1963 with Rolf Hochhuth's play *The Representative*, in
which Pius was depicted as a craven sympathizer of the Nazis. This was far
from the truth, despite some moral ambiguity in Pius's record. But Pius had
had a long papacy – some 19 years – and on his death was regarded rightly
as an energetic and great leader of the Church.

The conclave to elect his successor was one of the longest of the modern era, but the choice fell eventually (after 11 ballots) on Angelo Roncalli. It was a surprising choice. Unlike the minor aristocrat he succeeded, Roncalli (born in 1881) came from a large peasant family in Bergamo in northern Italy and had none of the sophistication and polish of his predecessor. No one had thought of him as a likely pope. He had served as an army chaplain in the First World War before becoming a papal diplomat. During the Second World War he was apostolic delegate – in effect, the Vatican representative – to Turkey and Greece, and helped thousands of Jewish refugees to escape from Europe. Made patriarch of Venice and cardinal in 1953, most observers thought he was too old to become pope. Roncalli was fond of emphasizing his peasant background, his simplicity and lack of formal education. This was a little disingenuous. He was evidently an intelligent and sometimes shrewd man. But he was not forceful in the style of his two predecessors. Many thought that was fortunate. But it meant that he sent out sometimes conflicting signals, leading some to think he was more progressive, and others to think he was more conservative than he really was. On dogma – the truths the Church proclaimed about the Christian faith – he was indeed conservative. But he had long before embraced a view of collegiality – the collective authority of the assembled bishops of the Church rather than of the pope acting alone – that in turn was to transform the Church's understanding of the nature of its own authority and to make him truly progressive in church affairs.

On his election he took the name John XXIII. He announced almost immediately three significant initiatives: the summoning of a synod of Roman diocesan clergy, the establishment of a commission to revise the Canon Law, and, most important of all, the calling of an ecumenical council to address the problems of the Church in the modern world. The spirit of the Council was to be pastoral rather than legislative. In other words, it was not to try to define and impose the will of the pope on the Church, or of the Church on the world, but to consider what the implications of change in the world were for the Catholic Church. This emphasis on pastoral care fitted exactly John's image of his own office and his humility. He was crowned pope with all of the trappings of the papal monarchy, including the fans of ostrich plumes and the tiara, but in manner and attitude he was far from behaving like a monarch. There were tensions within the Curia, the papal court, over what his real intentions were. It was difficult to say he had a policy as such, though formulating policy was in any event difficult given the resistance he encountered from leading Vatican officials. John's reign will be forever associated with the Council he called, but in fact many of the decisive changes in the Church's organization and life emerged after heated debate in the Council itself and not as a result of forward planning on his part.

Even his encyclicals do not quite add up to a consistent whole. *Ad Petrum Cathedrum*, issued in 1959, reiterated the traditional Roman line of hostility to communism and insisted on the well-established understanding of church unity as conformity to the Catholic Church. More momentous was *Mater et Magistra* (1961), which used the term 'socialization' approvingly and endorsed the development of the welfare state. *Pacem in Terris* (1963) pushed further the formulation of this 'opening to the left'. It distinguished between error and people who err, and made the perhaps unexceptionable point – except that it was not widely accepted in Catholic circles at that time – that systems of belief that were in error on fundamental points might nevertheless have some acceptable outcomes.

The tone of *Pacem in Terris* was positive, optimistic, world-affirming. But a year before, in his Apostolic Constitution (a solemn decree) *Veterum Sapientia*, John had confounded advocates of liturgical change and commended the use of Latin. All the same, taken together these statements signalled a new spirit. They were cautious but they were not focused defensively on the difficulties of the Church. A further symbol of that spirit of openness was John's developing of diplomatic links with Moscow, including an exchange of Christmas greetings with Nikita Khrushchev, the Soviet leader, in 1962. By then, John had effected a basic shift in Catholic attitudes to politics. In place of the absolute hostility to communism that had marked Vatican policy since 1917, John now emphasized the distinction between the religious jurisdiction of the Church and its role in public affairs. By implication Catholics were free to choose which party they supported. It is no surprise that this shift was deeply unwelcome to many Vatican bureaucrats and to conservative Catholics, and that rumours were to circulate after his death – completely unfounded – that John had in fact been a freemason, in an attempt to discredit his legacy.

John died of stomach cancer in 1963, after just one session of the Council. Giovanni Battista Montini, born in 1897, was elected after a short conclave to be his successor. He had been widely tipped as a future pope for years. Like John's predecessors, Montini (Paul VI) was from a noble family and had had a career of distinction in Vatican diplomacy and administration. But he was never a mere bureaucrat. He was a man of breadth of mind and great mental agility. Unlike the rough and ready jollity of John, there was something a little feline in Montini's ability to discern opportunities for pursuing more forward-looking policies than Pius XII's officials could countenance. He had risky theological friendships in the freeze that set in after *Humani Generis*, and one young English priest, a future archbishop, was taken to one side in Rome in 1953 and told by a cardinal that Montini was 'the most dangerous man in Rome'. Why was this so? He did not have John's strong pastoral instincts. He was fastidious and reserved, and gained a reputation (unfairly, in fact) in his last years for a certain querulous humourlessness. There was nothing in his personality to suggest danger. But there was in his views. More than anyone else among upper echelons of Vatican diplomats under Pius XII – more so even than Angelo Roncalli himself – Montini was aware that the Catholic Church had to change. And he had the political skills to ensure that it did. He was thus the perfect successor to John in the midst of the Council.

In his opening address to the second session of the Council, just three months after his election, Paul expressed complete continuity in spirit with John, when he restated the aims of the Council as the renewal of the Church, dialogue with the modern world and the search for unity with other Christians. When the Council divided over the question of collegiality, with some of the bishops and the Vatican bureaucrats resisting the notion of collegial authority in favour of the papal monarchy, Paul adroitly accepted the draft in favour of collegiality, but added a preliminary statement conceding something to the conservatives. This was a typical Pauline fix – it accepted most of what the 'progressives' were after, fundamentally, but had enough caution in it to take the sting out of conservative opposition.

The single most glaring example of Paul's caution was his encyclical on contraception, *Humanae Vitae* (1968). Paul had established a special commission to examine the whole question in the light of traditional Catholic teaching on marriage, and specifically withdrew consideration of the subject from the Council on the grounds that the commission was already at work. But the document that eventually emerged was a strong statement against artificial contraception which overshadowed the shift in Catholic understanding of marriage from something concerned primarily with procreation to something that also involved mutual satisfaction and fulfilment. The encyclical provoked enormous controversy, so much so that Paul did not issue another encyclical in the remaining ten years of his reign.

There were other limits to his willingness to countenance reform. Clerical celibacy was one. Though the Council took note of the provision made for priests to marry in the Greek-rite Catholic churches of the East (the 'Uniate' churches), Paul resisted extending discussion of this question to the remainder of the Church. And he insisted on inserting the title 'Mother of the Church' into the section on Mary in the Council's Dogmatic Constitution on the Church.

Paul's apparent inactivity in his last ten years belied a period of immense change as the influence of the Council spread. There was an increasing sense, as he grew older, that in parts of the Catholic world the results of the

Council ran far beyond what the Council fathers had foreseen or desired. Paul himself did not approve of all that happened. When he died in 1978 it was evident that the Council had changed the Catholic Church from top to bottom. But not all change was good. There was a widespread feeling that too much was changing too quickly.

Vatican II: a revolution in the church?

The idea of an ecumenical council was not a new one. Ever since the First Vatican Council had been interrupted in 1870, from time to time Catholic theologians had mooted the possibility of another council to complete its work. But Vatican II rapidly developed into something much more wide ranging than even Pope John had envisaged. It became clear in the course of the first session that its business was much too comprehensive to be concluded in a matter of months. One of the reasons for this was the growth of the Catholic Church worldwide in the twentieth century. In 1869 some 800 bishops and heads of religious orders had assembled in Rome. Now, in 1962, there were more than three times that number, with several hundred theological and other experts. By the time the Council ended, there were also almost 80 observers specially invited from other Christian communities. With so many present, it was hardly surprising that a wide range of views was heard on the floor of St Peter's. Most of the hard work of the Council was done in the various drafting sessions of the special commissions, but the texts of the conciliar documents then had to be submitted for discussion, and that was when tempers flared. Tensions were particularly acute between the old guard of the Vatican bureaucracy and the more progressive or independent-minded bishops and their experts from Europe, Africa and the Americas. The leader of the conservatives, Cardinal Ottaviani, Secretary of the Holy Office of the papal court, captured perfectly the sense of crisis he and his like felt when he declared, 'I pray to God that I may die before the end of the Council – in that way I can die a Catholic.'[2]

It would be impossible in a short book like this to give a full account of the proceedings of the Council and of the documents it issued. But it is worth highlighting two key documents in particular and then a number of particular themes. The most important document of the Council was the Dogmatic Constitution on the Church, *Lumen Gentium*. Though this repeated traditional doctrines about the Catholic Church, it also contained a number of significant new emphases. It introduced the concept of the 'whole People of God', and made this the leading theme of the Council. The Church was to be seen not just as an ordered hierarchy, a 'command' structure of descending ranks of authority from the pope, but as a whole assembly of the faithful before God, in which the laity also possessed an intrinsic spiritual authority. The language of the 'royal priesthood' of the faithful was used – language more commonly associated with Protestantism. Picking up an image from St Augustine's *The City of God*, *Lumen Gentium* spoke of the Church 'now sojourning on earth as an exile'. This was a very different view from the conventional one of the Church as a perfect society. It suggested that the Church was a mixed body, made up of sinners as well as the righteous and therefore always needing reform and renewal (another common 'Protestant' theme).

The Pastoral Constitution on the Church in the Modern World, *Gaudium et Spes*, complemented this more dynamic and reflective view of the Church with a greater openness to the world. If the Church was a pilgrim people in the world, it had to be open to receive critically developments within the world. It was 'pastoral' inasmuch as it proclaimed the Church's care not only for Catholics but for all peoples. The only explicit condemnation in the document was, tellingly, that of unlimited nuclear warfare. As the Pastoral Constitution began, 'The joys and hopes, the griefs and anxieties of the men of this age, especially those who are poor or in any way afflicted, these too are the joys and hopes, the grief and anxieties of the followers of Christ', for, as it went on, 'nothing genuinely human fails to raise an echo in their hearts'. What followed was an extraordinarily positive, humane evaluation of the Church's relation to human politics, economics and society. Just a few of the subtitles gives a flavour of the document: 'The Interdependence of Person and Society', 'Promoting the Common Good', 'The Excellence of Liberty', 'Reverence for the Human Person'. The document was necessarily short on specific policy. What mattered much more was the suggestion that the true vocation of the Catholic Church was engagement with the world and not withdrawal from it or defence against it.

Open to renewal from within (and so to self-criticism), open to the world around it – this double dynamic found expression in other changes in the policy, constitution and life of the Catholic Church. The Council abandoned the traditional position that 'error has no rights' and endorsed the principle of religious liberty. In its decrees on ecumenism and on the Eastern churches, the Council announced a new understanding of relationships with other Christian communities, which were acknowledged as fellow pilgrims, and opened the way for Catholic involvement in the movement for Christian unity. The Dogmatic Constitution on Divine Revelation, *Dei Verbum*, placed a central emphasis on listening to God's Word. Though it asserted the interdependence of church tradition and Holy Scripture, at the same time it announced a fundamental shift in the understanding of the relationship of the two, with the interpretation of tradition flowing from the authority of Scripture. All of the conciliar documents reflected a move away from a centralized papal monarchy towards a conception of the Church as a 'communion of communions' – a body of local churches held together through the collegiality of the bishops of the Church, with the pope as the first among equals. But the Catholic faithful were to notice the impact of Vatican II above all in the transformation of the liturgy. Now, in the spirit of *Gaudium et Spes*, the Council's document on the liturgy permitted the use of the vernacular as an alternative to Latin. Any cautiousness in the document itself was soon swept aside as Catholic churches throughout the world began to abandon the Latin Mass.

From Rome to the world

It was in Latin America that the most dramatic changes took place in the ten years after the Council. Even before 1962 there were signs of what was to come. In the years after the end of the Second World War, military dictatorships or quasi-fascist regimes were in power in many countries. Catholic opposition to communism often made the church hierarchy sympathetic to the ruling elites. But this was beginning to change. Popular Catholicism was beginning to find more sympathy with liberal or left-wing political movements. The Chilean priest Clotario Blest, as early as the late 1940s, was incurring the wrath of the Chilean hierarchy by his support for the cause of the workers. In the north of Chile, observers noted that various *Bailes* – groups who danced to the Virgin Mary as a mode of prayer – embraced socialist themes. There was even a dance called 'The Marxist-Leninist dance of the *Virgen del Carmen*'. In Brazil a movement of Catholic students by 1960 was calling for the abolition of multi-national capitalist enterprises. Similar movements – small-scale, admittedly – were cropping up all over the continent. Latin American Catholicism remained paternalistic and populist overall. But clergy were finding it impossible to ignore the struggles of the poor, and the Latin American bishops, who held one of the first regional episcopal conferences (CELAM) as early as 1955, were edging towards identification with the political aspirations of the poor. Vatican II gave a fillip to this trend. The difference can be seen in Argentina, Chile and Paraguay. In Argentina, in the final years of the Perón regime in the early 1950s, the Church was drawn into conflict with the regime, as Perón sought to extend his control over education. Arguably the Church's motivation was entirely defensive, seeking to protect the interests of the Church in religious instruction and church schools. In Chile and Paraguay, by contrast, by the late 1960s the Church's opposition to state policies was based on a positive identification with the interests of the poor. In Chile there was even talk of a 'Christian revolution', when the Church formed a temporary alliance with the moderate-left Christian Democrat party. In Paraguay the

Church began a long and difficult struggle with the Stroessner regime over the rights of indigenous peoples.

In 1968 CELAM met at Medellin in Colombia, and endorsed the 'preferential option for the poor' – the policy of deliberate alignment with the struggles of the poor against inequality and injustice. This phrase became the watchword of liberation theology, which emerged out of the efforts of Latin American theologians to construct a theology of positive, practical engagement with the needs of the poor. Encouraged by church leaders such as Archbishop Helder Camara of Olinda and Recife, theologians such as Gustavo Gutierrez and Leonardo Boff pioneered a theology that was both orthodox doctrinally and radical socially, drawing much on Marxism. By the beginning of the 1970s the Catholic Church across Latin America was undergoing a fundamental realignment of its social and political commitments, to the alarm of conservative clergy. This was happening locally as well as nationally, through the 'base ecclesial communities', groups of local Catholic people formed to sustain each other in the struggle against injustice. By the 1970s there were hundreds of thousands in the sprawling cities of Latin America. Social justice was the goal of liberation theology, but its form and its prompting ideas were thoroughly contextual, and therefore distinctively Latin American. Gutierrez, Boff and others were fond of pointing out the limitations of the European 'intellectualist' theology they had imbibed in seminaries in Europe. They thought it was essentially elitist, assuming a paternalist model of social relations. It had dissociated morality from social justice and considered the latter merely the effect of proper pursuit of the former. Traditional Catholic moral theology, so the liberation theologians argued, was entirely incapable of mounting a sharp enough critique of the structures of injustice and oppression experienced by the poor in Latin America.

The emergence of liberation theology was a sure sign that the days of neo-Thomist uniformity were at an end. The same was true elsewhere. In Africa, for example, it was to be some time yet before an African 'preferential option for the poor' would emerge in an equivalent 'liberation theology' for Africa. But that was because African priorities were different. Latin American countries had enjoyed independence from colonialism for 150 years already. Africa was just emerging from the shadow of empire. More urgent for African Catholics was the assertion of cultural and religious independence. Questions of social justice were at first subsumed under arguments against colonialism. Only in the 1950s, as African theologians began to criticize and reject the theology of mission imported from Europe, could it really be said that a true 'African theology' began, and this was encouraged again by the reforms of Vatican II and especially the adoption of indigenous languages for the liturgy, which in turn led to the creative appropriation of traditional symbols and ceremonies from African culture. African theologians – Protestant as well as Catholic – even began to articulate various forms of a theology of adaptation (sometimes called 'concordism'), which suggested that Christianity need not reject out of hand African traditional religions but see them as manifestations of grace. Through the concept of 'conscientization', African theologians sought to encourage the self-consciousness of African Christians as Africans, with all that implied by way of critique of Western theology and values. They acknowledged and celebrated African diversity. As one Catholic African theologian has put it, 'for a long time Westerners have not noticed that there is not one world that exists, but worlds; there is not one history, but histories; not one culture, but cultures; not theology, but theologies'.[3]

These were years of continuous growth for Catholicism in most parts of the continent. Not that Catholics necessarily were increasing their share of population overall; the population itself was increasing rapidly. By the mid-1970s there were over 52 million Catholics in Africa. Though the African churches sent just 311 church leaders to Vatican II, of whom only 60 were African themselves (the others were mostly European expatriates and missionaries), the Council was a great spur to autonomous development. In 1969 regional gatherings of bishops were brought together in the Symposium of Episcopal Conferences of Africa and Madagascar (SECAM), and African Catholicism at last had its own collegial authority.

The impact of the Council was also great in North America and Western Europe. It was here that conflict within the Church had been most acute in the last years of Pius XII, as more progressive theologians had faced censure and even dismissal. But for every progressive there was a conservative. Just as there was a brace of French theologians who had been marginalized or inhibited from teaching in those years, and whose influence was to burst out at the Council, so on the opposite wing of the Church there was the French arch-conservative Archbishop Marcel Lefebvre and his followers who strenuously resisted all of the innovations of the Council. This was a relatively new phenomenon in Catholicism – internal *conservative* criticism. Resistance to liturgical reform was a feature not only of Catholicism. Anglicans and Lutherans faced the same difficulties. For all that Vatican II represented a spirit of openness and renewal, its principle of *aggiornamento* ('spirit of openness') alienated some traditional Catholics as much as it excited and enthused others. Worryingly for the Church, the conservatives could point to one significant fact – *aggiornamento* did not necessarily lead to Church growth. Instead, in the 1960s, just as the conciliar reforms were beginning to take effect, both in Europe and America there were significant *downward* trends – fewer churchgoers, fewer candidates for ordination, fewer members of the religious orders. The conservatives conveniently ignored (for who could prove this?) the possibility that it all could have been so much worse without reform. And they also conveniently ignored the fact that by far the most controversial teaching of the Church in the 1960s and 1970s was the one point above all on which Paul VI had proved himself conservative too – contraception.

This brief survey of the Catholic Church on the eve and in the aftermath of Vatican II has left out much. In countries under communist control, it is extremely difficult to assess the real impact of the Council. The Catholic Church in Eastern Europe still experienced a suffocating oppression. The 'opening to the East' under John XXIII made it possible for some bishops from Eastern Europe to attend the Council. Josif Slipyj, Metropolitan of the suppressed Ukrainian Catholic Church ('Uniate'), was released just before the Council after 17 years of imprisonment, but he was forced into exile in Rome where he proved a rather embarrassing critic of the 'opening to the East'. Another opponent of compromise was Cardinal Josef Mindszenty of the Hungarian Catholic Church. Arrested in 1948, tortured and imprisoned, he was released during the Hungarian uprising in 1956 but was forced to take refuge in the American embassy when the Russians invaded. There he stayed for 15 years, until Pope Paul finally ordered him out and again into exile. The views of leaders such as Slipyj and Mindszenty were a kind of standing rebuke to what they saw as Pope Paul's softness on communism. Whereas Paul's policy implied a spirit of openness and cooperation in the West, its political connotations in the East were quite different. Particularly where Catholicism provided a medium of resistance to Soviet domination – as in Poland – it is not clear at all that the Council meant the same thing (a spirit of renewal, liberalization, progressivism, and so on) as it did in the United States. The year after the end of the Council, Poland celebrated the millennium of the coming of Christianity to the country. Incredibly convoluted and clumsy attempts by the communist authorities to ban or control the celebrations failed completely, as a copy of the icon of the Madonna of Czestochowa, the 'Queen of Poland', was paraded around the country, attracting thousands upon thousands of the faithful. This was much more in the spirit of ultramontane Catholicism – bracing, defiant, separatist, aloof, deeply traditional. But how else could one be a Catholic in an atheist state? Things were worse, admittedly, in China. There the Catholic Church had been driven underground, soon after the communist takeover. There was an 'official' Catholic Church, the Catholic Patriotic Church of China. But this was a puppet church and would have nothing to do with the universal church of Rome. Its bishops were appointed by the state and not by Rome, it could not recognize the authority of Rome and it did not accept the reforms of the Second Vatican Council. Though some of its clergy were recognized by Rome as having received valid ordination, they exercised no freedom to act as authentic Catholics. It was impossible to say what, if anything, *aggiornamento* meant in *that* context.

CHAPTER 8

The Orthodox Churches

The iron hand of communism

The extension of Soviet control in Eastern Europe at the end of the Second World War brought millions of Christians directly under the power of a militantly atheist regime. The Soviets avoided talk of empire, of course, but an empire it was. The newly occupied territories included around 12 million Orthodox believers, though the numbers are incredibly difficult to pin down with any degree of accuracy. Some were in Orthodox strongholds, such as key provinces of Romania, parts of Hungary and Bulgaria. Others were in religiously mixed territories, such as the Baltic states, Poland and Czechoslovakia. In these lands, the Orthodox churches now found themselves caught in a position of great ambiguity. Once Soviet rule had been firmly imposed, like all Christian communities behind the Iron Curtain Orthodox believers faced a difficult struggle for survival, as Moscow and its puppet regimes sought to weaken and erode religious belief. And yet the Orthodox were not quite in the same position as other groups of Christians. Stalin's partial rehabilitation of the Russian Orthodox Church in 1943 implied that Orthodoxy could be a useful mechanism of control over religion throughout the Soviet Empire. With the Vatican so strongly opposed to communism in the immediate postwar period, this was not an option for Roman Catholicism. And so the Orthodox found themselves reluctantly drawn into Soviet policy against other communities of Christian believers.

It was the Uniate churches that suffered the most. These were communities of Greek-rite Christians in communion with Rome – formally part of the Catholic Church and yet retaining a significant degree of local autonomy and tradition, including a married priesthood. Uniate churches were found in parts of the Ukraine, in Romania, in eastern Czechoslovakia and southern Poland, in Bulgaria and Hungary. The Soviet solution to the Uniate problem was simple and brutal. From 1946 their bishops were imprisoned or executed, and their synods pressurized into seeking union with the Orthodox Church. Orthodox leaders scarcely dared resist this policy, and absorbed the Uniates into their own numbers. Or so it seemed on the surface. In fact many Uniate Christians went 'underground', pretending to conform to state policy while actually continuing to harbour a desire to return to Rome.

The Orthodox churches thus gained millions of half-hearted new 'converts' who looked Orthodox in liturgical style and church organization but were reluctant members of the official churches. There was not a squeak of protest about the treatment of the Uniates from the Orthodox hierarchy. But then their own position was deeply compromised by the policy of the Soviet state. They were permitted freedom of worship, but within clearly defined limits. They were allowed to re-open churches, and by the mid-1950s in Russia there were some 16,000 in use again. But their activities were strictly controlled. Worship was practically all they could do. They were not allowed to teach the young or to aid the sick. They were subject to regulation by local state authorities and needed permission even to repair their own buildings – something that gave enormous scope to zealous party busybodies to interfere with, block or even wreck parish life. And they faced an endless barrage of anti-Christian propaganda from the official organs of the state. The young in particular were targets for atheist propaganda. Hostile observers were forever pointing out that it was mostly the old who attended church. Certainly the young were inclined – as in Western Europe – to stay away from church. And yet there was a further reason for their absence: they were simply not allowed to attend. A foreign observer of the Easter rites in a church in Novosibirsk right at the end of our period – in the mid-1970s – noticed the old age of the packed congregation. But then he observed the policemen and party pickets filtering the crowd as they pressed forward to get in: 'It was plain that all men and women under about 40 were not being permitted to proceed to the entrance or to approach the railings with the exception of some mature women who were accompanying old people.' All of this put the Orthodox hierarchy in a very difficult position. If they openly criticized the state, they were quickly retired or pushed out of the way. Provided they professed loyalty to the state, they were tolerated grudgingly and allowed to assume some responsibility for their people. What was the right way to behave? Was it courageously to defy the Soviet authorities, suffer as a result, and lose any chance to help church members? Or was it to remain silent, and suffer again, in order that some protection, some pastoral care, could remain in place for the Christian community? Towards the end of the 1950s, it must have seemed as if the latter was the better course. Stalin was dead, and Khrushchev had buried his reputation. Soviet society seemed to be moving towards a gentle thaw.

But Khrushchev was no friend of religion, and, motivated perhaps by internal party conflict, with Christianity to hand as a useful scapegoat, in 1959 another round of fierce persecution began. More than half of the churches now open again were closed or demolished. There were public denunciations of the corruption of monks and nuns. Local party hacks were encouraged to harass and goad clergy and churchgoers. Secret police infiltrated meetings and even services. Foreign visitors, and even Orthodox worshippers themselves, often commented on the coldness of Orthodox congregations, their unwillingness to speak to anyone or to welcome anyone. The reason was simple – they were afraid of the stranger. In 1961 there was a synod of the Russian bishops at the seminary of Zagorsk. It was called hastily by the patriarch, without prior warning. Its meeting was very short, and preceded by long, tiring services and by a very heavy meal. It had four items of business. Three were not controversial – one was to join the World Council of Churches, which the state was actually keen to see happen (assuming that the Russian bishops would be good propagandists for the Soviet Union). The fourth was very controversial. It was a decree to terminate the influence of parish clergy over the financial affairs of their parishes and to place parish finances under the control of a handful of laity, including representatives from the local communist party. Three bureaucrats from the central office that regulated church affairs were present in the room, sitting behind the bishops. None of them spoke, but everyone knew the threat they represented, and the decree passed without a single dissentient speech. The official report gave the impression of an entirely free decision, in response to concern about clerical corruption. Some time later, an insider's account filtered through to the West. It made no bones about what was really going on:

> They [the three bureaucrats] sat in silence and their faces were tense. It was the tenseness of a trainer in a circus watching the animal he has tamed. Will it do everything it has been ordered, or will it let him down and spoil the act?

The bishops said nothing because they knew that to speak out would simply make things worse for them, the patriarch and their communities.

It could have been much worse. In Albania a communist dictatorship set out to exterminate Christianity completely. The Orthodox community was a minority tradition in Albania at the beginning of the century, but still the largest Christian church in the country, with just under a fifth of the population as members. In 1922 the Albanian Orthodox Church had declared itself autocephalous, but this had not been recognized by the ecumenical patriarch himself until 1937. During the war Albania's clergy had mostly supported Enver Hoxha's partisans against the occupying Italians and Germans. Hoxha's communists took over government in 1945, and the 1946 constitution proclaimed religious liberty. But pressure mounted against the church to force it into line with the Russian Orthodox Church; when Archbishop Kristofor Kissi resisted, he was deposed and replaced, and in 1949 decrees were issued subjecting all Albania's religious communities to the state. For 18 years Orthodoxy was regulated closely, with a consistent attempt to undermine it through state-sponsored atheist propaganda – the Russian way. Then, in 1967, Hoxha switched allegiance and announced a new policy, following the 'Cultural Revolution' in China. All religious activity was declared un-revolutionary – 'To be a revolutionary means not only to have no religious faith but also to struggle continuously against religious beliefs, which are an expression of feudal and bourgeois reactionary ideology' – and party workers were instructed to go through the country forcing people to abandon their beliefs. Within a matter of weeks all churches and mosques in Albania were closed. It was a catastrophe for the Orthodox Church. Its archbishop, Damian, was put in prison, along with the rest of the hierarchy, where he died in 1975.

If Albania was an example of the worst that could happen under communism, Romania was a good example of more lenient treatment. Despite the presence of a strong Catholic community in Romania, the Orthodox Church there saw itself as the legitimate religious expression of Romanian nationalism. The signing of a concordat between the Catholic Church and the new Romanian state in 1927 had intensified the rivalry between the two, particularly over education. Orthodox resentment over what they saw as rising Catholic political interference was channelled into the movement of the 'Iron Guard' in the 1930s, a fascist organization suffused with a quasi-Christian mission for national redemption. On the accession of the communists at the end of the war, practically the entire Orthodox hierarchy were locked up. The price of renewed acceptance was the inclusion of the Romanian Uniate (Greek Catholic) Church into the Orthodox Church in 1948. The Catholic concordat was abolished. Orthodoxy now moved into line with state policy in Romania, and some Romanian Orthodox Church leaders were to be more accepting of elements of Marxist ideology than was true anywhere else in the Orthodox world. Numerically dominant, for much of this period Orthodox Church life was lively and relatively unrestricted, though it faced persecution in the 1950s. By the 1960s a more moderate state policy prevailed. Churches remained open, and the Romanian Orthodox Church was permitted a greater latitude in maintaining theological contacts with the West (especially through the World Council of Churches), in theological education, and in publishing its own journals than was true, for example, in Russia.

Even so, no one in Romania could be under any illusions about the communist vision of the future. It was not one that included religion.

Believers were still harassed, churches still sometimes closed and the life of the Orthodox Church still subject to petty constraints. That was the minimum condition of things in the communist bloc. And yet a strange kind of accommodation had taken place on both sides in practically all communist countries except Albania. On one side, it is true, leaders of the Orthodox churches were involved in some abject compromises, as the condition of survival. But on the other, the communist authorities had to come to terms with the fact that years of hostility and bursts of outright persecution had failed to eradicate religious belief. Though there is evidence that church-going was in decline in communist countries in this period, it was also in decline in the West. State persecution did not make much difference. And so communist regimes on their side had also compromised, recognizing that it was better to try to work through the Church, and to try to control it, than to alienate their people completely by suppressing it. It was an unstable compromise. It was led from the Soviet Union, which sought to make the autocephalous and autonomous churches of Soviet dependencies aligned to the policy of the Moscow patriarchate. Soviet imperialism, in other words, worked through the Church in the same way it worked through subject governments. There were many examples of heroic resistance to the state authorities, and the fact that the Church was never completely subjugated meant that the authorities were ever on their guard. Nationalism, time and again, was the medium of working compromise. But even that could not be a basis for long-term stability, for it sat uncomfortably with the universalist humanism of Soviet doctrine. The Soviets could not ultimately reconcile tolerance of nationalism with the maintenance, *de facto*, of empire, and so a religious policy that relied on working through national churches contained something of the seeds of its own destruction. In the era of détente, in the late 1960s and 1970s, when the Cold War eased, communist countries began to face internal challenges from dissident groups – some of them inspired by, or connected with, the Orthodox churches.

Orthodoxy in Greece and the diaspora

The Soviet Empire included within it a large majority of Orthodox believers – probably by the 1970s some 95 million out of a total of around 120 million believers worldwide – and so the impact of communist rule was far greater on this part of the Christian Church than it was on any other Christian tradition. But the Orthodox family of churches was, as we saw earlier, a diverse and scattered one. The very freeze in international relations during the Cold War meant that there were few dramatic movements in Ortho-dox demography in this period. Since migration from the Soviet bloc was strictly controlled, once the postwar borders were settled the geography of

Orthodoxy worldwide did not change substantially.

Greece contained the largest single Orthodox Church outside the communist bloc – nearly 10 million members. There were no more territorial gains, no more expansion of the Greek Orthodox fold, after the 1920s. Instead, as a legacy of Italian and then German occupation, there was a severely divided society, and a civil war which ran on from the war years until 1949. The Orthodox Church generally sided with the government forces (supported by America and Britain) against the communists, unsurprisingly, and emerged victorious. But the Church's position was more strongly rooted in popular support than this naked partisanship might suggest. Archbishop Damaskinos carefully cultivated a spirit of independence from the state, at the same time as strengthening state support for the Orthodox Church – a masterly achievement. As a result the Church received state funding for its ministry but was placed in a position of critical distance from the government.

The Orthodox churches of the diaspora were inevitably affected by the continuing oppression of their parent churches under communism. Setting to one side the Moscow patriarchate itself, and its few churches outside the Soviet sphere of influence, there were in effect three main jurisdictions of Russian Orthodox in the West – the Russian Orthodox Church Abroad (ROCA), the Orthodox Church of America (OCA) and the 'Paris jurisdiction' of churches under the ecumenical patriarchate. The Soviet policy of seeking to achieve hegemony over all the Russian churches in exile through the Moscow patriarchate merely served to exacerbate the tensions between these three jurisdictions and Moscow, and among them. The apparent subservience of the Moscow patriarchate fuelled ROCA's conviction that it had betrayed true Orthodoxy. In the sceptical words of one writer, ROCA lived in a 'prison of daydreams about the prerevolutionary Orthodox autocratic monarchy'; indeed it had canonized the last tsar.[1] Several attempts by the Moscow patriarchate to seek reconciliation with ROCA were bound to fail, then. The latest of these was made in 1974, in the years of the Brezhnev 'freeze' in Russia. Probably the patriarchate felt obliged to make these overtures in the interests of its relations with the Soviet state, but no one can have thought that much was ever likely to come of them while the communists remained in power.

But ROCA was not itself in a conciliatory frame of mind where the other jurisdictions were concerned. It claimed to be the true inheritor of the spirit of the Russian Orthodox Church. Therefore it could not countenance the existence of other jurisdictions. It was essentially caught in a defensive mindset, determined to protect what it took to be true Orthodoxy. It was not likely, then, to approve of the Paris jurisdiction's ecumenical contacts and spirit of engagement with Western theology. Sergei Bulgakov had been singled out for particular criticism by ROCA in 1936, though he was also condemned by the Moscow patriarchate which, however, had no access to his books, since they were banned in the Soviet Union. But ROCA also fell out with the Orthodox Church of America. OCA had a policy of unifying the various ethnic Orthodox jurisdictions in the interwar years, and by 1941 had over 400,000 members in eight dioceses. But the Moscow patriarch's overseas jurisdiction – called the Moscow 'exarchate' – failed in its attempt to secure the submission of the metropolitan of OCA in the apparently favourable conditions of the American–Russian alliance before 1945, just as ROCA failed in its parallel attempt to do the same. Moscow, in fact, could play these jurisdictions off against each other. Its admission to the World Council of Churches in 1961 intensified the rivalry with ROCA and brought a certain embarrassment into ecumenical circles accordingly, especially in relations with the American Church. To whom did one turn for the voice of authentic Orthodoxy if one wanted to open up a theological dialogue with the Orthodox Church? The position of the American Church was simplified by the eventual granting of autocephaly (i.e. effective autonomy) by the Moscow patriarchate in 1970, a move that naturally reinforced the gulf between OCA and ROCA.

The divisions masked the gradual worldwide growth of Eastern Orthodoxy. Some conversions to Orthodoxy in East Africa, and particularly in Kenya and Uganda in the 1940s and 1950s, and later in South Africa, marked the beginning of a small Eastern Orthodox presence in Africa under the patriarchate of Alexandria. Orthodox churches in Greek-speaking communities in Europe and Australia were consolidated in this period, especially at the end of the period in the wake of the Turkish invasion of Cyprus in 1974, when hundreds of thousands of Greek Cypriots were expelled from their homes and driven into exile. Over 145,000 Greeks had emigrated to Australia in the 20 years from 1947. As a result, the Orthodox Church in Australia underwent prolonged expansion, achieving the status of archdiocese from the ecumenical patriarch in 1959. Conflict rumbled on for years between the new metropolitan, Ezekiel Tsoukalas, and the older *koinotites*, the lay-run representative bodies that had dominated Orthodoxy in the Greek-speaking city communities of Australia, but the split was a marginal one: many of the *koinotites* submitted to Ezekiel, and the new churches of the suburbs in any case fell directly under his authority. Division seemed to be endemic to Orthodox Christianity, and yet it often thrived in spite of division.

Oriental Orthodoxy

The end of the Second World War did not bring a vicious round of blood-letting for the Oriental Orthodox churches as it had for those caught up in the aftermath of the collapse of the Ottoman Empire in 1918–22. But almost all of these churches were, nevertheless, in due course affected by the political changes the war accelerated. Islamic nationalism and the foundation of the state of Israel were like a pincer movement exerting pressure on Oriental Orthodoxy in the Middle East. Orthodox believers of the Syrian and Coptic churches had long been settled in Palestine. As Arab Christians they were trapped in the escalating tension and violence between Arab and Jew after 1948, and often ignored or reviled by Islamic Palestinian militants and Jews alike. Over the following decades, as Jewish migration to Israel rose and as Palestinian militancy and pan-Arab hostility to Israel grew, the Christian communities of the Middle East began to feel distinctly isolated. Tens of thousands of Palestinian Christians emigrated to America, Europe and Egypt, and their numbers in Israel itself and in neighbouring states declined.

In Egypt itself, however, independence under the presidency of Gamal Abdel Nasser brought its own complications for Christians. Nasser sought – like Atatürk of Turkey before him – to found a new state on a religiously neutral policy. But it made good political sense for him to court Islamic sympathies and therefore to tolerate Islamic revivalism. Pressure on the Coptic Church followed accordingly, and a determined defence of the Church's own traditions and of its patriotism in the face of hostility from Muslims became a daily fact of life for Egypt's Christians. In this situation it was perhaps not surprising that the period saw a self-conscious revival of Coptic life, culture and monasticism, and a succession of strong leaders, including Patriarch (or 'Pope') Cyril VI from 1959 to 1971 and Shenouda III from 1971.

In the case of Ethiopia, the ejection of the Italians by an Allied force in 1941 led to full acknowledgement of independence in 1942 and nearly three decades of relative peace for the Ethiopian Church. But the reigning monarch, Haile Selassie I, faced mounting difficulties by the 1950s over the mixed achievements of his programme of modernization. He also faced a growing Marxist opposition movement among students at Addis Ababa University and the army, and was eventually deposed in 1974. Strongly supported as he was by the Ethiopian Orthodox Church, of which he was a loyal member, the almost inevitable period of intense persecution – fortunately brief – followed. Land was taken away from it, its clergy were harassed, and its privileges disappeared. Yet once again – the common experience of Orthodoxy almost everywhere in this period – intense secular hostility got nowhere in the end. The Church grew in strength in these years, aided if anything by its new-found pariah status and by growing popular disillusionment with the new Marxist regime in the years of 'Red Terror' of the mid-1970s.

CHAPTER 9

Protestant Unsettlement

Postwar problems

The 30 years after the end of the Second World War was an era of almost uninterrupted American and Soviet ascendancy, leading to a superpower rivalry that effectively fossilized international relations. But for the historic denominations of Protestantism it was a period of re-evaluation and change that does not comfortably fit the chronology of the Cold War. In Europe the churches at first re-established themselves with amazing rapidity. In America and Canada, even though the time of Protestant ascendancy had almost gone, again at first there seemed little serious challenge to the older traditions' dominance, apart from the continuing growth of Catholicism. In Australasia much the same was true.

For nearly 20 years, confidence was high. The late 1940s and 1950s were a time when historic Protestantism could afford to believe that the Christian future was running its way. For a brief period, the Second Vatican Council confirmed that impression. Was the Council not in effect internalizing a Protestant critique of the Catholic Church by acknowledging its permanent need of reform? There was even talk of religious revival in historic Protestantism in the 1950s and early 1960s, with many of the signs of institutional affiliation, including churchgoing, showing a modest upturn. Writers such as W.H. Auden, Catherine Marshall, Dorothy Sayers and T.S. Eliot were unafraid to be identified (sometimes rather loosely) as Christian. The Christian apologist C.S. Lewis in these years built up an international following that has continued to rise since his death in 1963, with sales of his books reaching over 4 million a year by the 1990s; much of this success was for his Narnia stories, but his Christian apologetic works continued to sell well too. Church leaders were making inroads into the new medium of television also.

But in the mid-1960s confidence was to fade dramatically. In the words of one historian, writing a little too sharply of the situation in Britain, 'really quite suddenly' a formerly religious people forsook Christianity 'in a sudden plunge into a truly secular condition'.[1] Churchgoing plummeted, the young withdrew from Sunday schools and church youth organizations, and an older generation's moral values were challenged by an implacable combination of permissiveness and social radicalism. By the early 1970s historic Protestantism was mostly in retreat in the West.

If this were all that needed saying of Protestantism in this period, however, it would be misleading. The history of Protestantism is much more complex than the trajectory of confidence until the early 1960s and then collapse suggests. For in saying all of this, we have kept close to a Western view of things, and yet this was a time in which any notion that worldwide Protestantism could be adequately described in historic categories inherited from Western Europe had to be called into question. Western Protestantism's dominance was beginning to recede. The dismantling of the old European empires brought in its wake new challenges for the churches planted by the missionaries.

There have always been definitional problems surrounding the term 'Protestantism' – always some Protestants (such as Anglo-Catholics) who hardly liked to think of themselves as Protestants, always some Protestants (such as Unitarians) who were not even recognized as Christian by other Protestants, always some Protestants (Mennonites, Anabaptists) who thought the mainstream denominations had 'sold out'. Of its very nature, Protestantism was defined as much by what it was not – Papalist, Greek or Eastern Orthodox – as by what it was. And yet – as we saw in Chapter 4 – it is possible to identify major historic strands of Protestantism which remained, until roughly the middle of the twentieth century, the dominant force in worldwide Protestantism. But for a variety of reasons, what it meant to be Protestant was to become, from then on, infinitely more complex.

Both in Europe and in America many of the older historic denominations contracted sharply in the 1960s. But in America this loss was more than made up for by the growth of other churches, some predominantly white, such as the Southern Baptists, but others predominantly black. This did not happen in Europe. But there was also a growing tension between the ecumenical goals of the major denominations and the loyalties of many of their members. What came first – a common Protestant identity, or, say, Methodist identity, or Presbyterian identity, and so on? This often played itself out in divisions over liberal theology, with 'conservatives' fearful that their churches' identity and faithfulness to the Gospel were compromised by the insistence of 'liberals' that the churches had to adapt to change. Just as the Lutheran denominations of America were drawing together, culminating in the formation of the Evangelical Lutheran Church of America (ELCA) in 1988, the Missouri Synod Lutherans fell out with each other in the 1960s over biblical criticism. A further complication was the impact of decolonization and the emergence of independent and Pentecostal churches. In much of the world the older traditions represented a shrinking proportion of Protestant believers. The drift of all of this was clear by the early 1970s: growth and vitality in Protestantism lay mostly outside the historic denominations.

There was one country in which much of this had little impact. This was the one substantial part of the Soviet bloc that contained a majority Protestant population – East Germany, or the German Democratic Republic (GDR), where around 80 per cent were Protestant. Here the relationship between church and state was not unlike that between Orthodoxy and the state in some countries of the Soviet bloc, with the church receiving some official recognition despite the proselytizing atheism of the state. In 1948, in the absence of direct Soviet intervention, the churches of the eight states in the GDR were allowed to join the Evangelical church union for the whole of Germany (the EKD). The Communist Party of the GDR did not apply a militantly atheist policy, perhaps because the churches were socially useful, running welfare agencies, hospitals, homes for the elderly and kindergartens. The 1949 constitution permitted freedom of religion in theory, but the state policy in practice was to undermine the churches through informants, propaganda and party pressure – a familiar pattern. The climate became harsher for the churches in 1956 with the abolition of the church tax in response to strong criticism of the regime from some church leaders, including the veteran bishop of the Confessing Church, Otto Dibelius. The EKD's decision to supply chaplains to German NATO forces in West Germany from 1957 made the position of the GDR churches untenable, and they were forced finally to withdraw in the late 1960s. At this point it looked as if the state had finally subjugated the Protestant churches and isolated them from the rest of Europe.

The problems faced by Protestantism in the GDR were thus different from those facing Protestants elsewhere in Europe. They were not that different – though perhaps not so serious – from those facing Protestant churches in China, though there of course the Protestant churches had always been small in relation to the population as a whole. Both in China and in the GDR – and also, incidentally, in the Baltic states, now officially absorbed into the Soviet Union, in which there were some smaller Lutheran populations – persecution, whether mild or heavy, naturally put the struggles of the churches of the West in quite a different light. Even if numbers fell – as they did substantially in the GDR in the late 1950s – it is difficult to tell how one should account for that. Were people simply afraid of the authorities or were they becoming 'secularized' just like people in the West?

Secularization in the West

But was the West becoming secularized? That has certainly been the conclusion of many sociologists and social historians. Language about church decline had been around for generations, and reflected classic sociological theories about the role of religion in modern society. Put nineteenth-century anxieties about the absence of working-class people from church together with the increasing criticism of traditional Christianity articulated by philosophers and social critics of the period, and it is no surprise that a fashion took hold for describing religion as essentially premodern and bound to decline in modernizing, urban and industrial societies. Influenced by the founders of sociology such as Karl Marx and Max Weber, sociologists used the term 'secularization' to describe the gradual withering of religious commitment and identity in modern society. Some argued – following Weber – that modern society was intrinsically rational, instrumental and this-worldly, and therefore unsympathetic to the mystery and other-worldliness of traditional religion. If religion was to survive, it had to transform itself into something much more preoccupied with this world than with the transcendental realm. This was one of the reasons why radical theology became briefly fashionable in Protestant circles in the West in the 1960s. Others argued – following Emile Durkheim – that displacement was going on, with the traditional religion of the West fading as people transferred their 'gods' to other forms of social value and activity – political parties (witness the almost religious commitment demanded of communists and fascists), or entertainment and leisure (witness the rise of the Hollywood and TV 'star' culture).

There was some evidence to back up these theories. Long-term measurements of churchgoing in Europe since the end of the nineteenth century suggested a gradual decline, deepening into sharp decline in the 1960s. Regional patterns of churchgoing varied enormously in all countries, but there was much impressionistic and some statistical evidence to indicate that on the whole churchgoing was lower in the newer industrial cities than it was in smaller, older settlements and in the countryside, and lower among the working class than it was among the middle class. The rise of new forms of leisure clearly did affect traditional church life: the growth in car ownership encouraged people to use Sunday as a day for excursions or for visiting friends and family, and the cinema and television provided an alternative source of entertainment to the social clubs once supported by the churches. Things got much worse for the churches in the 1960s. The new youth culture of rock and roll, drugs and fashion pushed a wedge between the young and the old, and the young abandoned religious organizations with remarkable speed. The Student Christian Movement (SCM), the leading ecumenical organization for Protestant youth across the English-speaking Western world since the late nineteenth century, suddenly collapsed in the 1960s. Annual figures for confirmations in the Church of England fell by well over a third between 1960 and 1970. In the diocese of Brisbane in Australia, the Young Anglican Fellowship fell from 65 branches in 1965 to just 17 by 1971. These are merely a few random signs of the severe contraction that faced Protestant churches in the West. What many historians have called – aping China – the 'cultural revolution' of that decade had catastrophic implications for the historic denominations. Despite some variations, the figures do not differ significantly across Britain, Scandinavia, the Netherlands, Germany, Australia and New Zealand.

But they tell a different story in America. Both in Canada and in the United States, most of the historic denominations also contracted. In the United States the Episcopal, Reformed, United Methodist, Presbyterian, United (Congregationalist) and Disciples of Christ churches had all expanded between 1940 and 1960, and shrank between 1960 and 1980. Because of their prominence up until then, and because American society fully participated in the new 'permissive' culture, the impression gained ground that in America too religion was in retreat. But regular churchgoing overall remained buoyant, and certainly stayed at a level – put by some as high as 40 per cent of the population in the 1970s – well above that of Europe and Australasia. Other churches expanded to fill the gap left by the shrinking traditional denominations. The Southern Baptists, for example, expanded by almost 50 per cent between 1960 and 1980, to become far and away the largest Protestant denomination in the US, with over 13 million members. The Assemblies of God (Pentecostal) grew from just 200,000 members in 1940 to well over a million by 1980. Many other smaller churches grew too. The contrast between Europe and America has always been a puzzle for those who support the secularization thesis in its most general and abstract form; it has led some theorists in reaction to suggest that Europe is the 'exceptional case' of secularization in a general world history of continued religious affiliation. But in a way, both sides are right. In Europe and America historic Protestantism began to decline sharply in the 1960s, though its rate of decline subsequently has not fulfilled the most pessimistic predictions. There was a common religious experience across these denominations on both sides of the Atlantic in which the cultural changes of the 1960s played an important role. And yet in Europe nothing arose in terms of new churches to replace the gap left by the decline in the older denominations, even taking into account in Britain the black-led churches which came into being through migration from countries of the British Commonwealth. America also registered a higher level of general religious belief than Europe, with well over 95 per cent in the 1970s affirming their belief in God. The figure in Britain, for example, was nearer 75 per cent, as it was for Europe as a whole.

There is a vital caveat here. Much of the evidence for church decline in this period depends precisely on measurements for *church* decline – churchgoing, baptisms and confirmations, numbers of clergy, and so on. While there was some evidence of a decline in actual Christian belief among the general population, it was much weaker; as the figures quoted suggest, belief always remained at a much higher level than actual participation in church life throughout the West. One sociologist has used the phrase 'believing without belonging' to describe how many European people see religion. This shows that there is more consistency over time in people's actual beliefs than there is in what they do about those beliefs. A Christian substratum of belief remained in place at a high level for much of this period. It was probably thinning out, as people lost contact with church life and religious education. Surveys, by their very nature, are not sophisticated instruments for evaluating just how 'Christian' popular belief really is. The dilemma is neatly captured by a respondent to a survey of religion in Islington in London in 1968:

Do you believe in God?
Yes.
Do you believe in a God who can change the course of events on earth?
No, just the ordinary one.[2]

We have to be careful in using the data about decline, in case we jump too quickly from records of *church* decline to assumptions about the disappearance of religion in modern society. But the differences between North America and the rest of Europe are still marked. One explanation is that in Europe the troubled history of church–state relations made the public expression of Christian faith much more problematic than it was in America.

What the American data does indicate is that a different kind of religion was taking hold in North American Protestantism from that which had earlier dominated the scene. It was more conservative socially, religiously and probably politically. Even within the older denominations, conservative Evangelical groups were more likely to hold on to their congregations. This has been another difficulty for the secularization argument. The implication is that while many people evidently have been tempted away from church and from Christianity by the social changes of the 1960s, many others have been sufficiently alarmed by those changes to want to find their spiritual home in churches which offer a clear and familiar message. The theological roots of this conservative Evangelicalism were complex and diverse, but three different elements in particular stand out. One is the older strand of American revivalism, dating back well into the eighteenth century, and shaped also by 'holiness' movements in the nineteenth century. Revivalism has remained a key feature of American religious life, and one surprisingly adaptable to modern media through 'tele-evangelism'. Another is Pentecostalism, a movement that also had its roots in the holiness movements and proved particularly attractive to black Christians. A third is fundamentalism, with its forceful and clear system of doctrine elaborated from a principle of biblical inerrancy. Now these three elements could in theory be found equally present in one church, but that was quite rare. Some Pentecostal churches were and are fundamentalist, but many are not. Some fundamentalist churches were also revivalist in their church culture, but again many were not. Southern Baptists were not Pentecostal and were not all fundamentalist.

The representative figure in this upsurge of conservative Evangelicalism was Billy Graham. Born in 1918 and brought up as a Presbyterian, Graham was ordained by the Southern Baptists, and after a brief spell in pastoral ministry became a full-time travelling evangelist. His theology was conservative, but not fundamentalist. His evangelistic methods were steeped in the history of American revivalism – the big crowds, the carefully managed meeting, the powerful, emotional address, the calling forward of those who felt drawn to make a personal commitment to Christ, the 'follow-up' ministry to those who had presented themselves. But, aside from his obvious personal charisma which transferred well to television and radio, there was something distinctive about his evangelism – it was essentially ecumenical. Graham put conversion before denominational loyalty and called on all Protestant churches to assist in his evangelistic crusades. From 1949 on, he drew ever larger crowds – 105,000 came to hear him in Boston in 1950, for example. Like earlier American evangelists such as Dwight L. Moody, Graham's overseas reception was immense. In 1954 he came to London for the first time, where some 2 million people heard him in the course of three months. He went on to tour northern Europe in the same year, and thereafter rapidly expanded his overseas activity. In 1959 he had an outstanding success in Australia. The effect of his personal charisma was shown in the overheard comment of someone who attended one of the 'warm up' meetings in advance of Graham's arrival: 'I'm not getting converted tonight, I'm waiting until Billy Graham comes.'

Graham's effect can be exaggerated. The numbers who came forward to make their commitment of faith were always a fraction of the total attendance, and a large number of these – often well over 50 per cent – were in fact already churchgoers. But that still left significant numbers who were not.

Overall Graham's ministry was but a small part of the total effort made by Evangelical Christianity in these years to 'grow' new believers. Moreover it did suffer from the 1960s effect: though his crusades continued almost until the end of the century, they never again had the impact they had in the 1950s and early 1960s. But his success, and the high public profile he attracted, pointed to two things. The first was that by the 1960s the culture and values of popular Evangelicalism were beginning to draw apart from the mainstream of Protestant theology. The radical theology of the 1960s – exemplified in the extraordinary impact of Bishop John Robinson's book *Honest to God* (1963), which called for a rethinking of popular images of God, and of Harvey Cox's *The Secular City* (1965), which argued that a non-transcendent reinterpretation of Christianity was needed for the modern world – in the end was an elite theology, a theology for the educated and philosophically informed. It had some popularity at first, certainly, but with the middle class. For all its appeal to the challenge of modern society, it was not really a theology for the masses. Evangelicalism was. Its success, however, raised precisely those problems of wider credibility the radical theologians were trying to address.

The second point follows from this. If this was a period in which historic Protestantism in the West suffered significant reverses, so that the term 'secularization' has some force as a description of what was happening in the West, there are other features of the period that sit squarely against that view. Protestantism in the West was undergoing both secularization *and* revival. It was in decline in its historical denominational manifestations. But it was re-inventing and transforming itself into a much more diffuse form of Christianity, in which the emotional individualism and doctrinal conservatism of Evangelicalism (or Pietism on Continental Europe) and Pentecostalism would come to play a central role. Part of its decline was to move to the margins, to distance itself from the 'establishment' role it had often played hitherto. But at the margins it sought, not – paradoxically – marginalization, but the creation of a new sub-culture of Evangelical values, a new society, in effect, from which once again it could speak to society as a whole.

Protestantism in the Third World

The transformation of Protestantism in this period, facing the challenges it did in the West, should not be transferred too hastily to the Third World. If in Europe one could see a process of decline in the older historic denominations not matched by the growth of new churches, and in America the decline of the older denominations matched by new churches, in much of the Third World one could see a third pattern: the continued growth of the older historic denominations alongside the growth of newer churches. Putting it like this is putting it at its simplest. There were substantial variations between regions, and the implications of the growth of newer churches in particular were not to attract very much attention from Western observers until the 1970s.

In Africa the growth of the newer churches has drawn increasing comment from observers, and will be covered in greater detail in later chapters on independency and Pentecostalism. Historic Protestantism did not lose out, however, in most parts of the continent, with the exception of North Africa, where decolonization was eventually followed by the emergence of militant Islamic movements which made life difficult for Protestants and Catholics alike. The underlying reality for much of Africa in this period, however, was a steady and substantial growth in the Christian proportion of the population to around 40 per cent in the mid-1970s (about 144 million people). Thus there was space for both the historic churches and the independent churches to grow, and the loser was African traditional religion. The transition to indigenous churches took time. Numbers of foreign missionaries actually increased during the 1950s, supported particularly from the United States. The churches of the newly independent states therefore often inherited church structures in which overseas clergy and workers continued to play an important role, if shortly to be a diminishing one. In parts of the continent, the historic churches thrived alongside a multitude of independent bodies. In West Africa, and especially Nigeria, for example, this was a period of great Anglican expansion, which was sustained through to the end of the century. The same was also true in South Africa, where Methodism and Presbyterianism also prospered. The growing conflict between the churches and the white nationalist government of South Africa over apartheid highlighted the role of certain brave and prophetic white clergy, such as the English priest-monk Trevor Huddleston, but that should not deflect attention from the fact that, overall, South African Protestantism more and more was a matter of black congregations and black clergy. Here as elsewhere in Africa the traditional churches thrived because they too, as they became autonomous bodies within their denominations, found ways of adapting the Christianity they had received from the missionaries to their own culture. In Uganda in this period the influence of East African revivalism, the Balokole, arguably kept within the Anglican Church prophetic impulses that elsewhere led to independency. The first black archbishop of Uganda, Erica Sabiti, was himself a product of the Balokole movement.

A somewhat more mixed experience awaited Protestantism in Asia. Here on the whole the consequences of decolonization were more immediate and destructive for the churches. No one knows how many Christians

there were in China by the late 1950s. Most of the main historic denominations still existed in some form, but statistics are only available for those
bodies that had agreed to conform to the government's 'three-self' principle: self-government, self-support and self-propagation. Much the same
was true elsewhere in Vietnam and North Korea. In South Korea, the
churches' experience was closer to that of Africa. Here the churches were
free to work, albeit with some restrictions, and they certainly survived and
grew dramatically, though mostly not at the same rate as the independent
and Pentecostal churches.

The other continent of the Third World in which Protestantism was to
grow dramatically in the second half of the century was Latin America.
But here, little of the growth was represented by the historic traditions, as
we can see by looking at the situation over 50 years or so. By the end of the
century just over a quarter (44 million) of non-Catholic Christians were
from the historic Protestant churches; the rest, around 130 million, were
Pentecostals, and they had grown from just 12 million 25 years earlier. Even
then it is likely that a high proportion of the members of the older traditions
– one estimate is around 37 million – were Charismatic Christians. That
would leave non-Charismatic mainstream Protestants in Latin America by
the 1990s at around 7 million only, out of a total Christian population of 445
million. Their growth in the whole of the preceding half-century had been
steady, but not dramatic.

Latin America is thus yet another example of the changing character of Protestantism in this period. Here it was often difficult to discern
a direct connection between the European Reformation and the Protestantism of individual believers. Pentecostalism, sometimes called a 'third
force' in world Christianity (after Catholicism and historic Protestantism – a division somewhat unfair to the Eastern Orthodox churches), was
marked above all by an enthusiasm for new gifts of the spirit that many
more conservative and orthodox Evangelicals found hard to square with
the supreme authority of Scripture. In its interpretation of Scripture, in its
doctrine and in its moral values Pentecostalism has shared so much with
mainstream Evangelicalism that it is hard not to adopt the terminology of
the editors of the *World Christian Encyclopedia* and call them all, together,
'Great Commission Christians' – though their definition might leave other
Christians looking askance: 'Believers in Jesus Christ ... who have accepted
... [the] personal challenge in their lives and ministries [of Matthew 28.19],
are attempting to obey his commands and mandates, and who are seeking
to influence the body of Christ to implement it.'[3] Whatever the adequacy
of this description the point can be taken: Evangelicals within and outside
the traditional denominations were becoming ever more vociferous within

worldwide Protestantism, and in Third World Protestantism in particular. This was a trend clearly established in the years from 1945 to 1973, though it was to go further still in the remainder of the century.

Women in Protestantism

At this point it is worth briefly noting a dimension of church life we have already considered in relation to Catholicism earlier in the century – the changing role and status of women in Christianity. Women composed by far the majority of congregations. Yet there remained great discrepancies between numbers and influence. Very few women occupied positions of leadership in the churches (the heads of Anglican female religious orders were possibly an exception, but they were very few indeed), though increasingly they were influential in church educational and welfare agencies at the highest level, having provided the bulk of paid and voluntary workers in these fields for decades. Gradually the opening up of higher education and the learned professions to women – something that happened in European colonies as well as in the West – provided a growing body of female expertise on which the churches could draw. But the ethical and social teaching of the Protestant churches remained, on the whole, as conservative as that of the Catholic Church, emphasizing the importance of women's responsibilities in the home.

It was in the 1960s that the social situation of women in the West began to change dramatically, with the sexual freedom that came with contraception (especially the pill, which was legalized for sale in the US in 1960), with the continuing rise in the numbers of women working, and with the feminist movement that followed the publication of Betty Friedan's *The Feminine Mystique* in 1963. This was to effect a revolution in the relationship between women and the Christian Church in the West. It was to erode the conventional pattern of family relations that underlay church teaching on women's domesticity, and to make patterns of sexual relationship long condemned by the churches socially acceptable. It thus weakened the link between women's interests and church teaching and made the churches less hospitable places for the many women who embraced their new freedom with enthusiasm. Some argue that it was the withdrawal of *women* from the churches in the 1960s that led to the sudden contraction in church attendance and membership in the West. That is plausible, though the evidence is somewhat mixed. This sexual revolution had almost no impact at all, however, on the majority of Christians in the Third World.

Teaching on the 'separate sphere' of women's work – the home – did not by itself rule out the possibility of women's church leadership, and even if the Protestant churches of the West were slow to respond creatively to the social changes of the 1960s, in this period they were beginning to accept arguments for the advance of women to positions of church authority – above all for the ordination of women. It is true that arguments between progressives and conservatives ran through all the Protestant churches, wherever they were in the world. Evangelicals who were suspicious of liberalism in doctrine were not necessarily opposed to women's leadership. But nor were liberals necessarily in favour of ordaining women. But the general trend in the West was clear, and it was to open up another gap with many of the churches of the Third World in the last quarter of the century.

CHAPTER 10

Independent Churches and New Religious Movements

New wine and new skins

So far I have used three broad 'families' of Catholic, Orthodox and Protestant churches as my main system of categorization, and this is justifiable for the twentieth century as a whole, given the predominance of these families of churches in the Christian world for much of the century. But as the century progressed, the categorization became more and more fragile. It worked particularly well for the Catholic Church because of its sheer size as well as its organizational identity and coherence. But we have already seen that the categorization is none too neat in the case of the Orthodox and Protestant churches because the diversity within each of these large clusters of churches was considerable, and generalizations about 'Protestant' or 'Orthodox' life and theology in the period are therefore hazardous. But much of the spectacular growth in Christianity in the Third World after the Second World War occurred outside the traditional denominations of the Christian mainstream. Sometimes this was simply because new religious impulses caught on among people remote from missionary activity from the older traditions, and therefore developed in a largely independent way. More often than not, it was because of a deliberate reaction against the older traditions, not least if they were experienced through the medium of colonialism.

Independent Christian movements in the twentieth century were usually developments within Protestantism, if that term is interpreted in the widest possible sense to mean churches that reject the authority of Rome and are not descended from the Orthodox tradition. But a term interpreted that widely surely does not say very much. Many of the independent churches were – to Western eyes – deeply conservative, with a theological culture broadly consistent with Evangelicalism. Some remained closely identified with particular traditions of Protestantism, such as the Baptists or the

Methodists. Others practically invented new forms of church organization. Some were concerned to protect the Christian tradition they had received from an earlier generation of missionaries against the polluting threat of other cultural values and belief-systems. Others synthesized Christian faith with common cultural practices condemned by the missionaries. Some were extremely individualistic, offering their followers specific benefits such as healing or prosperity. Others were corporatist, subsuming the welfare of the individual in messianic ambitions for a whole people.

Acknowledging the basic family relationship to Protestantism, there are five important matters of clarification. The first is that in the very nature of the case it is unhelpful to have too rigid an understanding of what Protestantism is when thinking about independent churches in the twentieth century. Some of them had quite porous boundaries and received much from other religious systems. The present writer, in south London in the 1990s, encountered a West African immigrant church that had broken away from the Catholic Church earlier in the century and adopted a Charismatic Evangelical Protestantism, but had preserved concepts of Catholic identity and order, including the wearing of vestments by its deacons, who were composed of all of the male members of the congregation. Second, it is also unhelpful to have too rigid a notion of Christianity itself. Some of these independent churches departed from traditional Christian beliefs or introduced new and seemingly bizarre elements, in a way that many others regarded as deeply compromising. The older churches once had a word for these things – heresy. But social historians have taught us rightly that heresy is a word of abuse that tells you as much about your own values as it does about other people's. It is a loaded term, and one that is best avoided not least because of the shocking consequences in the past of labelling people in such a way.

Third, in order to get a little more precision in the use of the term 'independent church' in this chapter, it is necessary to except from consideration here various schismatic or autonomous churches in the West. All of the main Protestant denominations in North America and Europe have faced internal division over issues of theological principle or organizational change at some stage in their history. In a later chapter, I shall look briefly at the implications of division over liturgical change and modernization – a preoccupation of some 'conservative' believers in the West and itself a telling sign of the challenges facing Christianity there. But it is not helpful to put these issues in the same basket as the emergence of independent churches in the developing world. A fourth issue is the question of the relationship to Pentecostalism. Here I am frankly at a loss how to proceed, except to observe that the overlap between Pentecostalism and the independent churches is great, but there is a point in treating them separately. The independent churches were not all Pentecostal, though many were, and studying them separately highlights the Christian response to colonialism. Pentecostalism, on the other hand, is a theological and liturgical current that has run across many Protestant churches in the twentieth century, including those in the West as well as in the developing world. It has certainly marked the emergence of what is practically a completely new, dynamic strand of Protestantism, but as such its history deserves a chapter of its own later in this book.

That takes us to the fifth and final issue, and what is in many ways the most important one. The rise of the independent churches was both a cause and a consequence of the complicated history of decolonization. At the risk of overestimating one movement of world politics in this history of the Christian Church, the consequences of the ebb and flow of imperialism were enormous. Christianity was caught up in it all, sometimes as victim, but more often than not as the justification, the worldview, according to which the European colonizers in the first place did what they did. The emergence of the independent churches is a startling demonstration of the failure of the late nineteenth and early twentieth-century European project to create a dependent and derivatively 'civilized' world outside Europe itself. That is why it is appropriate to place this chapter at the end of our consideration of the era from 1945 to 1973. It is also why this chapter concentrates on Africa and Asia, the areas that underwent decolonization in the late twentieth century. In Latin America, which also has some independent churches, the rejection of Portuguese and Spanish rule long before the twentieth century and the near absolute dominance of Catholicism created a very different context. Nearly all the independent churches in Latin America are Pentecostal, and they began as Pentecostal churches.

Independent churches in Africa

Independency in African Christianity is much studied, if still not well known in the West. It was neglected for a long time because its ethos and growth were so complex as to defy generalization, and its preservation of elements of traditional African culture and belief were often an embarrassment to the longer-established denominations. Recently even the terminology adopted by those who have studied it has undergone revision, with a reaction against the term 'African Independent Church' in favour of 'African Initiated Church', retaining, however, the acronym AIC. The shift reflects unease at the suggestion that the Western traditions represent a norm against which African independency continues to be evaluated. No terminology is without its difficulties, however. 'African initiated' may be historically accurate, but it loses something of the political edge of the older term; while it reflects an understandable concern to stress the integrity of African Christianity, at the same time it is a little anodyne. The reaction against colonialism was not the fundamental cause of independency, but it was undoubtedly a powerful element of it.

A crucial determining factor in the geography of independency was the absence of a monopoly missionary church. This might mean either the absence of any missionary presence altogether or the presence of several competing Protestant missionary societies. In the first case – the absence of missionaries – autonomous, African-led movements came into being that did not usually seek the umbrella of one of the European or American societies. In the second case by implication the very existence of rival societies undermined their credibility in the eyes of African people. Above all, in both kinds of context a very strong motive was the desire to find a form of authentic Christian expression for African people that was free from the hierarchy, exclusivism and racialism that African people often experienced at the hands of the missionary societies. Where one Protestant tradition was particularly powerful, as in Uganda, independency remained weak, and the development of forms of African religious expression tended to occur within the dominant tradition. But elsewhere independency was a kind of religious parallel to political nationalism. It was usually without direct nationalist aspirations, but it was definitely an expression of African desire for an independent life, and it therefore qualified and challenged European rule.

Difficult though it is to describe African independency in clear categories, historians have tended to identify three main 'waves' in the twentieth century. The first began in the late nineteenth and early twentieth centuries. Independent African Christian movements began to appear in these years, usually led by ex-members of one of the missionary societies' congregations. The name 'Ethiopian' has been given to many of these movements, expressing the sense that Christianity had African roots. Mojola Agbebi, for example, was a Yoruba from Nigeria, born as David Brown Vincent, who became a teacher at the Baptist Academy in Lagos. In the late 1880s he quarrelled with the American Baptist missionary society, and led a movement out of it to found an independent Native Baptist Church. Progressively radicalized, he rejected his Western name and European dress in 1894 and took his church towards an entirely indigenous expression of Christianity. Out went the European missionary's hymn books, for example, and in came specially written African hymns. By 1913 he had become the first president of the African Communion of Independent Churches and a well-known international figure, though his church was never large. Independent churches appeared in South Africa too in the same period, with secessions from Methodism, Presbyterianism and Congregationalism provoked perhaps by the exceptionally aggressive form imperialist sentiment took in the region.

One of the earliest causes of independency was polygamy. The unyielding hostility of the Western missionary societies to this made it inevitable that some African Christians would take a separate path. After all, as many were quick to point out, Old Testament justification could be found for the practice. The white missionaries roundly condemned it, but often showed little real understanding of its role in African traditional society, nor sympathy for the wives who would be rendered practically divorced and without support by its rigid enforcement. The United African Methodist Church – in fact a small, Nigerian church – broke away from Methodism on this ground alone in 1917.

The early independent churches were relatively small, and even many unashamed advocates of 'Ethiopianism', or Africanization were convinced that the Western missionary societies were still a viable medium for African Christianity. But in the 1910s and 1920s a second wave of independency began. Led sometimes by churches that had been founded in the early years of the century, nevertheless this was to affect a much wider area of the continent. The 'Zionist' or 'prophet' churches marked the advancing development of Africa, drawing support as much from the newly growing urban populations as from the rural areas. The Zionist Apostolic Church was founded early in the century by P.L. Le Roux, an Afrikaner who had left the Dutch Reformed Church and who prided himself on his relationship with Africans. Through his influence the term 'Zionist' entered into wide use in Africa. Zionism spread fast in South Africa, especially among the Zulu, who had suffered harshly from British and Afrikaner policies. It was often tolerant of polygamy and open to the use of symbolism and ceremonies from African traditional religion. As it grew it diversified rapidly, according to the activity of particular local prophets: their special visions and gift of prophetic insight were even more central to Zionism than they have been to mainstream Pentecostalism. Isaiah Shembe, perhaps the most famous Zionist prophet, was called the 'liberator' by the Zulu people, and in his hymns cast himself as a John the Baptist figure, a forerunner and interpreter of Christ himself. Zionism appeared in other parts of Africa too around the same time. The millennialist teaching of Elliot Kamwana in Central Africa was originally influenced by the Jehovah's Witnesses, with their eschatological conviction that the end of the world was imminent and to be ushered in by a cosmic Armageddon.

In West Africa independent churches sprang up under the inspiration of William Wade Harris, a Liberian revivalist who had carried out a famously successful evangelistic campaign in 1913–14, and Garrick Braide. Harrist churches appeared along the Ivory Coast during the First World War, and churches following Braide in the Niger delta. At first these tried to keep good relations with the missionary societies, but they were not prepared to compromise their autonomy and so usually developed separately. A particularly tragic episode occurred in the Congo, with an independent church movement led by Simon Kimbangu from around 1918. Kimbangu exercised a healing ministry – something that was to recur constantly in independent churches. Though his message was not directly subversive, he had many imitators, some of whom advocated the non-payment of taxes. The radicalism and popularity of Kimbangu's message alarmed the colonial government, and in 1921 his fellow deacons and leaders were rounded up and imprisoned and he was sentenced to death – a sentence commuted to life imprisonment. Yet Kimbanguism thrived even in the absence of its leader and under constant repression. Many have pointed out that Kimbanguism was not in fact so much a threat to established missionary work in the Congo as a movement of mass conversion to Christianity. The Aladura movement in western Nigeria was similar. 'Aladura' means 'praying people'. Many of the followers of leaders such as Moses Orimolade had separated from the Anglican Church and practised as faith healers. Independency was more limited in East Africa, though in parts of Kenya it was active. It was in South and West Africa that, by the 1950s, its greatest concentration was to be found. In South Africa (including Southern Rhodesia, Botswana and Nyasaland) around 10 per cent of the black population belonged to independent churches, with over a thousand separate organizations. These included some 'Ethiopian' churches such as the African Congregational Church and the Bantu Methodist Church of South Africa, and also many newer bodies such as the Christian Apostolic Church of Zion of South Africa.

By their very nature most of these independent churches were local in their appeal. Local might mean here a really considerable area, a whole region or territory, defined by particularly strong bonds of cultural and ethnic identity. The Apostles of Johane Masowe, another prophet who modelled himself on John the Baptist, were drawn from the Shona peoples of eastern Rhodesia, and their strength remained in that region even when large numbers followed Masowe himself to the suburb of Korsten in Port Elizabeth in the Cape. Even there, where they were known as the Korsten Basketmakers (because they specialized in weaving and basketmaking), they retained a strong Shona identity and were a close, industrious and urbanized community.

In Kenya, among the Kikuyu, independency was especially strong, where 'Arathi', or prophets, appealed to the poorest and most marginalized members of society and often rejected Western culture completely, including dress, medicine and education. A few of the larger churches underwent a process of internationalization in the 1940s and 1950s, spreading far beyond their original territories. But specific ethnic identities were powerful, and so, in the era of decolonization, nationalist politicians were sometimes tempted to build alliances with independent church leaders. These could backfire. In the violent Mau Mau rebellion in Kenya in the 1950s, for example, the British colonial authorities saw the independent churches' schools as a threat, and closed them. In general, however, independent church leaders were politically quietist.

Colonial governments and white ruling elites, such as that which controlled South Africa until the 1990s, may have been unnecessarily heavy-handed at times in dealing with them. But they were surely correct in their suspicion that independent, black-led movements – however conformist – were inherently threatening to white rule. It is a measure of their fear that only 11 churches were ever recognized by the white Nationalist government of South Africa, despite the thousands there by the 1960s. It is also a measure of the connections between independency – after all a black-led phenomenon – and nationalism that many of these churches thrived and multiplied in the late 1950s and 1960s. Some already well-established bodies such as the Congolese Kimbanguist church now reached their peak. Other new bodies came into being and grew rapidly, such as the Mario Legio church, a movement in west Kenya that was unusual in being a secession from the Catholic Church. The non-prophetist churches, or 'Ethiopian' churches, did as well as the 'Zionist' churches. Whether churches thrived because nationalist sentiment prospered in them in parallel with political nationalism or because disappointed and frustrated nationalist hopes were diverted into religion is hard to say. This question – which has echoes of an argument over the relationship of religion and politics more commonly explored in the context of industrializing Europe – looks likely to be a fruitful one for historians of religion in Africa long into the future.

Independency was always regionally diverse, and despite its immense growth in the twentieth century there were always parts of Africa where it was weak. By the early 1970s some of the impetus seemed to be going out of it. There were few new large movements of independency in the immediate post-colonial era. Some of the governments of newly independent countries found independent churches an obstacle to their rule just as the colonial powers had done, and began to suppress them – as in Zambia under Kaunda, and Zaire (the Congo) under Mobutu. But in the 1970s a third wave of independency began, influenced above all by Pentecostalism – a wave that continues to this day. Independent Pentecostal churches were enormously attractive in areas already susceptible to independency, such as West Africa, and South and Central Africa. In Nigeria and Ghana, for example, independent Pentecostal churches had become the dominant form of Christianity by the 1990s. Though they too have absorbed many aspects of African tradition, including dress, song and dance, they have also been conduits for the 'globalized' religious culture transmitted through mass media. The use of sound amplification and visual media has enabled the construction of mega-churches, in which many thousands of worshippers can assemble. Healing is still an extraordinarily potent element of their appeal, but often it is accompanied by an emphasis on the 'prosperity gospel' that has an obvious attraction to the poor. The rise of these new Pentecostal churches – such as the Zimbabwe Assemblies of God, with over a million members – has led to accusations that there are subtle, continuing forms of colonialism exercised through the financial aid given to African churches from the West and through the ideological influence of consumer culture emanating from America. But this is to claim much too much for the West. Pentecostalism is not so very different from older strands of African independency. It may have had some American origins, as we shall see in a later chapter, but it stretched back into elements of popular Protestantism with a much wider and deeper history, and simply echoed features of African culture – the interest in healing, special revelations, prophet-like figures – that were already present in many of the independent churches. It is simply yet one more means by which Africans have explored a way of being Christian that is true to their own culture and sufficiently adaptable to enable to it flourish in many different contexts.

Independency in Asia

After Africa, Asia is the other major continent in which independency has proved itself a force to be reckoned with. Here too there is a recent history of colonial exploitation that has provided an ambiguous legacy for Christianity. Much of the growth of independent churches here is very recent – from around the 1970s – and Pentecostal. Independency in Africa has apparently provided a bridge between the religious experience of African traditional religions and the more formal, organized religion of the West. But it would be quite wrong to assume that this simply demonstrates the pre-modern character of popular religion. Independent, Charismatic and Pentecostal churches have proved as popular in the urban context as in rural areas in Africa. The same is true in Asia, and perhaps even more so. Here the newer Charismatic churches are particularly popular with the urban middle class – those who are most engaged in the practical, rational business of building the Asian economies. Their experience appears to disprove the assumption of many Western sociologists that Charismatic religion is a kind of throwback to pre-modern notions of miraculous healing and special divine inspiration. I say 'appears' because the problems of interpreting the very diverse religious experience of Asia are complex and it is possible to find evidence for and against most permutations of this argument.

South Korea is a country where there has been dramatic growth in the independent churches in the second half of the century, and where at the same time this has been through – and not against – the general process of urban and industrial advance. Korean Christianity was derived above all from American Presbyterian missionaries at the end of the nineteenth century, and experienced a series of revivals at the beginning of the twentieth century. During the years of Japanese occupation, Protestantism was attractive as an alternative national identity. Korean Protestantism retained its Presbyterian imprint, but schisms occurred from the original Presbyterian church of Korea, and there are now something like 200 different churches in South Korea. Methodism is also strong and has also produced various breakaway churches. In 1960 about 1.6 per cent of the population was Christian; by the end of the century that figure had risen tenfold, with much of the increase taken up by the independent and Pentecostal churches.

As in Africa, the motives for independency vary. Early schisms arose out of a definite desire to break away from the missionaries' churches. But in recent years a large number of indigenous churches have appeared harmonizing mainstream Christian beliefs and practices with traditional, non-Christian Korean culture, including reverence for the forces of nature, the use of healing charms, and divination. In extreme form this took religious groups well outside mainstream Christianity. The Olive Tree Church, founded by Pak T'ae-Son in 1955, for example, centred on the claim that T'ae-Son was himself the immortal Olive Tree and an oracle of God who could cure sickness because he was filled with magical power. Most of the independent churches did not go anything like as far as this. T'ae-Son's movement in fact collapsed in the mid-1970s after a series of financial scandals, just as Korean Pentecostalism was beginning its period of greatest growth.

More will be said about South Korea in the chapter on Pentecostalism. Another unusual example of Asian independency is China. Here, almost certainly because of the conditions of repression and because of the need therefore to emphasize distance from Western, traditional Christian denominations, in the 1950s and 1960s a huge variety of house churches appeared. For obvious reasons it is almost impossible to gauge the true extent of this

movement. Many of these churches disappeared in the Cultural Revolution. They were separate from the official Protestant Church formed in 1958
which forcibly united all the Protestant denominations. They were conservative Evangelical in character and yet radically localized in membership.
From the 1980s, during a period of liberalization, independent churches
began to thrive in China again, and continued to do so during the 1990s
even after a period of repression began again in 1994, when the Chinese
government attempted to insist once again on a process of forced registra-
tion of churches.

One final example of Asian independency will suffice. In Malaysia,
Christian churches have had to operate in the post-colonial era in a situation
in which Islam is the state religion, and their freedom is limited, especially
when it comes to trying to obtain permission to build new churches. There
are practical incentives for Christians to form free, independent churches,
and Malaysian church life has shown an amazing fissiparousness. Many of
the independent churches are Pentecostal, as in Korea, and once again the
distinction between independency and Pentecostalism is virtually meaning-
less. Some of the independent churches operate much as any other Christian denomination, with a proper church building and a formal ministry.
But many are house churches, meeting informally in people's houses or in
businesses or in cinemas, for example, and with little by way of permanent
organization. They have a mainly Chinese membership and so can help to
reinforce ethnic identities at a time of continuing conflict between Christianity and the state. On the other hand, many of the larger Charismatic
Christian churches are inter-ethnic and may well receive support precisely
because they offer a new and different kind of belonging to that on offer with
the house churches. One scholar's suggestion is that all these groups thrive
on an attempt to reunite the material and the spiritual against the rather
dessicated rationalism of materialism, in a thoroughly modern response to
the problems of modernization: 'Against the moral and spiritual vacuity of
western culture with its substitution of materialism for spirituality there is
a reassertion in this movement of an integration of modern materialist life-
styles and spirituality and the non-rational.'[1] Once again the conclusion is
that independent Charismatic Christianity works with the grain of modern
society and not against it.

New religious movements

No account of twentieth-century Christianity would be complete without
some discussion of the many movements that have existed on the margins
of the main Christian churches in the course of the century, but which have
had a doctrine and organization so different from that of the Christian

mainstream that the term 'Christian' can be applied to them only with difficulty. These movements cannot be aligned closely with independent Christianity in Africa and Asia, and their inclusion in this chapter is not meant to imply that they can be. They do at the very least, however, share with the independent churches the obvious fact that they are not classifiable under any of the three major categories of Christianity through which I have organized most of the chapters of this book, namely Catholicism, Orthodoxy and Protestantism. I have included them here under the general umbrella of 'New Religious Movements' (NRMs), but this commonly used term is hardly a precise one. Some of the movements I have included under it are not new, for one thing – the Jehovah's Witnesses go back to the late nineteenth century, and the Mormons, or Latter-Day Saints, go back further still to the mid-nineteenth century. But in any case the range of views, forms of organization and patterns of leadership among them is so great that no one label could do them justice. Nor can a brief account here do more than sketch an outline of their role in the twentieth century.

NRMs have been described as 'sects' or 'cults' by most of the mainstream churches as well as by non-believers. In both cases the term is used pejoratively. 'Cult' in particular usually implies that a group uses various methods of coercion, such as brainwashing, to keep its members in line. A series of horrific incidents have underscored this impression. Most notorious perhaps was the siege in 1993 in Waco, Texas, when 76 people were killed after a 51-day stand-off between the FBI and a group of Branch Davidians led by David Koresh. The Branch Davidians were a schismatic group from the Seventh-Day Adventists. Fugitives from Koresh's group had accused him of child abuse, polygamy and the stockpiling of guns, and spoke of his malign yet charismatic influence over his followers. But incidents such as this tell us little or nothing about accusations of brainwashing, and an ongoing controversy within psychiatry has raised much scepticism that it is practically possible for cults to influence people this way. A well-known British study of the Moonies concluded that the charge of brainwashing and physical coercion was unfounded: there were sociological and psychological reasons why particular people were drawn to the Moonies.[2] 'Cult' is therefore a misleading term. But the word 'sect' has a more respectable sociological pedigree. In the sociological literature, the term is used to indicate a group which is deliberately separatist and exclusive, usually small, and inclined to protect the purity of its own values over and against the temptation to loosen them in order to attract more members.

This is a pretty good description of many of the NRMs, but again it is not watertight. Some NRMs have avoided mass evangelism, and so they have remained small, tightly knit local groups. But many do seek to make new members. Two movements that would certainly regard themselves as Christian and who have a strong evangelistic culture are the Jehovah's Witnesses and the Church of the Latter-Day Saints, or 'Mormons'. Both are now international churches. The Jehovah's Witnesses originated in America towards the end of the nineteenth century and were influenced by the Adventist teaching that the coming of Christ's kingdom on earth was imminent. They deny the doctrine of the Trinity and predict a great cosmic conflict to end this world. Their radical pacifism and rejection of secular authority have made them particularly vulnerable to persecution. Several thousand died under the Nazis, for example. The Witnesses now have adherents in almost every country, with some 11 million followers worldwide at the end of the twentieth century. The Mormons began in the American mid-West in the 1840s and claimed to have received a second scriptural revelation in the Book of Mormon. They too have a strong Adventist eschatology, believing that the tribes of Israel will be gathered together physically before the reign of Christ begins on earth, and that this will happen in the West. Controversially, their founder Joseph Smith endorsed polygamy. Though less widely spread than Jehovah's Witnesses, Mormons too have moved well beyond their Utah heartland and now have churches in most European countries and in many larger countries of the developing world. They had some 8 million followers worldwide by the mid-1990s. Both these movements have seen dramatic growth in the last quarter of the century, more than doubling in size.

More typical of the common stereotype of the 'cult' are the Moonies, or the Unification Church, founded in the 1950s in South Korea by Sun Myung Moon. The Unification Church does not accept the traditional doctrine of the Trinity, and while it seeks to unify all religions, it does so through the proclamation of Moon as the Second Messiah. Given Moon's prominence in church doctrine, it is hardly surprising that the Unification Church became, in effect, a personality cult. Controversy dogged it for years over its method of recruitment, which hinged on intensive courses and 'love bombardment', leading to the charges of brainwashing. In Sun Myung Moon's home country of South Korea, where the church is based, it had half a million followers by the mid-1990s. This represented significant growth from the 300,000 noted for 1970, but not especially dramatic growth in comparison with Korean independent and Pentecostal churches. In America the Unification Church had actually declined from around 30,000 members in 1970 to 20,000 in 1995. Great staged events such as mass weddings, in which thousands of couples who had hardly met were married in one great ceremony, attracted huge media attention, but masked the fact that the Unification Church was small in world terms.

The decline of the Unification Church in America may suggest that in the free, pluralistic context of the West, many of these NRMs were destined never to break through the glass ceiling and become truly popular mass movements. In the Global South, their influence was patchy. There were areas of strength, but even then their influence was usually far outweighed by that of the mainstream denominations and by the more recent Pentecostal and Charismatic churches. In Central Africa, for example, the Jehovah's Witnesses have been active since the early twentieth century, and by the mid-1990s reckoned on some 300,000 members in the Congo. But they were a very small proportion of the 41 million or so who constituted the total Christian community of the country. The role of the NRMs in general seems to have been to absorb Christians disaffected with the traditional churches or those who were seeking a tight, enclosed form of spiritual discipline. They were truly sectarian in tending to emphasize a sharp divergence between their own value-systems and those of the world around them, including the mainstream churches. But they were never likely to attract more than a small proportion of the worldwide Christian community and would have had to change fundamentally in order to do so.

PART III
1973 TO 2000: THE RISE OF THE GLOBAL SOUTH

CHAPTER II

From Oil Crisis to Oil Wars

Towards a global economy

The coming of the nuclear age in 1945 had robbed all but the most naive of optimism about the future of the international order. The Cold War cast a long shadow over everything. It was impossible to think contentedly about peace and prosperity when at any moment the world could be pitched into a nuclear winter. Hungary in 1956, Cuba in 1962, Vietnam, war in the Middle East in 1973, Sino-Soviet tensions, the Soviet occupation of Afghanistan in 1980 – time after time, it felt as if international relations were on a knife edge. But for the West, after the years of postwar austerity were over, it was actually an era of unprecedented prosperity. Trade flourished and living standards rose, fuelled by previously unimaginable advances in technology. Economically the West could feel secure.

But in 1973 all that changed. The oil-producing states of the Middle East hiked their prices, and suddenly the West found that its loss of political hegemony in the region had serious economic consequences. It was a bold assertion of political power by states not so long before under colonial administration. There were other producers, of course – notably the US itself – and oil represented just one of the raw materials needed by Western industry (though a vital one at that); the ensuing era of economic instability in the West cannot be explained by the oil crisis alone. The higher cost of oil merely hastened the slow-down and contraction inevitable after such a prolonged period of growth. It certainly highlighted a crucial weakness of industrialization in the West, namely its dependence on a source of fuel and material over which it had no direct political control. This exposed the fragility of a system of economic management called by some the 'managed market'. It was paralleled by the state-managed economies of the communist world and by the economic policies adopted by many of the newly independent states in Africa and Asia. Everyone was confident that governments could run the economy. The managed market combined the welfare state with moderate economic control (such as measures to control prices and

interest rates), and was justified by economic theories derived from John
Maynard Keynes. But in the wake of the oil crisis, Western nations faced
rapidly rising costs, and thus high inflation, and rising expectations (chiefly
wage demands) caused by a long period of economic stability. Influenced
by neo-liberal economics, they began to cut back on public expenditure
and limit pay settlements in order to control inflation. Inevitably this led
to rising unemployment and social unrest. Conflict was often accelerated
by politics, with governments forced to face – and sometimes face down –
industrial action, such as strikes and go-slows. No new consensus emerged
out of this period of economic instability, since the aggressive free-market
policies of some governments (such as those of Ronald Reagan in the US
and Margaret Thatcher in Britain) were only partly successful in controlling inflation and public expenditure, and people were left wondering if the
struggle had been worth it after all.

The implications of all this for the Third World were dire. If Western
governments were abandoning economic regulation, they were not going to
support regulatory policies in developing countries. And yet an unregulated
market by its very nature could spell disaster for poor countries that had
little to offer the global market. International financial institutions such as
the World Bank were influenced by the economic orthodoxies of the West:
they would lend money at rates of interest and attach conditions to the loans
that it was impossible for developing countries to meet. In consequence
the poor were caught in a double-bind. Moreover the giving of loans by
Western banks merely meant an accumulation of debt by developing countries' governments. Internal political turmoil, economic mismanagement
and corruption often made matters even worse. Rampant inflation during
the 1980s pushed up the rate of interest. By the 1990s the accumulated debt
of Third World countries amounted to a staggering $1.5 trillion. Brazil alone
owed over $100 billion.

All of this was bad enough, but this was also an era of rapid population
growth in the developing world. Third World governments were required
by Western aid to cut back on public expenditure (though – strangely? – not
always *military* expenditure) just at the time when welfare spending was
needed more than ever. The structural imbalances in world trade just did
not favour the developing world, and particularly Latin America and Africa.
The consequence was that, far from seeing the disappearance of famine and
disease – something that medical technology, transport and forward planning should have made possible – the last quarter of the twentieth century
saw their resurgence. Westerners were transfixed by images of the famine
in Ethiopia in 1984, but this was just one crisis among many. The desperate
need of Third World countries to find ways of stimulating economic growth

made it very difficult for them to sustain the environmental policies urged
on them by the West, just as anxiety about the effects of environmental
damage and man-made global warming began to take hold. The rain forests
of Latin America, Africa and Asia were disappearing fast as the century
drew to a close.

By then the leading industrialized countries were taking some steps to
ease the burden of Third World debt, but they were too little too late for
the millions who died of starvation and disease. Everyone in the West in
the early 1990s seemed to be talking about the triumph of the market and
the coming of a new age of prosperity. The collapse of the Soviet Union
and its satellite regimes underlined this sense of self-satisfaction. The mood
was infamously caught by the American historian Francis Fukuyama, who
claimed that the triumph of liberal capitalism meant 'the end of history'.
How wrong that was, not because in an obvious sense history goes on but
because the triumph of liberal capitalism had not in fact occurred. The
inability of the world economy to address its structural inequalities of wealth
and trade did not suggest the arrival of a new period of stability. Instead it
fuelled resentment and desperation. Time and again the effects of economic
insecurity and a raging sense of injustice found their outlet in movements of
protest against established governments and against the West itself. They
undermined world peace and encouraged radical religion.

A new international order?

In the last quarter of the century, the single most significant political change
in the international order was the collapse of Soviet communism. Remarkably – given the speed with which conservatives the world over hailed this
new fact – scarcely anyone in the West had predicted it. A Hungarian diplomat in Vietnam in the closing years of the Soviet regime later admitted,
'We all knew the game was up.' But if that was true to an insider, outside
the communist bloc it suited everyone to go on thinking that the Soviet
Union remained a credible threat to world peace. The armaments industry
benefited, certainly, and hundreds of thousands of workers were engaged
in it across the Western world. In the era of détente, beginning in the early
1970s, there were some signs of the inability of the Soviet regime to prevent
Western aspirations from percolating through to their peoples. Pop music,
new fashion, films and other consumer goods were smuggled across borders
or cherished by the few party workers and bureaucrats lucky enough to get
hold of them. Václav Havel, the dissident writer and later first president of
post-communist Czechoslovakia, described the subtle corruption of values
the 'system' encouraged when everyone coveted what no one was officially
allowed to have: 'The worst thing is that we live in a contaminated moral

atmosphere. We fell morally ill because we became used to saying something different from what we thought.'[1]

The first really strong signs of failure came in Afghanistan, however. Occupying Soviet forces there from 1980 onwards were unable to impose a lasting military settlement on a country resentful of their presence. The Americans covertly assisted the various group of Mujahideen or 'holy warriors' who sprang up to fight the Soviets. This was to prove a short-sighted policy, since out of the Mujahideen, long after the Soviets left, emerged the Taliban, the radical Islamist movement that was later to provide a haven for the anti-Western terrorist network Al-Qaeda. The military, economic and social strains of the Soviet policy in Afghanistan took their toll. Mikhail Gorbachev became Soviet leader in 1985 and committed the Soviet Union to a new process of openness (*glasnost*) and reform (*perestroika*). The collapse of the system, however, first began at its western edge, in East Germany, Czechoslovakia and Poland, when movements of protest and non-communist organization such as Solidarity, the free Polish trade union, were able to survive attempts to suppress them. Gorbachev refused to commit Soviet troops to prop up the ailing communist regimes of eastern Europe. But the Soviet Union itself followed suit, as democratic reform spelt the end of the old party regime.

It was an extraordinarily rapid and complete collapse. In just two years – 1989–90 – communism fell in Eastern Europe and the Soviet Empire came to an end. Around this time, two further series of events confirmed what an era of sudden change it really was. In South Africa the release of the long-imprisoned ANC leader Nelson Mandela in 1991 marked the beginning of the end of the system of apartheid maintained by the all-white nationalist government for over 40 years. It had survived riots in 1960 in Sharpeville and 1976 in Soweto, and the subsequent emergence of a worldwide anti-apartheid movement, largely by intimidation and violence. With Mandela and other black leaders in prison, the role of the churches in providing a surrogate leadership for the opposition to apartheid was crucial. The Anglican Archbishop Desmond Tutu and the black Reformed minister Allan Boesak were among the most outspoken domestic critics of the regime, and their commitment to peaceful methods made a government conscious of its need to maintain economic and political links with the West wary of taking direct action against them. Perhaps the most surprising thing about the transition to democracy in South Africa in the early 1990s was that it was accomplished with remarkably little bloodshed. Mandela's political skill – exercised to the full while negotiating with the government before his release from a position of apparent weakness in prison – undoubtedly had much to do with this. It surely also owed something to the impact of

Christianity. Even so, what happened in South Africa was different from the post-colonial settlements in most of the rest of the continent. There was a kind of trade-off, not to put it too finely. Whites gave up their monopoly of political power but their economic status was left untouched. Of course even under apartheid, South Africa was not strictly a colonial power: it was already a sovereign state, and its ruling Afrikaans elite considered themselves (with a certain sleight of hand historically) every bit as 'African' as their black compatriots. Post-apartheid South Africa was still troubled by mass poverty and by black resentment at whites' prosperity.

Change came rapidly to China too, though not politically. In the spring of 1989 peaceful student protests, centred on Tiananmen Square in Beijing, against the restrictiveness of Chinese society were brought to an end suddenly and bloodily by the army. It is difficult to be sure about the numbers, but up to 2,500 people may have been killed and another 5,000 wounded. Severe repression of the student movement followed. Ironically the protests came some 13 years after Chairman Mao's death had led to some relaxation of communist control, and 11 years after Deng Xiaoping had begun to introduce moderate free-market policies. The protests and their suppression were, then, an example of the truth of Alexis De Tocqueville's observation (originally made of pre-revolutionary France) that states are never so weak as when they begin to reform themselves. Yet perhaps this 'truth' was itself an illusion. The Chinese Communist Party remained firmly in control in the aftermath of the protests – so much so, that the policy of economic liberalization continued almost unchecked. Indeed by the early 1990s China was sending many thousands of students abroad to study in Western universities – hardly a sign of insecurity. Economic liberalization was followed – slowly – by liberalization in social life and in the partial freedom Chinese people were now given to join churches even apart from the state-sponsored Christian movements. Hard statistical evidence of church growth in this period is hard to come by. By the late 1990s the government figure for the total number of Christians in China was 20 million, but another estimate from an informed source suggests there might have been as many as 80 million Chinese Christians of various denominations, including Catholics, Protestants, independents and Pentecostals. House churches particularly thrived during the years of persecution. Some continued state persecution even in this era of reform made the collection of hard data on Christianity in China very difficult. The rapid growth of the Chinese economy in the 1990s, augmented by taking back Hong Kong, a key financial centre, from the British under a long-standing agreement in 1997, was proof of the success of the policy. The China of 2000 was a long way from the China Mao had envisaged in the years of the Cultural Revolution.

The tensions that had run through the international order since the end of the Second World War had largely disappeared by the early 1990s. The break-up of the Soviet Union, as states formerly absorbed into the Union, such as the Ukraine, Azerbaijan and Georgia, chose independence, brought an end to the immediate threat of war between the West and the Soviet Union. Hardly anyone now talked much about imminent nuclear war. The peace movements which had appeared in the West in the Cold War, particularly in the late 1950s and the 1980s, found popular interest draining away from them. Within a few years Marxism had ceased to be the radical ideological force it had been among the young for the duration of the Cold War. But this did not lead to a new era of peace and stability. The collapse of Soviet communism merely removed what had been as much a restraining force in international crises over the previous 40 years as an aggressive one. The savage war between Iran and Iraq in the 1980s was a foretaste of what might happen if regional conflicts were allowed to escalate without super-power intervention. War in Central Africa throughout this period proved the point; its nadir was the genocide in Rwanda in 1994, in which over a million of ethnic-minority Tutsi people were murdered by armed gangs of the majority Hutus. There, and in the series of conflicts that emerged out of the collapse of the communist Yugoslav state from 1991 to the end of the century, it was clear that the power of the UN to prevent human suffering was negligible. There was a vacuum, filled by the one power which still did have the capability and will to launch military operations almost anywhere in the world – the United States. Thus it was the US that led the expulsion of Iraqi forces from Kuwait in 1991 and the air campaign against Serbian forces in Kosovo in former Yugoslavia in 1999. Were these interventions, and others like them, benevolent operations to protect peace, security and freedom? That was the American claim. Others argued that they were motivated by economic interests – especially oil in the Middle East. But to many Westerners an unnerving element of the new and unpredictable international order was a renewed sense of religious conflict.

Radical religion

In political circles both in the West and in the Third World, as well as in the Soviet Union, in the years after the Second World War it was axiomatic that religion had ceased to be a political force in the world. The major ideological fault-lines were economic and social, not religious – they ran between capitalism and socialism. In Africa and Asia as much as in the Soviet Union, America and Europe, religion was accepted as a cultural fact, but its power to motivate human beings, to influence their political and economic choices and to shape their lives, was rarely acknowledged by political elites. There was plenty of evidence to the contrary – savage Muslim–Hindu conflict during the partition of India, hostility to Christianity in newly independent Muslim states, the influence of Orthodox Judaism in the new state of Israel, for example – but as long as argument concentrated on economic systems, and religion itself was assumed to be part of dying traditional cultures, the fact that a very large number of human beings professed faith in particular religions was something which political leaders did not need to notice. What mattered was where your ultimate loyalties lay – capitalist West or communist East.

But what appeared good political common sense risked minimizing the continuing power of religion in the modern world. Perhaps too many political leaders of the postwar generations were brought up on the secularizing myths of both communist and liberal capitalist apologists. As we have seen, the big story about Christianity in the postwar world was not its failure in Western Europe but its flourishing elsewhere. And it did so in forms that most Western commentators failed to take seriously enough – Catholicism, and the socially conservative wing of Protestantism. To the Western liberal conscience – and that could embrace both right-wing and left-wing politicians and thinkers – religion was effete if it was modern-minded and dangerous if it was traditionalist. Such a view rested on an extraordinary oversimplification of religion. It reduced Christianity itself to a simple polarity of progressive and reactionary, and often assumed a hierarchy of value, with Christianity for all its faults generally a more sophisticated religion than Islam, Hinduism and Buddhism. In Europe, with its long history of religious conflict, it was perfectly understandable that politicians had evolved a necessary *modus vivendi* with the churches, which assumed the displacement of the churches from the main streams of public policy. But that view could not take seriously enough the social implications of Christianity. Even churchgoing politicians might strive to keep religion out of politics; but church leaders knew that was impossible.

The common view may have been simplistic. But it was religion in its more radical guise that forced politicians to take notice. A more extreme version of Islam had been gaining ground in the Middle East for several decades, largely unnoticed in the West. It was itself diverse, representing several different strands of Islamic resistance to innovation or development within Islam, and including the Muslim Brotherhoods, the traditionalist 'Wahhabist' Islam supported by Saudi Arabia, and elements of Shi'a Islam. So it was not one movement as such, and the common application of the term 'fundamentalism' by Western commentators (transposing a word originally used in a Christian context) has been unhelpful. There were certainly strong religious, anti-modern components of the resurgent radical Islam of this period, but there were also significant political and social elements too. That was true above all in Iran, where, in 1979, a popular uprising overthrew the autocracy of the shah and led to the creation of an explicitly Islamic republic. Iran became a watchword for extreme Islam in the West. But what that missed was the substantial differences between Iranian Shi'a Islam and the actually more aggressive and more narrowly 'fundamentalist' form of radical Islam emerging from Sunni communities. Two things jointly misled Western commentators in their view of Islam: the Arab–Israeli conflict (and in particular the unresolved question of Palestinian self-determination) and the pervasive anti-Western rhetoric of much of the Arab world. In the Soviet bloc, until its disintegration in the early 1990s, the suppression of religious conflict simply masked the presence of restless Muslim communities in large parts of the southern Soviet Union.

It was not only in Islam that radical religion was growing in the last quarter of the century. In India the 'Hindutva' or 'Hinduness' movement that had first arisen as a form of Indian nationalism in the British Raj emerged once again in the 1980s as a reaction against the secularism of the Indian state and in particular against what was seen as its appeasement of Indian Muslims. There were movements of Buddhist self-assertion, sometimes also called 'fundamentalism', in Vietnam in the 1960s, and then in Myanmar, formerly Burma, in the last decades of the century. In all these cases, the boundary between politics and religion was extremely fluid, if not non-existent. That was also true of Christianity. The most startling example to Western eyes at the end of the century was the rise of the 'religious right' in America, a coalition of conservative Catholic and Protestant groups that supported right-wing Republican politicians and was believed to have had a decisive influence on the administration of George W. Bush, president from 2000.

It was unfortunate that the pervasive secularism of political circles in the West meant that the only substantive category in which they were able to grasp the continuing influence of religion at the end of the century was the blanket term 'fundamentalism'. This was a poor description of what were among the liveliest elements of the great world religions. It did not inspire confidence that Western leaders – in whose hands, after all, so many of the world's financial resources were concentrated – were likely to understand well the complexities of countries of the developing world. It also did not inspire confidence that they would understand well their own societies. The collapse of the European empires had produced a reverse-flow of migration, bringing eventually millions from formerly subject peoples to Europe. They had brought with them their religions. By the end of the century as much as 10 per cent of the population of France was Muslim.

In Britain there were large communities of Muslims, Sikhs and Hindus, as well as African and Caribbean Christians. Racial tensions, sometimes erupting into rioting, had encouraged a desire to promote better community relations in the urban areas where the immigrants and their descendants lived. But the drawing in of religious leaders to this process was slow and patchy. There was a general recognition of the urgent need to encourage inter-religious dialogue but little clarity about how this should proceed. Leaders of the Christian churches were often much more aware of all this – not least because of the international nature of the great world Christian communions. Catholic church leaders, for example, could not but be aware of the difficulties of Christian–Muslim relations in Central and Northern Africa and in Asia. The resurgence of radical religion in the developing world, and in the Middle East, had sponsored the emergence of terrorist organizations in some places, but again the temptation followed by Western governments time and time again was to try to confront the symptoms of terror rather than tackle its deeper causes.

Religion and the global challenge

By 2000 the Christian churches across the globe could draw some comfort from three things that the last two decades had demonstrated beyond question. The first was the continuing force and relevance of popular religion in general, and Christianity in particular, throughout the world. There was little evidence that secularized Europe was going to be a model for modernizing societies in the Third World – and anyway, little sign of the disappearance of religion in America. The second was the failure of state-sponsored atheism. The collapse of the Soviet system and the partial liberalization of China suggested that religion was too tenacious a phenomenon to be destroyed by atheist propaganda and persecution. People could not be forced into programmes of ethnic and religious (or anti-religious) integration. The third thing was a negative observation. The end of the Cold War, and of the polarized networks of loyalty it had sustained across the world, had not given way to a more stable international order but to a more unpredictable and unstable one. In that context the churches were likely to be more significant representatives of popular opinion, and perhaps brokers in regional conflicts, than politicians had for long supposed.

But the end of the polarities of the Cold War also brought with it more significant difficulties for the churches. The growing strength of Christianity in the Third World was rightly reflected in a greater confidence and assertiveness for Third World churches in the international and denominational councils of the main Christian traditions. Issues that looked important in the West, such as homosexuality and the ordination of women, were often issues on which their fellow Christians in the Global South took an oppo-site view. Likewise church leaders in the West were often blind to the press-ing nature of things that preoccupied the Global South, such as the local conflicts with Islam, corruption in government, the HIV/AIDS epidemic and, above all, the endemic poverty of many Third World countries. Bitter divisions began to open up within the mainstream churches. But these divi-sions could be paralleled by further divisions within regional churches. And they were complicated by the revolution in information technology of the last quarter of the century, as the flow of information from one part of the world to the other was dramatically speeded up by computers, the inter-net and satellite systems. Dissident groups could organize with a facility never available before. Globalization could create something like a genuine world community in terms of information (though let us not forget that it was only a small proportion of Third World populations that had access to information technology), but it was very doubtful that it could change significantly the inherent inequalities of political and military power and economic resources that continued to afflict the world.

CHAPTER 12

The Catholic Church

The greatest pope?

The last years of Paul VI were a time of uncertainty. There were no encyclicals, and Paul's energy was fading fast. His oversight of the Second Vatican Council was his greatest gift to the Church. But that legacy was proving an ambiguous one by the mid-1970s. In some countries the conciliar reforms were being taken further and faster than the Council itself had surely envisaged. Even many of the theological architects of the conciliar reforms, such as Henri de Lubac and Yves Congar, lamented the unrestrained enthusiasm for change in some Catholic circles, especially in the West. There national churches were shedding key elements of traditional and ultramontane culture – the Latin rite, Marian devotion, Gregorian chant – so quickly that they were provoking movements of resistance and reaction within their own ranks. But Paul did not have the will to reassert papal authority and rein in the modernizers. He died in 1978 and was succeeded briefly by Albino Luciani, Patriarch of Venice, a humble, pastoral-minded man, who may have been chosen as a competent but cautious shepherd of the Church. Luciani took the joint name John Paul, marking his loyalty to the spirit of his two predecessors. But he died suddenly, probably of a pulmonary embolism, just a month after his election; the Vatican issued a series of inconsistent statements about his death, prompting totally ungrounded allegations of murder that kept conspiracy theorists happy for years.

The stunned conclave of cardinals was summoned again. In the circumstances they took an amazingly bold decision. For the first time since the early sixteenth century they elected a non-Italian pope, by eventually (nine ballots) the huge margin of 103 out of 109 electors. Their choice was the Cardinal Archbishop of Cracow, Karol Wojtyla – about as far removed as they could get from the background and life experience of all of the previous twentieth-century popes. They elected him young – he was 58 – and expected therefore a long papacy. They certainly got one. In fact they got someone whom some described as 'the greatest pope of all'. Taking the name John Paul II, Wojtyla's papacy was one of the longest in history, last-ing nearly 27 years until his death early in 2005. Born in 1920, he was a complex, brilliant, physically robust, multifaceted man, whose character had been formed in the face of early loss – his mother died when he was not yet nine, and he was brought up by his devout father, a retired Polish army officer – and the experience of the Nazi occupation of Poland. During the war Wojtyla had worked in a quarry and a factory, and had become one of the first seminarians in an underground seminary run by Cardinal Sapieha, the redoubtable leader of the Polish church who came to symbolize its spirit of resistance to Nazism.

There was no doubting Wojtyla's personal courage, not least when he survived an attempted assassination in 1981 by a Turkish hitman who may have been put up to it ultimately by the KGB, the Soviet secret police. A charismatic figure, he had a wide circle of friends in his youth, including Jews and women. There were girlfriends. Celibacy in his case was surely a great sacrifice – perhaps that was why he later upheld it so forcefully. He proved an immensely talented student, interested in existentialist philoso-phy and phenomenology. He had become a bishop at the young age of 38, and thereafter had a meteoric rise – a significant theologian at Vatican II, Archbishop of Krakow in 1963, cardinal in 1967. In these years he published philosophy, drama and poetry, but became known above all for the audac-ity and political astuteness with which, under the guidance of Cardinal Wyszynski, Sapieha's successor, he helped to steer the Polish church through communist persecution. Commentators would later say that the spirit of his papacy was quintessentially Polish Catholic – doctrinally very conserva-tive, strongly Marian, confident in its Catholic identity and uncompromis-ing. That assessment has to be held in place with the fact that, out of the experience of communism, he also strongly supported the principle of reli-gious liberty; this went against the spirit of pre-Vatican II Catholicism, and implied that the freedom of the individual was an absolute necessity for the full development of religious faith. So this was not *merely* conserva-tive Catholicism. And in fact Wojtyla had also apparently taken something from the social engagement with Marxism, however much he abhorred its philosophical materialism and its atheism. He was one of the drafters of the conciliar pastoral constitution, *Gaudium et Spes*, and a strong defender of the principle of social responsibility – something not always appreciated by his politically right-wing defenders in the West.

This mixture of doctrinal and ethical conservatism with social progres-sivism ran through his teaching as pope. In contrast with Paul VI, encycli-cals, apostolic exhortations and apostolic letters poured out of the Vatican during John Paul II's reign – over 60 of them. Many of them reaffirmed traditional Catholic positions, pulling the Church back – as progressive Catholics saw it – from the radical developments that had followed Vatican II. In the apostolic letter *Mulieris Dignitatem* ('On the Dignity and Voca-tion of Women', 1988) John Paul welcomed the new educational and social opportunities for women, but emphasized their God-given role as mother. In *Veritatis Splendor* ('The Splendour of Truth', 1993), perhaps the most important of all his 14 encyclicals, he sought to re-anchor Catholic moral teaching in the concept of absolute truth, criticizing the way in which 'even in Seminaries and Faculties of Theology' Catholic teachers had accepted implicitly 'currents of thought which end by detaching human freedom from its essential and constitutive relationship to truth'. This was typical of John Paul's method: no concession on the fundamental objectivity of Catholic doctrine and moral teaching, but within that a positive evaluation of human freedom and dignity and a passionate concern for social justice. This double-edged method caught many more simplistic Catholic thinkers – whether on the left or the right – off guard. Thus he criticized the libera-tion theologians' use of Marxism and yet endorsed the principle of libera-tion in terms similar to the liberation theologians in *Sollicitudo Rei Socialis* ('On Social Concern', 1987). Perhaps his crowning achievement, however, was the publication in 1992 of a comprehensive *Catechism of the Catholic Church*. Attempts to produce a modern catechism before had faltered. Now John Paul's authoritarian, centralized understanding of papal responsibility ensured that an agreed document was pushed through – one that mostly affirmed traditional Catholic teaching without reservation.

The scale and depth of John Paul's teaching emerged slowly; only by the late 1980s was it possible to see the true breadth of his engagement with the challenges facing the Catholic Church, and to grasp its limitations. What the world saw at once was the extraordinary energy with which he took up his responsibilities. Here was a pope who travelled as no pope had done before him. People had forgotten that Paul VI had travelled outside Italy in the early years of his papacy. John Paul proved to be a relentless traveller, often exhausting his entourage before he began to succumb to Parkinson's Disease in his 70s. The travel was not a luxury. It was a very personal interpretation of the universal primacy. It is tempting to put this in an ultramontane light, and many did: John Paul was reasserting papal authority in the most direct way possible, literally going to region after region of the Church, calling the faithful together, stirring them up and settling outstanding local issues. It sat uneasily with Vatican II's emphasis on episcopal collegiality, and undermined the freedom and autonomy of the local church. It was an extraordinary attempt to bind the Church together by sheer force of personality and will. The masses of Catholic faithful who flocked to see him were probably unaware of the theological subtleties of collegiality and primacy, however. What they saw was a strong Christian leader and father-figure, fearless in denunciation of tyranny and injustice.

Among the most memorable of John Paul's journeys was that in June 1979 to Poland, less than a year after his election as pope. Huge crowds followed him everywhere. He was welcomed by well over a million people in Victory Square in Warsaw, and made 40 public appearances in nine days. The communist regime's attempts to suppress news about the visit backfired badly. He was forbidden to extend the visit to the mining communities of Silesia, and so he held a Mass for them at the monastery of Czestochowa, home of the 'Black Madonna', the icon of Mary hailed as the historic heart of Polish Christianity. Some quarter of a million miners and their families managed to attend, and, in the words of one biographer, 'the government witnessed the humiliating spectacle of a quarter of a million miners singing "Christ has conquered, Christ is King, Christ commands our lives" at the top of their voices'.[1] This visit alone, followed by others in 1983 and 1987, is credited with stirring up Polish resistance to the regime, encouraging the independent trade union Solidarity. Another memorable visit came near the end of his pontificate in 2000 when, already frail, he travelled to Israel, spoke at Yad Vashem, the Holocaust memorial, and inserted a prayer of penitence for the sins of Christians against Jews into a crack in the Wailing Wall in Jerusalem. Probably no Christian leader in the late twentieth century had done more to atone for the past abuses of Christian people against the Jews than John Paul II.

In a papacy of such length, energy and determination, so much merits attention that it is impossible even to approach a comprehensive account here. What can be said in summary by way of evaluation of John Paul II? If not the greatest pope of all, he was at least one of the greatest Christian leaders of the twentieth century. His evident courage, his strength of personality, his forceful leadership, his humour and personal charisma, all produced an indelible effect on those who met him or attended the rallies and services he addressed in his years of travel. He personified a spirit of Christian integrity and compassion. He was a powerful symbol of religious freedom in Eastern Europe. He made a notable contribution to Jewish–Christian relations and was a powerful and critical Christian voice in many controversial questions of international relations. He was nobody's fool – and nobody's stooge. Whether it is to his credit or not, he certainly halted the pace of progressive change in many parts of the Catholic Church and reasserted the central authority of the papacy itself. And yet, despite his strenuous efforts, it is doubtful that he made significant strides in tackling the internal difficulties the Catholic Church faced by the end of the century, particularly in the West. His doctrinal and ethical conservatism attracted the hostility of progressive Catholics and probably did little to strengthen the faltering authority of the Church in parts of the West.

The after-history of the Council

The problems Catholics faced by the third quarter of the century were manifold, but they were strategic and institutional for much of the Catholic world. Only in the West could it be said that there was serious division within Catholicism and a consequent impact on numbers attending Mass. Elsewhere – and particularly in Africa – the Catholic Church continued its long, impressive expansion. But there were still difficulties for the Church overall. At the risk of oversimplifying, these could be summed up in competing interpretations of Vatican II. If the Council had rightly turned the Church outwards in its view of the world – as all agreed – should that lead the Church towards further change in its constitution, theology and life in order to respond to the needs of the world, or should it lead rather to the conversion of the world to existing Catholic values and practice? The first position was the one broadly taken up by a host of progressive Catholic theologians, including Hans Küng, Edward Schillebeeckx and Karl Rahner among European theologians, the Latin American liberation theologians, and Tissa Balasuriya, the Sri Lankan theologian excommunicated in 1998 for his book *Mary and Liberation*. The second position was that adopted by conservative theologians and church leaders, including Joseph Ratzinger (from 1981 to 2005 Prefect of the Congregation for the Doctrine of the Faith) and John Paul II himself. Both positions claimed to represent the true spirit of the Council.

Following these contrasting lines, the legacy of the Council was a contentious one. On the exercise of authority in the Church, regional conferences of bishops were now almost universal in the Church. But it was clear that John Paul did not altogether trust them. CELAM, the Latin American bishops' conference, and effective sponsor of liberation theology, was addressed by him on his first overseas trip in 1979 and told in no uncertain terms about the danger of mixing Marxism and Catholicism. John Paul's distrust of the radical anti-government stance of Oscar Romero, the Archbishop of San Salvador gunned down in church in 1980, was evident in his refusal to entertain the idea that Romero was a martyr for the faith. In Latin America, increasingly through his papacy, favoured conservative appointments were made to the episcopate to bring the Latin American church back into line. The same was true of appointments to the cardinalate; it was to be an overwhelmingly conservative electorate in the conclave after his death in 2005. Whatever the formal position in favour of collegiality and regional autonomy, the overall effect of all of this was the re-centralization of authority. Nor was there any definite progress in the inclusion of lay people in the affairs of the Church, except at the most basic, local level, where – particularly in the West – parish councils became more common. But there was no synodical structure for lay representation.

The legacy in the field of ethics was particularly controversial. *Humanae Vitae*'s ban on contraception was vigorously upheld by John Paul. It had two unintended but disastrous consequences, which affected different parts of the Catholic world unequally. HIV/AIDS had become a pandemic particularly in Africa and then Asia by the early 1990s, and put enormous pressure on Catholic clergy on the ground. The virus spread rapidly in high-density populations, where prostitution was common and medical aid non-existent. The refusal to countenance the use of condoms to protect women even in these extreme circumstances seemed especially cruel. Millions were infected and died in a 'holocaust' that, while obviously not as such the fault of the Catholic hierarchy, still made it vulnerable to the accusation that it preferred the consistency of its teaching to the alleviation of mass suffering. But in the West, where contraceptives were easily available anyway, and where anti-retroviral drugs were also available by the 1990s, the problem with the Church's condemnation of contraception was not that it was lethal but that it was simply ignored. By the late 1990s the European countries with the lowest birth rates included the predominantly Catholic countries of Italy and Spain. Possibly the figures elsewhere were distorted by differential birth rates between immigrant and 'native' communities. But the point nevertheless was clear: European families took no notice of Catholic teaching on sexuality. The same was true, incidentally, of the ban on abortion. To a rising generation of young Catholics, it was also true in the area of sexuality in general. A vivid if distasteful illustration of this was the reported scattering of used condoms found at the back of the area in Cologne where the newly elected Pope Benedict XVI, formerly Cardinal Ratzinger, held an open-air Mass for some 100,000 young people in 2005. The point worth making is not the failure as such of Catholic teaching, but rather that its failure to make significant headway in this area of life raised important questions about the seriousness with which it would be taken in others.

In ecumenism, where the teaching of Vatican II had been genuinely revolutionary in Catholic terms, the main lines of Catholic policy continued unchanged. John Paul's image of the 'two lungs' of the Christian Church, the West and the East, was a powerful illustration of his enthusiasm for ecumenical relations with the Eastern Orthodox, though it left many Protestants wondering what he made of them. The problem for Protestants was that they were susceptible to precisely the ethical and ecclesiastical changes that John Paul regarded as a capitulation to the materialism and secularism of the West – including women's ordination and more liberal views on marriage and homosexuality. These were significant obstacles. There were major theological advances – the Lutheran–Catholic Joint Declaration on Justification, the reports of the Anglican–Roman Catholic International Commission, creative work on Catholic–Methodist relations – but no tangible changes in relations between the Catholic Church and Protestant churches. Indeed to many Protestants the Catholic enthusiasm for ecumenism seemed to have cooled, even in the wake of John Paul's ecumenical encyclical *Ut Unum Sint* ('May They All Be One', 1995), since there was no repeat of Paul VI's use of the phrase 'sister churches' to describe the Protestant churches. The Orthodox welcomed the Pope's apology for the Western Church's treatment of the Orthodox (including the sack of Constantinople in 1204), but the revival of the Catholic hierarchy in Russia and the Ukraine and the restoration of the Uniate churches in Eastern Europe and the Ukraine looked like acts of ecclesiastical aggression. The truth is that the progressive/conservative polarity perhaps breaks down here. The Catholic commitment to ecumenism was unquestionable. But it was a new commitment, and its working out in practice required refinement and clarification. How flexible was the language of 'sister church'? What were the implications of ecumenical agreement for communion? Could the Catholic Church take steps to recognize the orders of Anglicans? There were very disappointing answers on these and other questions for Protestant ecumenists. But that should not cloud the fact John Paul did not take the Catholic Church back to the position before Vatican II – far from it.

Perhaps the most serious problems affecting the Catholic Church in this period were pastoral, however. Here the legacy of Vatican II is hard to assess. A growing shortage of priests and seminarians affected the Church in America, in most of Europe, in Australia and New Zealand, and even in Latin America and parts of Africa. The shortage was becoming desperate by the end of the century. An elderly priest in a small urban parish in Brittany – a French region in which Catholicism is traditionally very strong – very early in the twenty-first century simply said, when questioned about why he ran a mothers' club himself, 'There are no young priests here. We older priests have to do everything.' In much of Europe, behind the shortage of clergy lay a deeper crisis in the faithful, as congregations began to thin out. The fall was seen most dramatically in Ireland, until the 1980s a country of comparable Catholic strength to Poland. The Irish 'economic miracle', a sudden spurt of growth accelerated by Irish membership of the European Union, carried secularization with it, as young and old alike abandoned the Church. So severe was the shortage of clergy in Europe by the end of the century that the one country in which there was no shortage at all – Poland – by then was exporting clergy to the rest of Europe. In Latin America and Africa the shortage had perhaps a different explanation – the paucity and cost of suitable education, the rapidity of population growth outstripping the ability of the Church to train new clergy and also the stigma attached to celibacy in large parts of Africa.

Shortage of clergy in the West was compounded by the spectacular and desperate stories of child abuse that emerged from the 1980s on. Abuse of children had been going on for years, both in Catholic parishes and in institutions such as schools and homes for orphans run by religious orders. It was difficult to evaluate the real scale of this. But it was a situation where detail was damaging. In America an especially infamous scandal was that associated with Cardinal Law of the archdiocese of Boston, who was accused of having covered up serious cases of child abuse for years, and was eventually – after much resistance from the Vatican – forced to resign his position in 2002. In Ireland the case of Father Brendan Smyth, who abused hundreds of boys over some 45 years of ministry and who was protected by his order, the Norbertines, gathered equivalent notoriety. And yet there was no evidence that the Catholic Church was any worse than other Christian churches or some other voluntary organizations, which also had their child abuse scandals but somehow failed to attract as much attention. One estimate was that the incidence of abusing clergy in the Catholic Church was no higher than 1.5 per cent, and probably a little lower than it was in other denominations. Possibly obscure psychosexual popular fears around monasticism and celibacy have distorted the way people see the Catholic Church in particular on this issue. Nevertheless both the abuse itself and the apparent reluctance of church authorities to discipline the abusers were enormously damaging to the public reputation of the Catholic Church, and more than any other single issue in the West contributed to a loss of popular confidence in the Catholic clergy.

John Paul saw himself as a pope of the Council no less than his predecessors. But the Council had opened up strategic disagreements among Catholics. Some saw the solution to the Church's problems in greater decentralization and deregulation. That might include, for example, a loosening of the canonical regulations on clerical celibacy, or perhaps a different policy on the matter of contraception. Progressive single-issue Catholic groups came into being supporting, for example, the ordination of women. For others the very achievement of the Council was its reconciliation of much-needed reform with the traditional polity of the Catholic Church. Organizational change was not needed and nor was doctrinal reformulation. Opposition to progressive Catholicism came from a variety of sources, including Opus Dei, a Catholic order founded by the Spaniard Josemaría Escrivá in 1928 and dedicated to the pursuit of holiness in ordinary life and work. Opus Dei is controversial because of its conservative message and its close, centralized organization. It has been accused of Catholic 'fundamentalism' by some.[2] Its conservatism is matched by that of various other 'new movements' in modern Catholicism, including the Neocatechumenate, founded in 1964 as a direct response to the Council and which seeks to recover the early Christian Church's practice of forming adults in the faith through a defined process of teaching. Caught in the middle of all this was the Pope himself, wedded to a deeply traditional understanding of the Church's teaching and practice and therefore strongly sympathetic to Opus Dei and other movements like it, and yet temperamentally adapted to an expansive vision of Catholic engagement with the needs of the world. It was probably only a pope of the force of personality of John Paul II who could have held all this together.

The changing face of Catholicism

Many of the difficulties outlined above affected Catholicism particularly in the West. Elsewhere in the world, though not without its problems, the Church was flourishing. As in Protestantism, the Western churches struggled and declined while the balance of Catholic numbers was shifting inexorably southwards and eastwards. During the conclave that elected Benedict XVI in 2005, for the first time in the history of the modern Church there was serious discussion about the possibility of electing a pope from Africa or Latin America.

Africa certainly looked set to become the future heart of the Catholic Church. By the mid-1990s there were already some 106 million Catholics in the continent as a whole. Extrapolating from rates of expansion (always somewhat risky), by 2025 this number could rise to 228 million. The expansion of African Catholicism was partly driven by population growth, but it was also fuelled by the impressive efforts the Church was putting into education, mission and the training of indigenous clergy. Between 1975 and 1987 the numbers of African clergy nearly doubled from 3,700 to over 7,000, and the rise was continuing beyond that level into the 1990s. This was barely sufficient for the Church's needs. Serious shortages of clergy in parts of Africa prompted the exploration of alternative pastoral strategies – the attempt in Mozambique and Zaire, for example, to create base communities of around 40 Catholic families, similar to the base communities of Latin America, the training of lay catechists, the delegation of certain pastoral and administrative functions from clergy to lay workers, and so on. But the problem in Africa was not that of Europe: it was not that of finding sufficient clergy from a diminishing popular base, but of catching up with the upsurge in the Catholic population. There were tensions within African Catholicism over the direction of liturgical reform since Vatican II, and continuing arguments over inculturation and the possibility of an 'African theology'. Cardinal Ratzinger, with the ear of John Paul II, was known to be suspicious of the latter, though few authorities even in the Vatican would have put things as bluntly as one Catholic missionary in Kenya: 'Africans have no culture, so they must accept Christianity in its Western form completely.' In fact Catholicism on the whole had adapted and incorporated elements of African culture well into its liturgical practice. The problem with reform of the liturgy was not the use of the vernacular languages, but rather the tendency for modern Catholicism to streamline the liturgy, often cutting out elements of colour and ceremony that had proved attractive to African worshippers. John Paul's strongly Marian spirituality found an echo in the continuing Marian devotion of African Catholicism. Marian visions have continued unabated in Africa, it seems, with notable instances in southern Rwanda in the mid-1980s, and in the late 1980s in Nairobi. African Catholicism may have experienced difficulties in numbers of clergy, continuing arguments over celibacy and polygamy, and troubled relationships with various African governments, but its devotional life overall was a successful marriage of conservative Catholicism and indigenous culture.

This was perhaps less obviously true in Latin America, still at the end of the century the real heartland of Catholicism, with nearly 50 per cent of Catholic believers living there in the mid-1990s. Here too it was predicted that growth would continue well into the twenty-first century, to reach 606 million by 2025. But the growth of the Pentecostal churches was mostly at the expense of Catholicism and looked set to continue proportionately well beyond 2000. What this implied for the functioning of the Catholic Church on the ground was hard to say, however. There was an acute shortage of priests, both in rural areas and in the huge and rapidly expanding hinterland of cities like Sao Paolo, Mexico City and Rio de Janeiro. The development of the base communities had been trumpeted in the 1970s and 1980s as the continent's most creative answer to the problem. By the end of the 1980s there were probably over 100,000 of them in Brazil alone. But by the 1990s doubts were setting in about their effectiveness not only in Rome (where there had always been reservations) but in parts of Latin America itself.

The doubts reflected serious divisions within the Latin American churches over the direction of change since Vatican II. Possibly nowhere else in the Catholic Church had the legacy of the Council been interpreted in such a straightforwardly radical sense politically and socially as well as religiously. In retrospect the highpoint of this radicalism was reached in the early 1970s, some years before John Paul II's election, when a struggle began within the Latin American episcopate between conservative bishops, represented by Alfonso Trujillo, Secretary of the Conference of Latin American bishops (CELAM), and the more progressive group associated with leaders such as Enrique Angelelli and Oscar Romero. It was an unequal struggle, because the conservatives were supported from Rome, and by the late 1970s CELAM had lost much of its independence. Thereafter under John Paul II a succession of conservative appointments to the Latin American episcopate emasculated the progressive leadership of the Church. Side by side with that went the re-imposition of Vatican control on the training of clergy, with John Paul's criticism of liberation theology and the removal of Leonardo Boff's permission to teach in 1985. It was unfortunate – if perhaps not altogether a coincidence – that the reining-in of the liberation theologians and the progressive leadership of the Catholic Church in Latin America occurred at a time of renewed political reaction in the continent, supported often by a US fearful of communist influence there. The military coups in Bolivia (1971), Chile and Uruguay (1973), Peru (1975) and Argentina (1976) raised the prospect once again of right-wing dictators supported by the Catholic hierarchy. It did not always happen like that, not least because of John Paul II's readiness on occasions to condemn social injustice and the abuse of human rights, but it confirmed the liberation theologians' suspicions of their own Church. By the 1990s many of these governments had fallen, and in any event the collapse of Soviet communism had removed a major reason for US support of them. This somewhat eased the political context in which the Catholic Church now had to operate in Latin America.

The Catholic population of Asia was also growing rapidly towards the end of the century, though there were sharp regional differences in rates of growth. In the Philippines there were remarkable similarities to the situation of the Catholic Church in Latin America. The incidence of poverty, population density and the absence of political rights for the poor in the Philippines prompted Catholic leaders there in the late 1960s – particularly the Maryknoll Fathers – to imitate the Latin American base communities. These were used not only as ecclesiastical agencies but also as a means of promoting trade unions, welfare work and cooperatives. During the military dictatorship of Marcos from 1972 to 1986, the Church was one of the few bodies able to lead opposition to the regime. The Catholic Church in the Philippines thus became much more closely identified with social justice and human rights than it had been in an earlier era, and that has surely aided its reception in the rapidly growing population of the Philippines.

All the same, there has been a significant growth of Pentecostalism, though the new Charismatic Catholic movement El Shaddai, founded by Brother Mike Velarde in 1984, has also grown rapidly to over 7 million followers and has probably kept many Catholics from defecting to Pentecostalism.

In China, on the other hand, despite the temporary recent thaw in relations between the government and Christian churches, the situation of Catholicism remained somewhat uncertain. In 1994 the Chinese government sought to re-impose central control on the churches in China. The Chinese Patriotic Catholic Church remained in being, but the Vatican had been able to pursue a policy of rapprochement tentatively here, appointing bishops but submitting them to the required process of state authorization. All the signs were that, despite continuing tensions between the Catholic Church and the Chinese government, Catholicism was growing quickly in the new China. Overall in Asia, as in much of the developing world generally, the shortage of clergy and the acute financial and other difficulties of the Catholic Church do not seem to have been practical impediments to growth.

CHAPTER 13

The Orthodox Churches

The collapse of communism

If there was one event that completely dominated the history of Eastern Orthodox Christianity at the end of the twentieth century, it was the fall of Soviet communism. The sheer number of Orthodox believers living under Soviet rule made it inevitable that the sudden disappearance of the Soviet system would have profound consequences for the life of Orthodoxy throughout the world. The 1970s and 1980s were later called 'the years of stagnation'. The conditions under which the Orthodox Church could function within the Soviet Union gradually eased, but it was only in the period of *glasnost* initiated by Gorbachev (the non-believing son of a devout Orthodox mother) in the late 1980s that serious steps were taken to give greater freedom of expression and worship to religious believers.

Persecution continued up until then, often working through the Moscow patriarchate itself. The career of Dmitri Dudko, a charismatic Orthodox priest willing to encourage criticism of the regime, was a case in point. Having served eight years in a labour camp, in the early 1960s he was appointed to St Nicholas of the Transfiguration in Moscow, where in 1973 he began to hold public question-and-answer sessions on religion and public affairs. Identified as trouble by Patriarch Pimen, he was dismissed in 1974 and then harassed continually as he moved through a series of parishes, until finally he was arrested in 1980 and forced to make an abject recantation of his opposition to atheism on Soviet television. But it was not an isolated incident. There were many other Orthodox dissidents in the gulags among the 300-odd prisoners specifically charged with religious crimes, including some who would come to prominence in the 1990s as reformers within Russian Orthodoxy. Their experience of internment made them suspicious of the compromises made by the patriarchate.

The survival of Orthodoxy despite persecution surely contributed to disillusionment with the Soviet regime, but did not play a leading role in the sudden collapse of the system in 1989 to 1991. Perhaps some inkling of what was to come could have been felt in 1988, with the celebrations of the thousandth anniversary of the coming of Christianity to Russia: the honour accorded the Orthodox Church was a sign of the beginning of a new freedom for the Church. In 1989 Gorbachev suddenly legalized the Ukrainian Catholic Church, ending at a stroke the Stalinist policy of forcing the 'Uniate' church into the Russian Orthodox Church. One of the last acts of the Soviet state was to pass a new law on religious freedom late in 1990, which guaranteed freedom of religion before the law, including full freedom of worship. But this new law had only a year to run, before the disappearance of the Soviet Union itself in the new Russian Federation led to the abrogation of all Soviet legislation. In 1993 the Russian Federation finally enacted a law that went even further than that of 1991.

In these conditions of new-found liberty, Orthodoxy discovered new energy and zeal. Churches and monasteries were handed back to the Church with alacrity. All restrictions on worship and on religious association were at an end. An entire religious culture, long suppressed, suddenly emerged into the light of day again. A priest in the diocese of Novgorod described the changes of just three years, from 1990 to 1993. In 1990 there had been just 25 parishes. Now the 'famous St Sophia Cathedral, closed in 1929, is again opened for believers; dozens of churches are being restored and rebuilt. There are four cloisters, numerous Sunday schools and a children's choir in the St Sophia Cathedral.' People spoke of a religious boom. The number of monasteries increased dramatically, passing 250 by the mid-1990s. Seminaries were reopened – nearly 30 of them after 1993 alone. By 1994 there were 14,000 parishes functioning, and the number was rising rapidly. By the end of the century there were well over 10,000 registered Orthodox organizations in Russia – that is, excluding parishes, but including schools and welfare and devotional associations. Nor was the boom measurable only institutionally. Many of the symbols and devotional paraphernalia of traditional Orthodox worship began to reappear – something inconceivable a few years before. In 1991 the remains of the last tsar, Nicholas II, and his family were disinterred from their graves near Yekaterinburg. After some controversy they were reburied in the cathedral of St Peter and St Paul in Nicholas's former capital of St Petersburg in 1998, 80 years to the day after they were shot by the Bolsheviks. In 2006 the hand of John the Baptist, which had been smuggled out of Russia after the revolution for safe-keeping, was welcomed with due pomp and ceremony at Christ the Saviour in Moscow and then taken on a tour of churches in Russia, Belarus and the Ukraine.

What did all this signify – that Russia was returning to the Orthodox faith at last? Certainly the collapse of communism left a vacuum in Russian life, and particularly in its sense of national self-identity, that Orthodoxy rushed to fill. Patriarch Alexei II, elected in 1990, was thrust into a position of public prominence. Many Orthodox clergy spoke of theirs as the Russian faith. But it would be a mistake to think that the religious boom pointed unerringly to a profound connection between the Orthodox Christianity and the Russian people as a whole. Those who called themselves Orthodox far outstripped the number of practising believers. By 2000 there were probably around 80 million self-identified Orthodox in Russia. That was only about half of the population, and other believers of all religions probably made up only around 15 million in total, leaving some 65 million or so Russians professedly without any religious belief – an astonishingly high proportion compared with countries outside the former communist lands. But of that 80 million Orthodox, somewhat less than 15 million at most actually attended church at least once a year, and the real figure may have been as low as 3 million. The disparity between practice and professed identity has led some to suggest that Russia is in fact among the most secularized societies in the world.

But the revival of Orthodoxy in Russia also faced a variety of other difficulties. The sheer speed of its expansion posed problems for the Church. It had too little money to restore or rebuild the churches returned to it, too few clergy to run them and low levels of theological education. The shortage of money was particularly crippling and led to a series of scandals throughout the 1990s as Orthodox clergy and laity alike, transfixed by Russia's chaotic experiments in the market economy, dabbled in hare-brained schemes to raise funds. One diocese produced bottled water under the name 'Saint Springs' to pay for the restoration of churches and monasteries; the label carried a blessing from Patriarch Alexei, but this did not stop the impression of scandal as the profits disappeared into secret funds. Investigation of the Moscow patriarchate's source of funding by the late 1990s identified a complicated web of banks, leisure investments and secret bank accounts, as well as a 40 per cent share in one of Russia's giant oil companies, with rumours of shady connections to the criminal underworld. More to the point, little of this money had reached the parishes. Another difficulty was the reappearance of the Uniate churches in Eastern Europe, and especially of the large Ukrainian Greek Catholic Church, which had many millions of adherents and represented a major rival to the Moscow patriarchate in the region. Sensitivities over the existence of the Uniates were reinforced by the Protestant groups which began to flood into Russia in the early 1990s.

These rivalries, arising at the same time as Russian Orthodoxy was reasserting itself, had the effect of igniting more extreme nationalist elements within the Church, and by the mid-1990s pressure was building from various Orthodox sources, including the patriarchate itself, for a modification of the 1993 law on religious freedom. In 1997 a new law put the Orthodox Church in a constitutionally privileged position, and limited the freedom of other religious groups. As if to cement the new alliance of church and state, the Orthodox hierarchy was courted by politicians, including the Russian President Boris Yeltsin, and his successor, the former KGB officer, Vladimir Putin. One English academic, visiting St Petersburg at the end of the century, was amazed to see an Orthodox priest blessing army recruits filing into a lorry destined for the war in Chechnya, the south Russian province which had tried to declare itself independent and faced a desperate conflict from 1999 to 2002. It was eerily reminiscent of 1914. And it opened up divisions within the Russian Orthodox Church itself, between reformists suspicious of the patriarchate, and traditionalists. Among the reformists was the highly controversial figure of Gleb Yakunin, a priest who pursued a campaign of denunciation of the patriarch himself, and who eventually founded a schismatic Orthodox Church in Russia in conjunction with a schismatic Orthodox Church in the Ukraine.

Yakunin's role in fomenting schism was, as the century drew to a close, perhaps a sad sign of what lies in store for the Russian Church in the future. There were many different strands within reformism as well as within traditionalism in the Russian Orthodox Church, and Yakunin was as much a symbolic figure, repudiated by many reformists themselves, as a typical one. But everywhere in Eastern Europe after the fall of communism the Orthodox churches faced a bewildering variety of external pressures and internal conflicts. In Yugoslavia, for example, the disintegration of Tito's fragile federation in the 1990s exposed the Orthodox Church of Serbia to allegations of a too cosy relationship with Serb nationalism. This made relations with the Catholic Church in Croatia particularly complex, since Serbian nationalism ostensibly sheltered behind the residual Yugoslav state in its attempt to prevent Croatian and Bosnian independence. It also placed renewed pressure on the Serbian Church's relationship with the autocephalous Orthodox Church of Macedonia, which had been encouraged to seek its ecclesiastical independence under the communist government as part of a characteristic policy of divide and rule. Macedonian autocephaly had never been accepted by the Serbian Church. The Serbian Church was also to stand accused of acquiescence in the savage brutality of Serb forces against the Bosnians and Croats. In these circumstances Orthodoxy in the Balkans could hardly serve as much of a force for peace.

Relations between Orthodox churches

Relations between Orthodox churches in the post-communist era were problematic because of the Soviet attempt to use the Moscow patriarchate as a means of controlling Orthodoxy in the Soviet Empire and in the diaspora too. Initially the patriarchate seemed to want to rediscover the role it had briefly assumed in 1917–18, when at last the Church had broken free of the bureaucracy of the tsars and reconstituted the patriarchate as an authority for all the Orthodox churches within the Russian Empire. During the Soviet era it had never formally renounced this role, which in any case served Soviet policy admirably. The fact that the state persecuted the Church meant that the adequacy of the patriarchate's understanding of its role as almost a pan-Orthodox one was openly called into question only by those churches of the diaspora which had deliberately broken with it or which had never fallen under its jurisdiction. But as soon as the authority of the Soviet state had gone, this 'greater Russian' role also began to falter. For those alert to the question, the history of the Orthodox Church in Finland was a good example of what might happen. When Finland had seized the chance of turmoil in Russia to secure its independence in 1918, its small Russian Orthodox community had promptly underlined its national loyalty by declaring itself a national Church under the jurisdiction of the ecumenical patriarch of Constantinople. It has developed a distinct national ethos since then, following the Western date for Easter, for example, rather than the later date favoured under the Gregorian calendar in other Orthodox churches.

The collapse of the Soviet state presented a paradox, then, for the Moscow patriarchate. It led to far greater freedom of worship and life than it had had at any time since 1917–18. But this came at the expense of its ability to influence many of the churches once under the Soviet sway. It was the same in formerly communist countries which had churches not integrated into the Russian Church, such as Romania. The tensions resulting from this conflict between freedom and authority were evident in three main areas. The first was the Moscow patriarchate's relations with the diaspora churches. The problem for the patriarchate was that there were several different jurisdictions. There were churches in the West that had always accepted the authority of the Moscow patriarchate. In the Soviet era these were few and far between, but they provided some continuity at least for the patriarchate's role. Then there were churches under the jurisdiction of the ecumenical patriarch at Constantinople. These were also small but intellectually influential. They were among the Orthodox most open to theological relations with Western churches and active in the ecumenical movement. By the end of the century there was no particular reason why these churches

– which had often lost a distinctively Russian ethnic flavour – should seek to transfer allegiance from Constantinople to Moscow. Finally there were the churches of the Russian Orthodox Church Abroad (ROCA), founded by those who had fled Russia in 1917. ROCA was committed to a pre-Revolutionary understanding of the role of Orthodoxy in Russia, even to the extent of being pro-monarchical. In 1990 ROCA began proselytizing in Russia, establishing the Russian Orthodox Free Church (ROFC). Inevitably this intensified mutual antagonism between the Moscow patriarchate and ROCA/ROFC, especially because parishes disillusioned with Moscow began to affiliate to ROFC. By the end of the decade ROFC had 37 parishes in Russia. In the scale of things, this was not a large number, but it was enough of a threat to prompt Patriarch Alexei II to begin preliminary negotiations with ROFC in 2003. In this context the revival of traditional Orthodox and nationalist sentiments in Russian political life in the 1990s was highly significant: it suggested that one part of the post-1917 breach in Russian Orthodoxy could be healed by a common culture of conservative Orthodox nationalism. But to the degree that Moscow took a step towards ROCA/ROFC, it was in danger of alienating the churches of the diaspora aligned to Constantinople.

A second area of potential discord concerned Moscow's relations with the Greek churches. During the Soviet era, the Greek Church, almost uniquely, was an established Orthodox Church outside the Soviet zone of influence. Until 1975 it was completely dominant constitutionally, with proselytizing by non-Orthodox churches forbidden. But its position was weakened by its cooperation with the military dictatorship (the rule of the 'colonels'), and the fall of the regime was a prelude to a period of reassessment which included the granting of qualified freedom to other religious bodies. But the Church is still in a more constitutionally entrenched position than any other church in Europe. This has the potential to be an enormously attractive constitutional model for other Orthodox churches, as is evident from the restrictive legislation passed in Russia in 1997. The twenty-first century may see further moves in that direction in other Orthodox countries. By the end of the 1990s there were signs that many Russian Orthodox hoped for a pan-Orthodox 'empire' of churches under Russian hegemony. But where would that leave the Greek churches and the ecumenical patriarchate itself?

But third, there were also evident tensions *within* the Orthodox churches that were not formally part of the Russian Orthodox Church, often provoked or exacerbated by the situation in Russia. One example was the Orthodox Church of Estonia. Part of the Russian Church before 1918, like Finland the Estonian Orthodox had sought autonomy from Moscow in 1920 and aligned themselves with the ecumenical patriarchate in 1923. But this was never officially accepted by Moscow, and Soviet occupation in 1940 effectively ended the Estonian Church's autonomy. No sooner had Estonia regained its independence in 1991 than the Estonian government attempted to reaffirm the Church's autonomy and allegiance to Constantinople. The Estonian Church now divided into pro- and anti-Moscow factions. A schism began in 1996, with 54 parishes aligning themselves with Constantinople and the remaining 30 with Moscow, though these latter were by far the more numerous as they consisted mostly of ethnic Russians. Similar tensions existed in the Ukraine in the 1990s, where – even apart from Orthodox/Greek Catholic rivalries – the Orthodox Church itself was divided between those who sought the jurisdiction of Constantinople and those who wished to remain under Moscow.

The Estonian and Ukrainian church disputes led in 1996 to a major breakdown of relations between Moscow and Constantinople. Schisms were by no means confined to Orthodox churches once claimed by Moscow. One of the most bitter post-Soviet schisms has been in the Bulgarian Church, which divided in 1992 into two factions over the Church's subservience to the former communist regime. Recognized as an autocephalous church in 1945 by the ecumenical patriarch, the Bulgarian Church was never formally under Moscow. But the end of communism merely produced a period of great domestic instability. A reformist faction within the Bulgarian Church gained support from the non-communist United Democratic Forces (UDF), whose election victory in 1991 led to an attempt to force Patriarch Maxim and the Holy Synod of the Bulgarian Church to step down and give way to a new patriarch and a reformed structure. Whatever the religious merits of this proposal, even to many critical of Maxim it looked like unwarranted state interference; the pro-reformist group failed to carry most of the Church with them. The schism was still unresolved 14 years later.

The Bulgarian situation aside, it would be easy to see these difficulties as springing simply from Moscow's quasi-imperialistic ambitions. That is often how the patriarchate's critics saw things, citing the reinvigorated relationship between Russian nationalism and Orthodoxy in the post-Soviet era. But there was a deeper question behind this, and it concerned Orthodoxy's status in the world at large. Was the re-emergence of Orthodoxy in Russia and the former Soviet world as a whole a providential sign that Orthodoxy was a uniquely blessed way of Christian belonging, indeed the *only* authentic way? There were plenty of Orthodox who thought so and who were horrified by the Western churches' compromises with contemporary culture. The fall of communism had opened the eyes of many Orthodox to the weaknesses of the Western churches, and they were determined to fight against the influence of Western culture. For some, the Moscow patriarchate was an alternative Christian centre to the West; others from non-Russian churches were equally suspicious of the West and wary of the aspirations of Moscow. Unsurprisingly, during the 1990s lingering Orthodox unease at the policies and procedure of the WCC came to the fore. In 1998 the Orthodox delegations to the WCC's Harare assembly refused to participate in joint worship or to vote until the basis of Orthodox participation had been resolved. But Orthodoxy was divided on ecumenical matters, and its divisions highlighted further complexities within Orthodox theology.

Theology and life

In an earlier chapter I traced the impact of Orthodox theology on Western Christianity through the dispersion of Russian Orthodox theologians after the Russian Revolution. By mid-century the educational institutions, societies and publishing houses through which Orthodox theology had been promoted in the West were well established. Orthodox participation in the ecumenical movement may have been controversial, but it brought with it a further range of contacts with other Christian churches. Orthodox theology was particularly influential in the area of ecclesiology, the doctrine of the Church, a matter central to ecumenical concern. The ending of what one scholar has called 'the constantinian *symphonia* between Church and State' in Russia in 1917 drew renewed attention in Orthodox circles to the study of the constitution and purpose of the Church – a question of pressing relevance in the scattered Orthodox communities of the diaspora.[1] If the Church no longer acted as the national conscience, hand in hand with the quasi-sacral office of the tsar, and therefore could no longer be said to be the Church of Russia, what made it what it was? Were there distinctive doctrines, or distinctive forms of organization that – in Orthodox eyes – 'made' the Church?

Like the Protestant churches lacking a centralized authority, Orthodoxy has never produced a definitive answer to that question. It has never abandoned its insistence on the principle of apostolic succession, for example, and yet different Orthodox theologians have laid slightly different emphases on it. One answer that did gain credence in the late twentieth century, however, was that it was above all the Eucharist that made the Church what it was. The Church was a union of inner and outer elements, the inner consisting in the God-given love that binds Christians together, and the outer in an objective act, participation in the (also) God-given celebration of the Eucharist. This 'Eucharistic ecclesiology' was famously summed up in an article published in 1960 by the Paris-based Russian theologian Nikolai

Afanasiev, 'The Church Which Presides is Love'. Afanasiev's view was not necessarily typical of Orthodox theology as a whole, but it was highly influential. It certainly had ecumenical potential, because it suggested that agreement around the Eucharist might be a key to church unity. It also found some parallels in new trends in Catholic theology. The Jesuit Henri de Lubac, writing around the same time as Afanasiev and influenced in part by Orthodox theology, conceived of the relationship between the Eucharist and the Church in strikingly similar terms. Another Orthodox theologian, the Greek John Zizioulas, in his widely read *Being as Communion* (1985), criticized and developed Afanasiev's Eucharistic ecclesiology in terms that made ecumenical convergence between Orthodox and Catholics even more attractive. This was all the more so given the prominence of the concept of *koinonia*, or 'communion', in ecumenical theology since Vatican II. In this direction, then, Orthodox theology promised much for the ecumenical movement as a whole.

But Orthodox ecclesiology could work in a different direction. Afanasiev's insight need not imply ecumenical potential. Instead its emphasis on the local church – where the Eucharist was celebrated – could strengthen existing local identities. Orthodoxy could not dispense with a concept of universality or catholicity: it could not be congregational, seeing the local congregation as the only ecclesiastical authority (otherwise it would be Protestant). After all it had its bishops, its patriarchs and its understanding of a common faith and tradition. But placing a very strong local ecclesiology together with a fixed understanding of what marks the universality of the Church (the episcopate, the common faith) produces a recipe for complete withdrawal from active relations with other churches. Since the universal church is present fully in the local church, and there is no possibility of change or development in the marks of universality, the local church has nothing to learn from others. Put a further factor into that – a certain determined nationalism, for example, or a suspicion of Western liberalism, or hostility to perceived Catholic 'aggression' – and the development of extreme Orthodox conservatism is understandable. That has been the experience of some of the Orthodox churches of the former Soviet Union. It is unclear how strong the anti-ecumenical impulse really is in these churches, because it is a matter of church policy that the opinions of different groups have to be balanced or reconciled. In the case of the Georgian Orthodox Church, which suspended its membership of the WCC in 1997, the main anti-ecumenical impulse came from the monasteries, which accused the WCC of heresy. Withdrawal was reluctantly adopted by the Patriarch, Ilia II, as a way of keeping the Georgian church together; it was a prelude to disciplinary measures against the leaders of the anti-ecumenical faction.

These contrasting paths within Orthodox theology indicated a cultural division fast developing within the Orthodox churches after the fall of communism. In the West many of the churches of the Orthodox diaspora were at last beginning to lose their ethnic exclusivity. This was true above all of Russian Orthodoxy, which became a refuge for disillusioned Catholics, High Anglicans and others. After all, Orthodoxy had much to commend it to spiritual seekers in the West who might be disappointed by the ordination of women or who might see Western Christianity as hopelessly shallow – a revered theological tradition, discipline, mystery, the saints, a distrust of regimentation and rules, a colourful (if rather long) liturgy, a somewhat decentralized system of authority. Some of these new converts embraced a rather rigid vision of Orthodoxy in the way converts can. Their numbers were few but they were an exotic and affluent group. They represented just the beginning of a process of indigenization of Orthodoxy in the West – a process carried further in America than in Europe. This was hardly much of a threat to the mainstream Protestant and Catholic churches, since the numbers involved were small. But they were vocal and influential, even if they sometimes tried too hard to adopt Orthodox habits. One English convert claimed he could always identify other converts by the way they imitated what they thought were proper Orthodox dress and attitudes: 'I remember in one Russian church in Belgium, you immediately knew who the converts were; the men had nineteenth-century Russian peasant beards and the women wore dowdy long skirts and seemed to be wearing tablecloths on their heads. You knew who the Russians were because they dressed normally.' Yet non-Russian converts did not turn themselves into Russian nationalists. Their Orthodoxy may have been a rather romanticized one, but the whole point in a sense was that they were adapting it to suit their own civic and national identities. Intermarriage obviously helped this process too. The very word 'diaspora' began to seem quite inappropriate in this context.

But in the East the situation was very different. Here Orthodox believers had had to profess their loyalty to state socialism, knowing that their religious beliefs were thought to undermine those of the new socialist society. No wonder they were fed up with doublethink. When the restraints were lifted at the beginning of the 1990s they naturally expected to be able to reassert their own vision of an Orthodox Christian society. This did not make them receptive to other views. Moreover what constituted the true Orthodox way was now itself a question of intense reflection and often of painful self-examination. Should the actions of the Church during the whole of the Soviet era be seen as irredeemably tainted? Or should Church leaders be forgiven for doing the best in the circumstances? If their actions were tainted, should Orthodoxy turn itself back 70 years to rediscover the true way of being Orthodox? But then how should changes in the worldwide church and in society in the intervening period be received? The ensuing divisions were reminiscent of the Donatist schisms in the North African churches in the fourth century, when Christians were bitterly divided over how to treat those who had abandoned the faith during the last great Roman persecution of Christians. Although the rigorists, the Donatists – those who refused to accept the apostates back into the Church – were ultimately branded as heretics, the question who had truly preserved the spirit of the faith in time of trial evidently touched on very deep resentments, since the Donatist schism rumbled on for well over a century. It remains to be seen if contemporary divisions trouble Orthodoxy for such a long period too.

The Oriental Orthodox

It remains only to touch briefly on the non-Chalcedonian churches. Here the most dramatic reversal of fortune has occurred for the Armenian Orthodox Church. The Armenian Church is a very old church indeed, claiming a foundation right back to the third century, and it is very much an 'ethnic' church, being virtually coterminous with the Armenian people. It experienced periodic bursts of persecution and disruption over the centuries. By the beginning of the twentieth century it was spread over parts of the Middle East and had four ecclesiastical jurisdictions, based in Yerevan, in Jerusalem, in Constantinople and in Sis in the Lebanon. The Constantinople jurisdiction was virtually obliterated by the Turkish massacres of the Armenians after the First World War. During the Soviet era, the Soviet Republic of Armenia, bordering on Turkey and with Yerevan as its capital, followed a similar policy of official toleration but practical repression as occurred elsewhere in the USSR. But it did at least provide a haven of sorts for the Armenian Church after its appalling experiences over the border, and Yerevan was in any event the spiritual capital of Armenian Orthodoxy. The end of the Soviet Union brought independence for Armenia in 1991 and a new era of stability and freedom for the Church. By the mid-1990s its numbers, in Armenia itself, had risen to some 2.5 million – more than twice the figure available for 1907. The small Syrian Orthodox Church – which renamed itself the *Syriac* Orthodox Church recently in order to distinguish itself from the Syrian state – has also thrived in recent years, though it remains scattered across several countries in the Middle East. Its communities in the Lebanon, along with other Christian churches, suffered particularly in the civil war and through Israeli and Syrian invasions that lasted from 1975 to 1990. An English priest visiting churches in Syria itself in 1992 noted strong attendances at the cathedral church of Mar Girgis (St

George). He also observed that there were friendly relations with Islam.

This was not the case for most of the Oriental Orthodox churches living in close proximity to Islam. In the new Palestinian authority established in 1994 under the Oslo agreement, and in Israel itself, Orthodox Christianity has continued to decline. The sheer volatility of the political situation there has made issues of identity particularly problematic for Palestinian Christians, who represent a disproportionately large percentage of emigrants and exiles: currently perhaps over 50 per cent of Palestinian exiles are Christians. Similarly in Egypt the Coptic Church continues to find itself struggling with Islamic militancy and with calls for the establishment of Shari'a law, even though it remains – at some 9 million members in 2000 – a substantial proportion (around 13 per cent) of Egypt's population. Hostile relations with Islam also afflict the Ethiopian Church, which has a higher proportion of the population, around 36 per cent, than any other religious group including Islam. Since the fall of the Mengistu regime in the early 1990s, after the collapse of Soviet military aid, the Church has begun to operate more freely again, but local and religious tensions remain. This has been a region fraught with conflict in the last quarter of the century, however. Following a prolonged rebellion against the Ethiopian government, Eritrea finally achieved independence in 1993, and the following year Pope Shenouda of the Coptic Church agreed – against Ethiopian wishes – to grant separate status to the Orthodox Church of Eritrea. This was at the outset of an Ethiopian–Eritrean war that lasted until 2000. With neighbouring Sudan to its west, a country itself bitterly divided between a Muslim north and a Christian south, it is hard to avoid the conclusion that the Ethiopian and Eritrean churches will continue to face a difficult time for many years to come. Thus most of non-Chalcedonian Orthodoxy, at least in its historic heartlands, finds itself facing a fraught and precarious rivalry with militant Islamism.

CHAPTER 14

Protestantism and Its Tribulations

Decline or transformation?

In the last quarter of the century, worldwide Protestantism was changing rapidly. In the West most of the older traditions continued their decline; in the Global South, or Third World, they prospered. But they changed as they prospered, and they were often outstripped by the Pentecostal and independent churches. At last the chickens of colonialism came home to roost. Not only did numbers increasingly favour the Global South but so did the balance of moral accountability. Now the traditional Protestant denominations in former colonies became more assertive, more conscious of their strength and more sceptical of the Christianity of the West. The permissive revolution of the 1960s and 1970s in the West merely convinced them that Western Christianity was effete and in danger of betraying the Gospel. Western church leaders often felt embarrassed about the legacy of colonialism and their churches' role in it. But church decline in the West opened up fissures within traditional Protestantism, encouraging conservative resistance movements on particular issues such as sexual ethics or women's ordination which began to build alliances with Third World churches. A vivid illustration of this came at the 1998 Lambeth Conference, the worldwide assembly of Anglican bishops, when conservative Western bishops and bishops from the Global South combined to defeat a moderate declaration on homosexuality and instated a much more conservative one.

Let us look briefly at the numerical reality underlying this marked shift in power within Anglicanism. In 1970 there were about 47.5 million Anglicans worldwide. But more than half of this number (about 27.6 million) came from the Anglican churches of the United Kingdom alone. Add to that the other 'Western' provinces of the Anglican Communion – the churches in Canada, Australia and New Zealand – at a total of 5.9 million, and the numerical dominance of Western Anglicanism within the Communion as a whole in the post-colonial years is evident. But by the end of the century the total of Anglican 'members' had risen to over 70 million, even though Anglicanism in the West was mostly in decline. The growth in the Anglican Church of Nigeria alone was staggering, from 2.9 million in 1970 to 17.5 million in 1995. Projections (always to be taken with a pinch of salt) were that by 2050 Anglicanism worldwide would have over 150 million members, of whom a small proportion – maybe no more than 20 million or so – would be from the West.

The growth of Anglicanism in the Third World was completely changing the culture and balance of power of the Communion. But the same thing was happening in other Protestant traditions. The World Alliance of Reformed Churches was another example. By the end of the century it had over 200 member churches from across the world. More than half of these were from Africa and Asia. Between 1970 and 1995, the 'affiliates' of the United Reformed Church in Britain fell from 350,000 to 187,000; the Church of Scotland from 2.5 million to 1.2 million; and the Reformed Church of the Netherlands from 3.1 million to 2.7 million – to take just three examples. But in Africa in the same period, again taking just representative examples, the Presbyterian Church of Ghana rose from 279,000 to 814,000; the Presbyterian Church of South Africa from 122,000 to 300,000; and the Reformed Church of East Africa in Kenya from just 6,000 to 110,000. The priorities of the Third World churches were not those of the West. They were neatly summed up in a document, 'The Alliance Beyond 2004', presented to the General Council at Accra in Ghana in 2004:

> Christianity in many African countries is growing. Many Christian churches seek ways to proclaim the gospel faithfully. They raise prophetic voices to challenge undemocratic governments and other social evils. They play a leading role in reconciliation and peace-building. ... WARC member churches in Africa look to the Alliance for a fellowship of solidarity and support: in standing up against economic injustice and poverty; in development projects and in rebuilding destroyed homes and missions; in providing appropriate theological education; in their women's initiatives and in linking with international agencies.[1]

The final outcome and implications of this far-reaching change were far from clear by the end of the century. Would historic Protestantism in the West shortly disappear? The figures pointed to serious contraction. Take the example of Methodism. In Britain and America, its historic heartlands, it was evidently in retreat. In Britain its number of affiliates (members and more occasional attenders) fell from about 2 million in 1970 to 1.2 million in 1995; in the US over the same 25 years the United Methodist Church declined from 14.3 million affiliates to 11 million. Methodism in both countries by the 1990s was a depressing tale of church closures and mergers. Or take the example of Lutheranism. In the US the Evangelical Lutheran Church declined from 5.8 million affiliates in 1970 to 5.2 million in 1995; in Sweden the Lutheran state church slipped from 7.9 million to 7.6 million; in Germany, the Evangelical Church (including Reformed as well as Lutherans) fell from 33.4 million to 29.2 million. Both in Sweden and Germany, however, the number of affiliates was buoyed up by the fact that membership was determined constitutionally and not by voluntary association: numbers of actual *attenders* declined more sharply. These figures could be matched for most denominations. Anglican figures – to take one more example – demonstrated an almost consistent pattern of decline. In Britain from 1970 to 1995 it was from 27.6 million affiliates (as in the case of Sweden and Germany a highly misleading measure) to 24.5 million; in the US from 3.2 million to 2.4 million; in Canada from 1.2 million to 800,000; in New Zealand from 870,000 to 800,000. Only in Australia was there an increase – from 3.8 million to 4 million.

The overall pattern of decline concealed interesting details. Comparatively, Lutheranism still looked much stronger in Germany than it was in the United States. But all church affiliation in America is associational: it is a choice made by particular people (or families) unconstrained by legal requirement. Inasmuch as Protestants in America inherit their church membership, it is through the emotional ties of the family: children may be baptized in their parents' churches, but the variety and informality of American church life encourages a free decision about churchgoing in adulthood. There is one significant, wider element of loyalty – the ethnic criterion. Lutherans in America are often descendents of German or Scandinavian migrants, and their Lutheranism remains an important element of their remembered European roots. This may help to explain why the contraction in American Lutheranism was relatively small. On the other hand, in Europe the residual influence of state religion is still marked. In Germany and in Scandinavian countries, church identity is determined through the legal requirement to pay church tax and through the 'folk' practice of baptizing children in the local church. These things are not to be dismissed as no indicator of true religious affiliation, but they clearly do not mean much in terms of conscious religious practice. Estimates of attendance in Germany suggest that only about 1.1 million people go to church weekly. It is certainly possible that there may be more churchgoing Lutherans in America than there are in Germany.

The trajectory of decline would probably have been much steeper in the 1980s and 1990s were it not for the fact that churchgoing tended to hold up well in the more conservative or Charismatic parts of historic Protestantism.

All of the main denominations by the 1990s had strong Evangelical or Charismatic wings which were increasingly vociferous in their churches' affairs. We noted in an earlier chapter the tendency of Protestant traditions to fragment. Arguably in the 1980s and 1990s the historic Protestant churches were discovering a new and more potent source of internal division even than those questions of doctrinal difference and of church government that had split churches in earlier ages. This was in ethics, where disagreement was particularly intractable – especially when it came to the moral behaviour of clergy themselves. The effect increasingly was to marginalize historical aspects of denominational identity. In the West this was underlined in any case by the gradual dilution of historical memory, as people seemed to cross denominational barriers with ever greater ease. What did it mean in these circumstances to be a Methodist or to be a Lutheran? It was not evident that even regular churchgoers really knew. On the other hand, it was a common perception of many churchgoers that their leadership was weak and had capitulated too readily to contemporary fashion. Protestantism's historical roots were ever more remote, its contemporary malaise ever more pressing.

A further sign of the crisis in traditional Protestantism was the growth of independent or free Protestant churches in the West that were not Charismatic but still markedly different in their organization and order from the mainstream denominations. Perhaps the best known by the end of the century was the theologically conservative Willow Creek Community Church. Founded near Chicago in the mid-1970s, this rapidly became a 'mega-church', attracting thousands of worshippers to its Sunday services. The source of Willow Creek's success was its ability to fuse clear organization and orthodox Christian theology with an informal style of worship and a strong emphasis on church growth. But Willow Creek was not unique; it represented a common mode of adaptation to contemporary culture.

All this did not necessarily mean that historic Protestantism would completely disappear in the West in the near future, however. The historic Protestant traditions still represented a substantial and vociferous segment of public opinion. More to the point, even where (as in America) state religion had long ceased to exist, like the Catholic Church the Protestant churches had centuries-old traditions of public service and social welfare that gave them continuing relevance in public discussion about social well being. In the late twentieth century their representative role was particularly sustained by the rise of significant religious and new ethnic minorities in all of these countries and by the rise of Islamic political radicalism. Postwar prosperity and the post-colonial bonds of obligation drew large numbers of people from the Global South to Europe. Even in America this was a period of continuing massive immigration, facilitated by the passage of the Immigration Reform Act in 1965. By the end of the century over a quarter of the population of the US were Hispanics and Asians. The operation of Islamic terrorism in particular often fed off the existence of significant minority Islamic communities in the West. What this all amounted to was the rise of a greater degree of religious and ethnic pluralism than Western society had experienced for centuries, and at the same time a perplexing reappearance of radical religion as a force for social instability. This was much more evident in Europe, where the Muslim minorities were proportionately much more powerful than they were in America, and yet it was American foreign policy – especially after the collapse of the Soviet Union – that time and again was to be used as a scapegoat by radical Islam. For that reason it was America and Americans that were often the target of terrorist atrocities.

Islamic extremism affected Africa and Asia as much as it did Europe and America, and made life particularly problematic for Christian minorities in predominantly Islamic states. African Christians, for example, commonly complained that the Western churches were preoccupied with trivial and incomprehensible questions of human sexuality while their people faced the threat of disease, hunger and violence daily. Other Christians faced this challenge too. But the historic, denominational bonds provided a conduit for African issues to be heard – if often ignored – in the West. Frustration from the churches of the Third World over the Islamic threat, over AIDS and over poverty and famine was an ever more insistent theme of international Protestantism in the 1980s and 1990s.

For this reason the Protestant denominations displayed a greater degree of awareness about issues of social justice, including resistance to racial discrimination, now than at any time in their previous history. There were some specific contexts for this. One was the apartheid regime in South Africa. Protestant churches, through the South African Council of Churches, were highly visible and active proponents of change. In 1985 the Institute for Contextual Theology issued the *Kairos Document*, a critique of the excessively pacific theology articulated by some church leaders in South Africa, which called for a more 'prophetic theology', in effect an appeal for a liberation theology for oppressed blacks in South Africa. Controversial as it was, the *Kairos Document* was a decisive development in the church struggle against apartheid because it exposed the fragility of arguments that rested on an appeal to the good conscience of the oppressors. More to the point, the willingness of church leaders and theologians ultimately to take the side of the oppressed was to prove vital in helping whites to accept peacefully the dismantling of apartheid in the 1990s.

Another specific context was East Germany, the GDR. Although the communist regime had apparently subjugated the Protestant churches by the mid-1970s, this was an illusion. Despite falling numbers of churchgoers, the churches were the one significant, symbolic area of public dissent available to ordinary East Germans, and as the authority of the Communist Party began to crumble in the mid-1980s, increasingly dissidents operated under 'the roof of the church'. Ecumenical gatherings of church leaders were emboldened to criticize the regime explicitly, and the churches were instrumental in organizing the mass protests that led, in the autumn of 1989, to the opening of the borders and the final collapse of Honecker's government. There was a popular saying in East Germany in 1989–90 that 'Jesus had triumphed over Marx'. Behind the specific commitments of the Protestant churches lay a wider Christian awareness of the need to fight oppression, linked to a growing realization of the urgent nature of the ecological crisis.

The pursuit of Protestant unity

Given the emergence of these ethical priorities in the 1970s and 1980s, it is hardly surprising that Protestants increasingly were convinced of the need for common action. The real achievements of the ecumenical movement were more evident between Protestant churches, however, than they were between Protestants and Catholics or Orthodox. The ecumenical vision was powerful in the 1960s and early 1970s: after Vatican II, Protestants could at last feel that there were real prospects of realignment and unity. By the 1990s, however, the original enthusiasm was fading. There were certainly gains, if not dramatic ones. The Catholic Church's entry into the ecumenical movement strengthened the role of the Protestant world communions, because the Catholic Church, as itself a worldwide communion, sought dialogue with corresponding worldwide institutions. By the late 1970s all of the main Protestant denominations were involved in ecumenical dialogue with the Catholic Church through their world communions. The most prominent of these were the World Alliance of Reformed Churches (WARC), the Lutheran World Federation (LWF), the Anglican Communion, the Baptist World Alliance (BWA), the Pentecostal World Fellowship (PWF) and the World Methodist Council (WMC), but there were equivalent bodies for most of the other historic Protestant churches too, such as the Quakers, the Salvation Army and the Churches of Christ. Leaders and representatives of the world communions were often accused of 'confessionalism' – a tendency to prize their own common tradition above wider concerns of evangelism and social justice – by their own church members. However unjustified the accusation, the development of common modes of action and even of fledgling worldwide forms of authority risked hardening denominational organizations – something at odds with the goal of unity. It was the old tension between 'Faith and Order' and 'Life and Work' all over again.

If the real achievements of the world communions were in the field of ecumenical dialogue, they were not matched by schemes of organic church unity in practice in more than a few cases. In 1970 WARC united with the International Congregationalist Council, a venture that reflected other more local mergers between Congregationalism and the Reformed churches. In 1972, in Britain, the United Reformed Church came into being through the merger of the Presbyterian (but not Church of Scotland) and Congregational churches. There were parallel developments in Australia in 1977, in Belgium in 1979 and in Jamaica and the Cayman Islands in 1992. Sometimes these church unions also involved Methodists; only rarely (the Churches of Bangladesh, North India, and Pakistan, 1970–71) did they also involve Anglicans. Lutherans also generally remained aloof. The uniting church movement was thus more significant on paper than it was in practice, since it mostly reflected a union of churches from a relatively narrow band of Protestant opinion. Still, important steps were made towards a modest convergence of traditions in historic Protestantism. There were other ecumenical ventures that crossed denominational or geographical boundaries within Protestantism more radically than the uniting churches. The Leuenberg Fellowship, concluded by agreement in 1973 between most of the Lutheran and Reformed churches of Europe, did not lead to a new 'church' as such but created a relationship of full communion between all these churches; in the early 1990s the Evangelical–Methodist churches also joined. The Porvoo agreement of 1992 between the British Anglican and the Scandinavian and Baltic Lutheran churches, and the Episcopal–Lutheran concordat of 1999 in the US (see Chapter 5) were other examples.

The most notable developments within Protestant unity movements in these years were in North America, Australasia, Europe and Asia. Notably absent from this list is Africa. Though there were some uniting church initiatives there, the spectacular nature of church growth in Africa even in the historic denominations made unity schemes less of a priority. It is a commonplace of secularization theory that the explanation for ecumenism lies principally in the fact of church decline. The suggestion works to a limited extent for Europe and America, where it was true that the Protestant churches most active in the ecumenical movement in the twentieth century were generally those undergoing decline. At the local level, shrinking congregations found it difficult to maintain their buildings and pay their contributions to central church funds, and so it often made sense to join together with other local Protestant churches. The very wide network of Local Ecumenical Partnerships (LEPs) in Britain owes much to this. The theory has its limits. It does not readily explain ecumenical initiatives in Germany and Scandinavia, where churches are better resourced through the church tax system. Nor does it readily explain the uniting churches of Asia, which, rather than declining, have faced instead the pressure of indifferent or positively hostile governments.

But it does perhaps cast some light on the role of historic Protestantism in Africa. There certainly have been significant ecumenical initiatives in Africa. They include the founding of national or regional councils of churches in 1960s and 1970s, such as those for Sudan, Swaziland, Lesotho, Liberia, Namibia, South Africa and Uganda. They also include some continent-wide bodies, above all the All Africa Conference of Churches (AACC), founded at Kampala in 1963. These were bodies that, however, included Orthodox and Catholics as well as a few independent churches. They were not strictly parallel to the uniting churches or to the regional agreements between the historic Protestant churches elsewhere in the world. One apparent exception is the united Protestant Church in the Congo, or the Église du Christ au Congo-Zaïre (ECCZ). But this is an exception that proves the rule. The ECCZ was not formed as a result of a unity scheme put forward by various churches themselves after a process of negotiation, but a state-imposed union in 1970 that encompassed all of the Protestant churches in the country, with just a handful of exceptions, including the Kimbanguist church. Some 76 different denominations were herded into it, including Mennonites, independents and Pentecostals. The member churches kept their own distinct forms of organization but were all equally subject to state regulation. Since Mobutu's regime was one of the harshest and most vicious on the continent, this was bad news for them. The one thing that the ECCZ most certainly was not was the result of a patient search for church unity.

But the underlying reality for African Christianity in the years after decolonization has been a double process of constant growth combined with the struggle to combat poverty, famine, the effects of civil war and HIV/AIDS. The complicated process of negotiation required by any scheme of church unity looked like a luxury the churches could not afford. Furthermore, in the conditions of rapid growth, Protestantism's very diversity was more of a strength than a weakness. No wonder the number of Christian churches in Africa is remarkably high, just as it is in North America, and no wonder that there are such immense regional variations. The Anglican Church in Ghana at the end of the century was very small, with around 200,000 members only, whereas in its near neighbour Nigeria it was large and growing at dizzying speed. All of this perhaps simply reinforced the ambivalence the African churches felt towards the 'parent' denominations – a term itself redolent of colonial dependence. The theologian John Gatu's 1974 proposal for a 'moratorium' in support sent from the West was meant to apply to the mission situation, to stop Western countries sending missionaries to Africa, in order to enable the African churches to forge their own identity; but it was widely misinterpreted to mean a simple suspension of the Western churches' financial aid, and was rejected by many African churches themselves because of this. And so the flow of money through the denominations continued almost uninterrupted, even as the flow of human resource finally drew to a close. Whatever opportunities the African Protestant churches had to begin to organize an independent ecclesial life were overshadowed by the deepening crises affecting much of Africa in the 1980s and 1990s, the era of what some called 'de-development'.

Inevitably different sets of circumstances affected Asia. In India and the Muslim states of Bangladesh, Pakistan and Indonesia the very embattled context of Christianity was a spur to common organization. But there was a similar ambivalence over the role of the 'sending' churches to that in Africa. The United Church of Christ in the Philippines (UCCP), an early uniting church (formed in 1948) that included Methodists, Congregationalists, Presbyterians and various free Evangelical churches, but not Anglicans or Lutherans, constituted the largest church in the Philippines after the Catholic Church by the 1970s, but was riven by disagreement over how to relate to the historic Protestant denominations of the West. There too there were calls for an effective moratorium, for, as one of the UCCP's leading theologians argued in 1971, 'the most *missionary* service a missionary under the present system can do today in Asia is to go home'.[2] Calls for a formal ban on missionaries from overseas here and elsewhere came to nothing, but in any event the flow of missionaries from the West was drying up as the historic denominations contracted sharply. Within a matter of years the whole nature of Protestantism in the Third World was to undergo a dramatic change, as the Pentecostal churches surged in size. Korea is a good example of the effect on traditional Protestantism. Practically all the mainstream Protestant denominations in South Korea saw their numbers rise substantially in this period. The Presbyterian Church in Korea, for example, almost quadrupled its membership from 534,000 to 2 million from 1970 to 1995. Over the same period the Korean Methodist Church doubled in size from 600,000 adherents to 1,230,000, and the smaller Episcopal Church in Korea increased from 32,000 to 100,000. But even those rates of growth, substantial as they were, paled beside that of the Korea Assembly of God, a Pentecostal church, which grew from just 10,000 adherents to 400,000. The Muslim state of Indonesia was another case in point. The Methodist

Church there remained fixed at around 70,000 adherents. Although the Protestant Church in Indonesia, the successor church to the state church of the former Dutch colony, surprisingly grew from 1.9 million to 2.7 million, its rate of growth again was far outstripped by that of many of the Pentecostal and independent churches.

In these circumstances the pursuit of wider Protestant unity was marginalized by the new, dynamic forms of church springing up particularly in the Third World. Some Pentecostal churches from across the world, like some of the older independent churches, have joined the WCC, and so are committed to common processes of discussion and action with the historic denominations. But inevitably their participation will bring new questions to the fore and will have the effect of creating a new set of challenges for dialogue and agreement, so that the hard work the historic denominations have already put into the pursuit of unity can only represent the first stage of what looks like an ever-widening circle of relationships.

Internal change and division

In other respects, too, historic Protestantism saw a further development of trends already evident by the 1970s. The most visible of these were almost certainly the growing movement to admit women to the churches' ordained ministry and leadership, and the divisions opening up within and between the churches over questions of sexual morality. The movement for women's ordination naturally had its wider context in the promotion of women's rights, education and professional development, something spurred on by the widespread employment of women in the West in the two world wars and by the granting of women's suffrage. But it also drew on long-standing traditions of women's ministry and work in many of the Protestant churches – especially Methodism – and on the very prominence of women in most congregations.

In general terms it was easier for churches which had dispensed with the threefold order of ministry (deacons, priests and bishops) to include women in their official or ordained ministries, since they had mostly abandoned the attempt to follow a traditional view of ministry shared with the Orthodox and the Catholic Church. Moreover they could mostly take these decisions on a local or regional basis. Presbyterian and Methodist churches decided to ordain women in 1956, long before there was any substantial pressure on them to do so. But Congregationalists in England had decided to do it as long ago as 1917, and were followed by the Congregational Union in Scotland in 1929. Other Reformed churches followed suit in due course – the French Reformed Church in 1965 and the Church of Scotland in 1968. Meanwhile the Lutheran churches – at least those amenable to 'modern' developments

– were also going through similar discussions, and by the 1970s practically all of the Scandinavian, German and US Lutheran churches had agreed to ordain women. So too had many Baptist churches and the Disciples of Christ.

It was a different matter for Anglicans, for they had retained the three-fold order of ministry and had an Anglo-Catholic wing that contained many sceptical that women's ministry could be reconciled with church tradition. The ordination of Florence Li Tim-Oi as priest in 1944 in Hong Kong was an emergency measure during Japanese occupation which caused immense controversy, and was not repeated for a generation. Hong Kong, however, did decide formally to ordain women in 1971 and was followed closely by other Anglican churches, including those of the US, Canada, New Zealand, Brazil, Kenya and Uganda, and in due course by many other provinces of the Communion. The Church of England did not follow suit until 1992. By then, not only had women been admitted to the ordained ministry in principle in most Protestant churches, but in the West they had become an increasing proportion of the numbers ordained – so much so that some male ministers began to talk fearfully of the 'feminization' of the ministry. But this was absurd. Men remained the dominant gender in church leadership, and these changes were more in evidence in the declining Western churches than they were in the growing Third World churches. Moreover even in the West the strongest opposition came from the more conservative elements of Evangelicalism, again the sector of Protestantism apparently most resistant to decline.

Even more bitter divisions opened up over the question of sexual ethics and in particular homosexuality. The sexual revolution of the 1960s in the West transformed the sexual habits of young people particularly. By the 1980s and 1990s cohabitation before marriage, or in place of it, was very common indeed in the West. But though it was met with regret by the churches it did not attract anything like the controversy that homosexuality did. Here changes in church policy mostly followed changes in wider society. Until the mid-twentieth century active homosexual relations were illegal in most Western countries. The legalization of homosexuality by states in the second half of the century inevitably raised tensions with the churches. Some responded in due course by adopting a more tolerant view. Usually this came in three phases – first, a general tolerance of homosexuality among church members; second, a readiness to ordain practising homosexuals; and third, adoption of some sort of service of blessing or marriage for same-sex couples. Few churches got further than the first stage. The ordination of women had not directly confronted Protestants with the challenge of reinterpreting Scripture, though opponents could draw some support from

St Paul. But homosexuality did, given Paul's teaching on sexual behaviour in the Epistle to the Romans. It became a litmus test of a church's biblical orthodoxy, and Evangelicals in particular dug their heels in over this question. By the 1990s all of the mainstream Protestant churches in the West faced internal division, and their disagreement was fuelled by the general incomprehension and abhorrence with which proposals to adopt a more liberal policy were met by Protestants in the Third World. No issue looked more likely to force a split in the historic denominations. No issue served to focus so sharply the divergence between traditional Christian teaching and the social values of Western society.

In Anglicanism the debate over homosexuality broke open in the years after the 1998 Lambeth Conference. Conservative movements within many of the Western provinces of the Anglican Communion sought support from the leadership of Third World Anglicanism. The Diocese of Sydney in Australia formed almost a separate conservative stream of Australian Anglicanism, but it encouraged and garnered support in other Anglican circles. The election of a practising homosexual as bishop of New Hampshire in the Episcopal Church of the United States in 2003 triggered a Communion-wide crisis and threatened to force the break-up of the Communion. Presbyterianism in America was also seriously divided over homosexuality, with a 'Confessing Church' movement in place – adopting a title deliberately from the German churches' struggle with Nazism – with over 1,300 congregations committed to defence of the teaching 'That God's people are called to holiness in all aspects of life' which included 'honoring the sanctity of marriage between a man and a woman, the only relationship within which sexual activity is appropriate'.[3] The Church of Sweden, a Lutheran church, had a conservative dissident movement called the 'Free Synod'. It had originated in opposition to the ordination of women, but became equally hostile to the moves the Swedish church made towards ordaining practising homosexuals and countenancing the blessing of same-sex couples.

By the beginning of the twenty-first century there were dissident or schismatic groups within most of the denominations. Sometimes these divisions had broken out over liturgical change rather than ethics. Churches that had been content to leave their vernacular services unchanged for centuries, now, under the pressure of falling congregations or of new mission challenges, sought to translate them into more familiar, everyday language. This was a process echoed in the increasing frequency with which new, up-to-date translations of the Bible were appearing. But the trend towards liturgical reform in Protestantism (paralleled in the Catholic Church's post-Vatican II reforms) encountered bewilderment and resentment from a significant proportion of existing church congregations. This was clearly a 'no win' situation for the churches.

At least when it came to questions of liturgical style, compromise was usually possible. In general terms it was ethical disagreement that was by far the most bitter source of church division. But there were strategic divisions as well. Most supporters of change on women's ministry, sexuality and various other issues such as interfaith relations assumed that the unity of the Church was an absolute good, which should not be compromised by principled disagreement on particular matters. Of course this was somewhat disingenuous when the change of policy for which they argued might represent a fundamental betrayal of principle for their opponents – they were asking their opponents to abandon the Gospel and yet adhere to the Church, so it was alleged. But their view was articulated within a broad consensus on the desirability of toleration and out of recognition of the provisional nature of human reception of truth. Opponents of change, on the other hand, often considered church unity at best a secondary issue, subservient to the true proclamation of the Gospel. For conservative Evangelicals and Pietists in particular, the problem with homosexuality was that it was symptomatic of the Western churches' abandonment of biblical standards of morality and therefore of the Gospel itself. An International Congress on World Evangelism was held at Lausanne in 1974, inspired by Billy Graham, and this gathered together representatives from Evangelical churches throughout the world. It distanced itself from the ecumenical movement and appealed to a broad range of Evangelical opinion. Though it was to have little official standing in the churches, it represented a formative moment in the consciousness of the modern Evangelical movement. Coming as it did just a few years after the traumatic changes of the 1960s, it reflected a determination to reassert traditional Evangelical principles and signalled the way in which, increasingly through the last quarter of the century, the decisive alignment in contemporary Protestantism would not be along denominational lines but along the fault-line of conservative versus liberal positions on ethics.

CHAPTER 15

Pentecostalism

The character and roots of Pentecostalism

The remarkable growth of Pentecostal Christianity is surely the most start-ling fact about the Christian Church worldwide in the last quarter of the twentieth century. It overshadowed the more traditional forms of Protes-tantism in the Global South, and even the growth of Catholicism. Its surge in popular support was so great in just 30 years or so that in the early years of the twenty-first century scholars who had failed to notice its advance for years suddenly began to hail it as the future of Christianity. The only detailed figures currently available for the whole world suggest that from around 980,000 adherents in the early years of the twentieth century, or about 0.1 per cent of world population, it soared to over 425 million by the end of the century, or about 8 per cent of the population – fully one-quarter of world Christianity. As usual it is almost impossible to be confi-dent about the accuracy of these figures: the true figure could be anything between a quarter of a billion and half a billion. When we try to estimate the numbers of Pentecostals or Charismatics *within* the longer-established churches, we really have almost nothing firm to go on. The same source of figures for Pentecostalism worldwide – the *World Christian Encyclopedia* – also reckoned on some further 125 million Evangelicals in the mainstream Protestant churches at the end of the century, taking its total of 'Great Commission' Christians up to 561 million, or about 10.6 per cent of world population, or almost a third of world Christianity. As if these breathtaking figures are not enough, the impact of Pentecostalism was even more strik-ing in the Global South, given the continuing decline of most mainstream Protestant churches in the West, and the fact that Western Europe has generally proved the least fertile soil for Pentecostalism.

Difficulties about measuring numbers pale by comparison with the problems of defining exactly what Pentecostalism is. One common defi-nition is theological. Pentecostalism emerged out of the 'holiness' move-ments of Protestant revivalism in the nineteenth century and emphasized a further stage beyond conversion, baptism in the Spirit, which was exemplified in speaking in tongues following the description in Acts 2.1–13. To this basic doctrine one should also add belief in the inspiration of the Bible, in salvation through conversion and revival, in instantaneous sanctification and in divine healing. But the difficulty with this is that it relies excessively on a concept of 'Spirit baptism' and on what is often called a doctrine of 'initial evidence' of that through speaking in tongues, which is not widely shared by all Pentecostal churches and indeed is typical mostly of 'classical Pentecostalism', the Pentecostalism that originated in America in the early twentieth century and has spread to some parts of the world.

One of the pioneering historians of Pentecostalism, Walter Hollenweger, has proposed a much looser definition based on practice and experience. His description of the key elements of early African American Pentecostalism could stand as fairly typical of the movement worldwide: oral liturgy, narrative theology and witness, maximum community participation in worship, the use of dreams and visions in worship and a special understanding of the relationship of mind and body demonstrated through liturgical dance and healing by prayer.[1] But even this does not cover all cases. Many of the Asian churches have moved towards a form of written liturgy, for example, in order to cater for vast gathered congregations. Some, there and elsewhere, are developing a fully 'professional' ministry, with distinctive training, clerical dress and more formally defined leadership, with a corresponding limitation on community participation.

We should note certain widespread if not universal dimensions of Pentecostalism: conviction of the presence and power of charismatic gifts of the Spirit (tongues, prophecy and healing), the belief that these demonstrate a new state of grace for the individual (usually following conversion as a later stage), a vibrant, lively and usually spontaneous form of worship, and the absence of a corporate understanding of the Church as mediating grace. This last point is a vital one. Much of the language of Pentecostalism highlights the believer's direct experience of the power of God, as if they are exposed directly to the scorching heat or emotionally overwhelming nature of God's love. It is a language of individual prostration before God, leading to an almost ecstatic conviction of personal calling and of privileged possession of God's love. In this way it has a lot of resonance with much older traditions of Christian mysticism, and yet it is profoundly democratic and non-ascetic: it requires no sustained contemplative practice. The term 'Pentecostalism' is really an umbrella concept which cannot be reduced to a single definition, and which may even at times be profoundly misleading. It is performative Christianity – ecstatic (but disciplined), informal (and yet predictable), spontaneous (but still planned in broad terms) and strongly participatory (but with charismatic ministers as leaders). It shares with historic Protestantism belief in the inspired authority of Scripture and in justification through faith. But its use of charismatic gifts makes it vulnerable in the eyes of many traditional Protestants to the charge of inventing a new authority or second revelation to rival Scripture. It is instinctively non-doctrinal and non-confessional in its understanding of the Church (which is not to say that it has no doctrine). One British scholar, David Martin, has called it 'a protean indigenous Christianity … indifferent to the agenda of the Western theological intelligentsia'.[2]

Pentecostalism is marked above all by extraordinarily vibrant and exciting worship. A research student working in Argentina recently described the experience of going to the church of a well-known Pentecostal preacher in Buenos Aires, Claudio Freidzon:

> My hope for a seat evaporated instantly; the old cinema was completely full and people were already standing at the back. A smartly suited young man took the stage and suddenly the hall erupted into applause. A deep drum roll led into the bouncy beat of 'La única razón para vivir'. The floor vibrated with hundreds of tapping feet. … Freidzon arrived to more applause. He took the microphone, a stream of incomprehensible words followed, people joined in with praise tongues, the loud music continued, the auditorium was filled with music and the hum of human voices praising God.[3]

Evidently Pentecostal worship is fun and requires little or no formal preparation. That does not by itself explain why Pentecostalism has grown so rapidly. One plausible reason is that Pentecostal belief is a way of channelling divine power directly into the lives of believers. The charismatic gifts as such are almost incidental: they are striking testimonies of the believer's possession of God's grace rather than a means of procuring it. Like healing, they are fruits of grace – powerful and immediate signs of God's approval. The attraction this has for the poor and marginalized, and for those who have experienced disappointment or loss or acute pain, is very great.

At its loosest, then, the term 'Pentecostal' simply means a conviction of the return of the charismatic gifts of the first Pentecost, the Pentecost described in Acts 2. Put this way, it is not so much a new movement as another wave of the charismatic experience and spirituality that has always surfaced from time to time in the history of the Christian Church. Its immediate precursors lay in the great Evangelical and Pietistic revivals of the eighteenth and early nineteenth centuries and in particular in Methodism and the various 'holiness' movements. These were churches which had taken John Wesley's teaching about 'entire sanctification' to a logical conclusion, connecting the sanctification of the believer after justification to the reception of gifts of prophecy, healing and tongues in the manner of the first Pentecost.

Pentecostalism's decisive moment, according to the conventional accounts, came in 1906 in Azusa Street, Los Angeles, when William J. Seymour, an African American preacher, began preaching on spiritual gifts, and practising Spirit baptism, with speaking in tongues. Seymour had been a follower of Charles Parham, a white Methodist minister who had also preached tongues and healing. But Parham did not favour mixed-race meetings and did not openly evangelize. Seymour's initiative was completely open to all races, and energetically expansive. The numbers of worshippers at the Apostolic Faith Mission in Azusa Street rapidly increased. News about it travelled quickly in a country now united by telegraph and rail. People on the 'holiness' circuit came to Los Angeles out of curiosity, and many took Seymour's message back to their own communities, founding or transforming new churches.

The movement split as rapidly as it spread. Theological divisions opened up between those who held to the Wesleyan holiness view of 'Spirit baptism' as a third stage following justification and sanctification, and those who emphasized the 'finished work' of Christ on the Cross. For the first group (sometimes called 'Holiness Pentecostals'), 'Spirit baptism' was intrinsic to the salvation of the individual believer. For the second group (sometimes called 'Reformed Pentecostals'), salvation was a finished work of grace; the sanctification of the believer was an ongoing process following conversion which freed the believer from the effect of sin, and so a second baptism in the Spirit was not a necessary stage of salvation. This division became practically a racial one, with white pastors in particular following the 'finished work' line, rejecting the emotional chaos they thought ensued from urging 'Spirit baptism' as necessary to salvation. The largest African American network of Pentecostal churches, the Church of God in Christ, is a Holiness Pentecostal movement; the largest white American network, the Assemblies of God, founded in 1914, is a Reformed Pentecostal movement. A second major division occurred over the doctrine of God in 1916, when a group of Pentecostal churches adopted what they called a 'Jesus only' theology, and their opponents a 'Oneness' theology. Rejecting the traditional Christian doctrine of the Trinity as three persons in one God, they asserted the one person of Jesus Christ, who had different titles as Father, Son and Holy Spirit. This group were seen as heretical by the Holiness Pentecostals in particular, though the split from the Reformed Pentecostals was also bitter. Holiness, Reformed and Oneness Pentecostals were to constitute the three major divisions of American Pentecostalism, though the number of actual churches or denominations multiplied to over 300 by the end of the century.

There are some difficulties in the conventional account of Pentecostalism as springing from Azusa Street. First, it is a romanticized, heroic reading of history, overemphasizing the role of one minister, William Seymour. Seymour was certainly influential in the early history of Pentecostalism, but there were many others who were developing theologically along much the same lines, such as Charles Harrison Mason, founder of the Church of God in Christ. Though later influenced by Seymour, much that was characteristic of Seymour's ministry and preaching was already commonplace in Mason's congregation as early as 1897. Seymour's ministry was a crystallizing moment, drawing together various strands of theology and experience that were part of a seething spiritual world on the edges of conventional Protestantism in late nineteenth and early twentieth-century America. Second, it overemphasizes the importance of American Pentecostalism in the global context. The American churches sent missionaries around the world, and many of the larger American Pentecostal denominations today have churches in several continents. There were European Evangelicals who came to America to experience Pentecostal worship and were transformed by it, such as Thomas Ball Barratt, an Englishman who was instrumental in founding Pentecostal churches in Scandinavia after experiencing Pentecostal worship in New York in 1906. But there were also parallel movements in worldwide Evangelicalism that did not owe anything directly to the American connection. A revival in Korea, for example, broke out within the Presbyterian and Methodist churches there as early as 1903. There was a revival in 1905–7 in India, at the Mukti Mission in Poona run by Pandita Ramabai. Here young women were baptized in the Spirit, fell into a trance and began speaking in tongues. The Mukti Mission in turn had a profound impact on Latin America, through the influence of Minnie Abrams, a Methodist missionary who experienced Spirit baptism in Poona and was instrumental in revival in Chile in 1909. There were other independent revivals in Africa, more or less unconnected with American Pentecostalism. The origins of Pentecostalism are therefore diverse. They indicate a series of more or less spontaneous eruptions within worldwide Evangelicalism, linked by the rapidity with which news about revival circulated in these Evangelical circles and by the amazing activity of Pentecostal missionaries sent out from many of the new churches with the conviction that speaking in tongues gave them a divine gift of evangelism.

Pentecostalism in the Global South

Summarizing the growth of Pentecostalism worldwide is no easy task. Every continent is different and every country is different, it seems. Like the seed in Jesus's parable, some Pentecostal churches have hardly grown at all, some have grown rapidly and then collapsed suddenly, some have grown fitfully and split often, some have started slowly and then suddenly surged in numbers, and some have grown slowly but consistently – there is no overall pattern discernible. What follows is therefore nothing more than a brief sketch of some of the more striking instances of Pentecostal history, which cannot pretend to be anything other than highly selective.

Latin America is usually hailed as the most startling example of the recent growth of Pentecostalism. This is partly because the sheer dominance of Catholicism in the continent's religious history until recently has thrown into sharp relief the unexpected nature of this development. And yet many of the Latin American Pentecostal churches have their roots in the early twentieth century. The largest Protestant church in Latin America, the Assemblies of God in Brazil, came into being through the work of two Swedish American preachers, Gunnar Vingren and Daniel Berg, before the First World War. Its healing ministry proved particularly attractive, and by mid-century it was adding 10,000 converts a year. By the end of the century it had churches in every Brazilian state, with over 4 million followers. Its membership came mainly from mixed-race (European and African) people, particularly the poor. The tendency to recruit from the poor is a common feature of Pentecostalism in Latin America, where the Catholic Church so often has the appearance of a semi-official religious establishment. The Assemblies of God in Brazil echo the Catholic Church's social provision, through their schools, literacy schemes, homes for the sick, aged and orphaned, and day nurseries – all without the hierarchical organization of the Catholic Church. In Brazil as elsewhere the Pentecostal churches are rivals to the base communities lauded by the liberation theologians, and much academic ink has been spilt about whether they are truly a movement *of* the poor or a movement *for* the poor led by outside (North American, it is alleged) evangelists. In fact there is little evidence of deliberate intervention by American outsiders; the vast majority of Brazil's Pentecostals are poor people who run their own churches. By the end of the century it was reckoned by some authorities that almost a quarter of the Brazilian population were members of Pentecostal churches.

In some parts of Latin America the political allegiances of Pentecostal church leaders have been controversial. In Chile, for example, in the 1970s one of the largest Pentecostal denominations, the Methodist Pentecostal Church (MPC), was led by Javier Vásquez Valencia, who regularly courted the favour of Augusto Pinochet, the dictator who had overthrown Salvador Allende's elected left-wing government in 1973. The MPC, however, was another church that traced its origins back to the beginning of the century, in the work of Willis Hoover, who in turn was influenced by Minnie Abrams. Courting dictators was not a characteristic part of its history, and the vast majority of its members even in the 1970s were drawn precisely from those sections of the poor most hostile to Pinochet's regime. Pentecostalism in Chile has suffered, ironically, from the same charges sometimes laid at the door of the Catholic Church, namely that it preaches acceptance of one's station in life and therefore reinforces existing structures of injustice. But its social implications have to be understood in the context of its radically empowering message of divine favour and prophecy for the poor and outcast. Pentecostals too have a social conscience and can adopt what by any standard are radical programmes of social improvement in areas in which their influence is great.

If the growth of Pentecostalism is hard enough to outline in Latin America, that task is even harder in the case of Africa. Here the question of how to define 'Pentecostal' is particularly difficult, because there is an enormous range of churches which share many features of American 'classical' Pentecostalism, but which would not necessarily regard themselves as Pentecostalist. It is impossible to describe a clear line between the independent churches and the Pentecostal churches, and so this chapter has to be seen as complementary to that on the independent churches.

Difficulties of definition are perhaps illustrated by a simple question that is crucial to the context of Christianity in Africa – how should one regard the cult of the ancestors? Veneration of the ancestors is an almost universal feature of the non-Christian, traditional religions of Africa, and still a powerful element of African culture. The ancestors, having died, inhabit an often undefined realm, from which they may appear in visions or dreams and exercise influence (benign or otherwise) in the lives of their living descendants. Some AICs and Pentecostal churches are surprisingly open to the ancestor cult. One historian quotes an archbishop of the Christian National Apostolic Church in Zion, in South Africa, as saying, 'Whoever forsakes his ancestors is also forsaken by his ancestors and he becomes an easy prey to diseases and to all his other enemies.'[4] Others – especially those churches found in the cities and descended from 'classical Pentecostalism' – entirely reject the cult as adoration or appeasement of demons. The spectrum of opinion in the African churches runs from acceptance to outright rejection; all responses on this spectrum are a tribute, however, to the continuing power of the ancestor cult.

As in Latin America, although the growth of African Pentecostalism has really only attracted scholarly attention in the last 30 years or so, it goes back to the beginning of the century. In 1907 a group of preachers who had travelled through America and experienced the Azusa Street revival began to work in black churches in South Africa. John G. Lake and Thomas Hezmalhalch were among them. They founded the Apostolic Faith

Mission of Africa in Johannesburg in 1908. The church grew quite quickly, but divisions occurred over the question of race, especially when the white leaders tried to block black members from exercising any real influence over the Church. One of these schisms, the Zion Christian Church formed in 1925 by Engenas Lekganyane, had over 4 million adherents by 2000. But hundreds of much smaller churches were formed in South Africa during the century. Similarly the Pentecostal churches of West and East Africa had much older origins, and the overlap with the 'independent' churches is very great indeed. In Kenya, for example, what came to be called the 'Roho', or 'Spirit', movement began with a revival in 1912 among the Luo people. For 20 years the followers of Alfaya Odongo Mango were held within the Anglican Church, but the relationship was tense, and in 1934 they were finally banned from Anglican churches. West African Pentecostalism really began with the revivals of William Wade Harris in 1913 and 1914 (already recounted briefly in Chapter 10), but Harris's policy was to encourage people to stay with the existing mission churches. But in time dissatisfaction with the mission churches led to the emergence of independent Pentecostal churches. Three of the largest in Ghana by the end of the century stemmed from the ministry of a Ghanaian evangelist, Peter Anim, and a Northern Irish missionary, James McKeown, in the years between the two world wars. Both men remained actively involved in their churches' affairs into the 1970s and 1980s, but they disagreed over the question of healing, something central to the experience of many African Pentecostal churches. Anim and his followers rejected Western medicine and made much of the healing miracles that accompanied their work. In an African context the healing ministry of many Pentecostal churches has provided a powerful element of continuity with the magic and oracles of African traditional religions. Even when a church has adopted an attitude of outright rejection of the cult of ancestors and insisted on its members avoiding contact with local witches or 'medicine men', the healing and tongues that go with many Pentecostal churches' worship provides an obvious substitute for the benefits of the traditional religions. McKeown did not deny healing miracles, and indeed encouraged them, but like many Western Pentecostals was able to reconcile them with use of Western medicine. The rejection of Western medicine by some churches has of course become particularly difficult in the context of the HIV/AIDS crisis across Africa.

African Pentecostalism has seen an explosion in numbers in the last 30 years or so of the century. In this movement of 'New Pentecostalism', as it is called, the use of electronic music and mass media in worship has been central, and startling success has been achieved among a more affluent section of society in the rapidly growing towns and cities of Africa than the older and 'classical' Pentecostal churches were able to attract. In Nigeria, for example, the Deeper Life Bible Church was founded as recently as 1982 by William Folorunso Kumuyi, a former lecturer, though its origins lie in Bible classes he held from the early 1970s. The Church's growth has been so rapid that it claims to be the fourth largest church in the world, though it is hard to know quite what the claim means, since it does not refer to numbers of members as such. It is certainly a large and rapidly growing church. By the end of the century it had almost a million adherents. Churches like this have attracted the affluent partly through creating community in the anonymous context of the sprawling cities. But some have also proclaimed what its critics call the 'prosperity gospel' – the argument that God's favour towards his faithful will include showering material blessings on them. Encountered particularly in the mid-West 'Bible Belt' of North America, this is highly controversial, firstly because it seems to imply that God's generosity can be coerced, and secondly because it leads to the presumption that the possession of the 'trinity' of health, wealth and happiness by a Christian is a sign of the quality of their faith.

The 'prosperity gospel' is unlikely to account for the success of 'New Pentecostal' churches in Africa overall, given the prolonged economic, political and social difficulties of many African states since the world economic recession of the 1970s. It is true that this may be a good example of what sociologists have called 'cognitive dissonance' – the idea that so powerful and all-encompassing may be the believer's worldview that their failure to acquire something the value system promised (such as healing, or a good crop or a gift) merely reinforces the original conviction, because the believer accounts for the failure in terms of their own inadequacy rather than thinking that the system is unfair. Here there may be parallels between, for example, the medieval cult of the saints, with the healing stories attached to saints' relics, and modern Pentecostal healing practices. It is hard to prove or disprove such an argument. The American theologian Harvey Cox offers a different perspective. He sees Pentecostal religion as an expression of 'primal spirituality', an instinctual and experiential form of practice that engages the believer at a deeper level than that of theological systems – or, in his words, 'that largely unprocessed nucleus of the psyche in which the unending struggle for a sense of purpose and significance goes on'.[5] According to Cox, this has been lost in the formalized, doctrine-determined religion of the West and rediscovered in Pentecostalism in the threefold form of primal speech (speaking in tongues, or alternatively 'praying in the Spirit'), primal piety ('trance, vision, healing, dreams, dance'), and primal hope (the millennial hope 'that a radically new world age is about to dawn').[6] Cox's own description of a night gathering of the African

Apostolic Church in Zimbabwe before Holy Communion offers a vivid example:

> [At] first quietly, but then more and more volubly, the adults begin to pray, both singly and in little knots of four or five. Some of the prayers are sobs and groans. As the evening wears on toward midnight people begin to walk around the fires, then to run and jump, shouting out their prayers in resounding cries and wails ... as the sun rises, the crowd becomes quiet. With great dignity and composure they line up to pass through what they call the 'gates of heaven'. Each of these gates consists of twelve 'prophets', the title given to ministering priests of the church. ... As the worshippers pass through these 'gates', each makes his or her confession. When they get to the inside, they are symbolically entering the Kingdom of God.[7]

Contrast this with the much more formalized worship of mainstream Protestant and Catholic worship – even in its anyway more exuberant African form. Here there is an extraordinary sense of freedom, hope, gathering and catharsis.

In Asia there are many similarities to Africa and Latin America. The rise of Pentecostalism there has been rapid and has easily overtaken the growth rates of other forms of Christianity. By the end of the century, there were supposedly 135 million Pentecostal and Charismatic Christians there. But in general terms – with the notable exceptions of India and Korea – Pentecostalism has been of more recent origin in Asia. In India, Evangelical revivals among the Christianized populations of the south in particular occurred from the mid-nineteenth century, and provided the background to the 1905–7 'Spirit' revival in Poona. Korea is perhaps the most startling example of recent Pentecostal growth. Christianity arrived there only in the 1880s, but there was a well-established tradition of revivalism in the mainstream Protestant churches by the 1900s. 'Classical' Pentecostalism arrived somewhat later, in the 1930s, and the Assemblies of God were constituted in Korea in 1953. In time they included the church of David Yonggi Cho, who began with just five members in 1958 but became so successful as a pastor and preacher that by 1969 he built a 10,000-seat church in Yoido – technically the largest church building in the world – to cope with rising numbers. Built on an island, the Yoido church was opened in 1973, but by the early 1980s had to be enlarged to seat 25,000. By 1993 the Yoido Full Gospel Church had over 700,000 members, with 700 pastors (many of whom were women) in what was technically still one congregation. The sheer size of the church building is staggering – it is monumental, like the cathedrals of Europe must have seemed to medieval citizens. An assembly on such a scale would obviously be impossible without sound amplification. Perhaps because of the building's size, but also because of the strength of the Methodist and Presbyterian roots of Pentecostalism in Korea, Yoido actually uses a regular written liturgy – an unusual development for a Pentecostal church. Elsewhere in Asia, it was in the 1920s and 1930s, or later still, that Pentecostal missionaries began to arrive. Churches were disrupted by the Japanese invasions and by the civil war in China and the imposition of communist rule, and have had to cope accordingly with political situations of enormous diversity. In China some estimates put the numbers of Pentecostals and Charismatics as high as 50 million by the end of the century.

A Charismatic revolution?

For all its diversity and its widely different contexts, there is a basic element of continuity in Pentecostalism, and that is faith in the present power of the Holy Spirit manifested in extraordinary gifts, usually healing and some form of tongues. This is paralleled in the 'Charismatic movement' within the mainstream Protestant churches and the Catholic Church, highlighting yet again the difficulty of defining Pentecostalism closely. Rather than assuming Pentecostalism was a separate development, we should perhaps see *one* movement of Charismatic renewal rippling through Christianity from the early twentieth century, at first outside the older churches, but increasingly within them. There is no sharp distinction between Pentecostalism and Charismatic Christianity in terms of doctrine or practice. The Charismatic movement ultimately has deep roots in the history and experience of Evangelical revival too, and there were many 'Pentecostal' preachers in the early years of the century who remained committed to the churches in which they had been nurtured, difficult though that often was. Even so, these preachers would often call themselves Pentecostal. There were also Pentecostal leaders willing to dialogue constructively with non-Pentecostal churches, who thus carried news about Pentecostalism further afield. The most notable of these was the indefatigable David du Plessis, who became a regular attender at the assemblies of the World Council of Churches.

The emergence of a distinct Charismatic movement can be traced to the early 1960s. In America the influence of Dennis Bennett, an Episcopalian who declared publicly his Spirit baptism in early 1960, was vital. Bennett turned a small, failing church congregation in Seattle into a large and vibrant church and became a personal inspiration to many other ministers within the historic Protestant denominations who followed his lead. In Britain it was again an Anglican church that became the conduit for Charismatic Christianity – All Souls', Langham Place, in London, where the well-known Evangelical John Stott was rector, and his curate Michael Harper received Spirit baptism in 1962. Other Charismatic Evangelical Anglicans were David Watson at St Cuthbert's, York, and John Perry at St Andrew's,

Chorleywood, though other denominations were also quickly involved. Harper helped to found the Fountain Trust, an organization devoted to propagating and organizing the Charismatic movement. In West Germany the Lutheran minister Arnold Bittlinger also received Spirit baptism in 1962 and was instrumental in encouraging Charismatic renewal in churches across Germany and in establishing an ecumenical Charismatic community at Schloss Craheim. The Charismatic movement also rapidly spread to the Catholic Church, under the influence of the Second Vatican Council. Initially appearing in America under the aegis of a group of students and lecturers at Notre Dame University in the late 1960s, it was encouraged by Cardinal Suenens of Belgium and endorsed by Paul VI at a congress for Catholic Charismatics at Rome in 1975. What is particularly striking about this wave of Charismatic energy in the Western churches is its chronology – the 1960s, the time of cultural revolution in the West, when churchgoing began to plummet. Whatever the precise relationship between the Charismatic movement and wider questions of church attendance, it is plausible that the vitality of the movement helped to slow down church decline. The fact that it was an area of growth in church life at a time of general decline naturally helped it to achieve a certain credibility more quickly than might otherwise have been the case. By the end of the century, one statistic was even claiming that there were some 120 million Catholic Charismatics throughout the world – around 10 per cent of world Catholicism.

But the Charismatic movement also prompted the development of new churches and organizations on the penumbra of the old. In America the 1970s saw the rise of 'tele-evangelism', with preachers such as the Methodist Oral Roberts and the Southern Baptist Pat Robertson (later a contender for the Republican vice-presidential nomination) wielding immense influence through their broadcasting networks. Though both of them remained within their denominations, their impact was felt well beyond them, and they helped to set the scene for the development of a new wave of independent Charismatic churches in America and elsewhere in the last quarter of the century. These included various churches which adopted a controversial emphasis on 'shepherding', involving the submission of members to spiritual leaders. The 'shepherding' movement grew rapidly into the early 1980s but collapsed in mutual recrimination. Other organizations preached the 'prosperity gospel', which we have already encountered in Africa. One of the foremost exponents was Kenneth Hagin, founder of the Rhema Bible Training Centre in 1974. Another development was the so-called 'Third Wave' (classical Pentecostalism and the Charismatic movement were supposed to be the first two waves) associated with names such as John Wimber of the Vineyard Christian Fellowship, whose advocacy of 'power evangelism' proved as influential in Britain as it did in America. Critics have pointed to the ambiguities surrounding this notion of power. According to one, for example, the concept of divine power in Wimber's songs and worship is 'quasi-Monarchian': it emphasizes Christ's reigning in glory, 'at the expense of Christ in his risen humanity, who has known weakness'.[8] An emphasis on power and empowerment does run through the Charismatic movement, and is evidently open to abuse. This was underlined by occasional scandals involving abusive or grasping Charismatic ministers. But there was nothing unique about Pentecostal or Charismatic ministers in this respect, and if there was a temptation sometimes to overemphasize the overwhelming nature of divine power, charismatic experience surely gave back to the believer a vital sense of being affirmed and accepted.

That may provide a clue to the extraordinary transcultural appeal of Pentecostalism and Charismatic Christianity. It is perhaps too soon to say with any certainty if it represents the future of Christianity as a whole – a revolution in Christian piety. The fact that it has flourished within the hierarchical system of the Catholic Church, as well as in extremely informal independent churches, suggests that the experience of the gifts of the Spirit and doctrines such as birth in the Spirit are sufficiently flexible to accommodate many different theological convictions on the spectrum of Christian belief. That supports Harvey Cox's contention about primal spirituality, even if the term itself is somewhat vague. But there is a sense in which this powerful wave of Christian experience and practice has touched a deep personal vein for millions of Christians and evidently given them something powerful by way of affirmation and fulfilment, something unavailable to them in the more conventional patterns of Christian worship. Its very emotionalism may be part of its appeal, then, not only for the poor and marginalized of the developing world but also for the privileged and rich who feel their lives have been emptied of ultimate significance by modern consumerism. It is telling that Pentecostalism and Charismatic Christianity have mostly been conservative in ethics and in biblical interpretation, and in the case of some churches even fundamentalist. The sheer excitement and risk of Pentecostal worship has mostly co-existed with a desire to inhabit the world of the Bible as if it was exactly coterminous with the world of today. Pentecostal preaching and spirituality is one of immediacy, as if Jesus and the Apostles are present vividly to believers as friends and guardians. This leaves little scope for a more cerebral reception and interpretation of the biblical texts, and is a daunting contrast with Western churches' preoccupation with the impact of science, history and modern philosophy on the traditional faith at the beginning of the century.

The Christian Church at the Beginning of the New Millennium

Extravagant celebrations in towns and cities throughout the world marked the beginning of the new millennium on 1 January 2000. But eras in human history do not begin neatly on 1 January in one year and end on 31 December in another. If we take August 1914 as the real beginning of the twentieth century, when should we look for an ending? Probably in the West most people would look to the terrorist attacks in America on 11 September 2001. Nearly 3,000 people died in the assaults on the World Trade Center. Images of the hijacked planes crashing into the two towers are etched on the memories of those who were anywhere near a television that day. There were many other instances of mass suffering in the closing years of the twentieth century. But the atrocities of 9/11 struck at the heart of a superpower and stirred up a major new offensive against Islamic extremism. A 'war on terror' was declared by the US President, George W. Bush, who even used the provocative language of 'crusade' to describe it. The world suddenly seemed much less secure, much less stable than it had even under the shadow of the Cold War.

What is interesting about the West's reactions to 9/11, for our purposes, is what it tells us about the West and religion. The atrocities prompted feverish speculation about a clash of civilizations and the fanatical underbelly of immigrant Muslim communities in the West. Puzzled media stories about radical Islam expressed a profound sense of dislocation from the human experience of religion. There was a sense of incomprehension, as if the apocalyptic worldview reflected in the notes found in the baggage of Mohammed Atta, one of the leaders of the 9/11 terrorists, came from another planet or another universe. There were agonized, self-referential columns in newspapers from writers who posed as the conscience of their society and wondered if they could ever write again after 9/11. Nothing showed up the West's growing blindness about religious belief so well as its confusion about the motives and values of the terrorists. Not that, in saying this, one need believe that the terrorists' worldview was an acceptable or adequate expression of Islam. But the assurances of the vast majority of Muslim scholars and leaders that Atta and his companions did not represent the authentic, peaceable voice of Islam rang hollow to a class of journalists who had largely given up paying attention to the religious traditions of the world.

For most of the developing world the real story about religion at the end of the century was not its eccentricity, or its fanaticism, or its lack of contact with the material things of life, but its relevance to ordinary life. This was true for Christianity as much as Islam. Neither the prophets of doom nor the apostles of Christian progress could explain adequately what had happened since 1914. The total Christian population of the world had more than tripled, from 558 million in 1900 to 1.747 billion, but its percentage share of the population – if these figures are accurate, which is admittedly a big 'if' – had marginally slipped from 34.5 per cent to 33.2 per cent. The slight fall, given all the caveats about the figures, is probably insignificant. But the basic point is obvious: as a world religion Christianity had maintained its position throughout the century. It had not significantly advanced, but neither had it declined. A pessimist – or a secularist – might conclude that the immense effort Christians had poured into evangelism had run to nothing in the end. All the hope of Edinburgh 1910 that the evangelization of the world was just around the corner had evaporated. An optimist might conclude that the doomsayers had been proved wrong. Christianity had found ways of adapting to new situations so that decline in any one part of it was matched by revival and growth elsewhere. So diverse, so complex was the modern history of the Christian Church worldwide that both generalizations were true.

Yet certain important conclusions do stand out from the century as a whole. One is the failure of sustained efforts to suppress Christian belief. Churches did not on the whole offer heroic examples of resistance to tyranny, though there were many significant exceptions. Ten of them were commemorated in statues filling empty niches on the West Front of Westminster Abbey in 1998. Their names read like a roll-call of conflict over Christianity in the twentieth century, and included Martin Luther King Jr., Archbishop Janani Luwum (murdered by President Idi Amin of Uganda in 1977), Archbishop Oscar Romero, Elizabeth of Russia (an Orthodox nun murdered by the Bolsheviks in 1918), Wang Zhimin (a Chinese Christian killed during the Cultural Revolution) and Dietrich Bonhoeffer. But in general in Nazi-occupied Europe, in the Soviet Union and elsewhere, churches reacted to persecution with the usual mixture of fear, self-interest and muted defiance. And yet even during the most savage and sustained onslaughts against believers, when Christianity was driven underground, it stubbornly survived. If that is a conclusion that stands generally in favour of the churches, it is offset by the reflection that Christians did little to prevent or contain the colossal scale of human suffering in the course of the twentieth century. Worse, they participated in some of its most terrible crimes. Christians defended apartheid in South Africa, supported the Nazis, turned a blind eye to murder and mayhem and propped up totalitarian regimes the world over. That is a serious debit balance. It is perhaps countered by the role many Christians played in the development of human rights, social justice and international aid. But the record of the Christian Church overall, in the context of world war and the slaughter of millions, was definitely a very mixed one.

When we turn from the general contribution of Christianity to world history and look instead at the churches themselves, two further conclusions stand out. The first is the massive institutional resilience of the Catholic Church. On any reading, the Catholic Church by the end of the century was a colossus in world Christianity, a doctrinal system and ecclesial body of such scope and diversity that it dominated the Christian landscape in every continent. At its heart was a papacy that had recovered from the weakness and turmoil of the mid-nineteenth century to become – quite unexpectedly even for many Catholics – an unchallengeable source of authority and status within the Catholic Church as a whole. This had happened controversially, and as John Paul II's papacy drew to a close there were plenty of Catholics who lamented the bureaucratic centralization that had occurred since he was elected pope, or who accused him of authoritarianism. The difficulties the Catholic Church faced by the 1990s were immense – acute shortages of clergy, falling congregations in the West, the widespread ignoring of Catholic moral teaching, significant internal dissent, the problem of squaring teaching on contraception with the pastoral needs of countries where HIV/AIDS was rife – but there were no clear signs that the break-up of the Catholic Church, predicted by some, was more than the remotest possibility.

The second conclusion concerned the persistence of 'primal religion' (in Harvey Cox's words) in the twentieth century. The more restrained, cerebral form of Christian piety that by the end of the nineteenth century was typical of the Western Protestant churches had been overtaken by Pentecostalism and Charismatic Christianity, and reached the limits of its cultural adaptability. If there was one thing no one foresaw at Edinburgh in 1910 it was this. The specific context for the flourishing of primal religion in the developing world was the dismemberment of the European overseas empires, but Pentecostalism and Charismatic Christianity crossed all denominational, social and geographical boundaries. This was a salutary reminder that religion is not a matter of reason alone, but of emotion and of mystery, and that the deepest longings of human beings for some sense of purposefulness cannot be fulfilled through rationally articulated systems of doctrine alone.

Given all this, what were the prospects of the Christian Church at the beginning of the new millennium? A spate of books appearing in the 1990s and 2000s highlighted the growth of Pentecostalism in the Global South and reached startling conclusions. By 2050, it was claimed, the largest Christian countries in the world would be the United States, Brazil, Mexico, the Philippines, Nigeria and the Congo. America apart, the leadership of the Christian world was moving south. Religion in Europe would continue to decline, though it would not disappear. Within countries of traditional Catholic strength – such as Brazil and Mexico – a steadily increasing proportion of the population would in fact be Pentecostal. This global trend would merely intensify Christian rivalry with Islam and prolong cultural conflict between these two world religions, especially because the growth of Christianity would occur precisely in those parts of the world – Asia and Africa – where Islam would also advance. It would also sideline the Western churches' preoccupation with issues such as women's ministry and homosexuality.

There were two problems with this analysis. One is that it depended on forward projection from uncertain historical trends. As we saw earlier in this book, the statistics of Christian church membership are not precise. They do not measure the same thing across different traditions, making comparison difficult. But even if we could be sure that the historical data was accurate, we could not predict all the variables that will affect the growth of churches over the next half-century or so. It may be that the birth rate will decline in parts of the world, or that social improvements in some developing countries will fulfil needs currently met by religion, or that new forms of religious belonging will arise, or that new conflicts will decimate populations. None of this can be foreseen. Even so, allowing for much uncertainty about future trends, the basic outline of growth summarized above is likely on the present evidence. But the second problem is structural. In suggesting that the leadership of the Christian world was moving southwards, the most pessimistic analyses neglected the fact that this would open up a widening breach within Christianity itself between the numerically static or shrinking but affluent Western churches and the numerically growing poorer churches of the Third World. What effect this would have on the course of church controversy it is impossible to say. But it does suggest that the Christian–Muslim conflict need not be the only one, or even the most serious one, likely to afflict the worldwide Christian Church in the future.

Nevertheless, accepting the likelihood that something of this forward projection of Christian growth will happen, what might be the major problems ahead for the Church? This survey of the Church in the twentieth century, put alongside the current predictions, suggests to me three specific challenges. The first is the need to resist the assumption that numerical growth is a sign of theological correctness. At the end of the twentieth century there were plenty of critics of Western liberalism crowing over the decline of liberal Christianity and the startling growth of Pentecostalism. But they argued as if numbers alone resolved all disputes and as if the controversies of the last 200 years in Western theology could be ignored as unimportant. Western guilt about colonialism reinforced this perception. Such a view risked forgetting that Western theology had considerable achievements on its side as a mediation of faith in the modern world. Not to take seriously the nature of these arguments would put Christianity into an essentially reactive position at odds with the intellectual and spiritual needs of a large proportion of the population.

The second challenge will be to find ways of continuing and renewing the ecumenical movement. For all its shortcomings and disappointments, the emergence of a worldwide movement of Christian cooperation and mutual understanding was a major achievement. It helped to mitigate the mutual hostility between different Christian traditions that had built up over centuries. It provided a means by which different Christian cultures could talk to each other. It was also a means by which misunderstandings could be corrected and stereotypes exposed. One of the most heartening developments in the second half of the century was the fact that some of the independent and Pentecostal churches joined the WCC. In turn the WCC sought to expand its range of commitments to encompass these new Christian communities. Ecumenical dialogue required years of patient listening, and sometimes this led to no concrete developments on the ground. But it was not a luxury. It was a powerful symbol of Christians learning to live with each other and recognizing each other's needs. Its potential contribution to world peace was immense, if yet to be fulfilled. Against the possibility that the growth of powerful, conservative Charismatic movements in the Global South might bypass the ecumenical instruments of the WCC and the Catholic Church, the value of Christians meeting each other, getting to know each other, worshipping together when possible, and attempting to understand what might constitute real unity between them, would need to be asserted forcefully.

In turn that opens up a third challenge, interfaith relations. At the end of the twentieth century Christians were far from agreed on how to regard the other world religions. Some advocated an 'inclusive' approach: Christian faith did not exclude true believers in other religions from salvation. Others were 'pluralist': faith was contextual and all the great religions in their own way contributed to the human search for God. But these views were typical of the Western churches, and even there they almost certainly represented a minority. By far the majority of Christians followed an 'exclusivist' line: for them the Christian revelation was uniquely true, and salvation was found only through faith in Jesus Christ. And yet even the 'exclusivist' position could emphasize the elements of wisdom and truth to be found in other religions, the impossibility of prejudging the mercy of God and the practical importance of respect for other people. All Christians, then, had much to offer the world, potentially, by way of an appreciation of the ways of religion. This was a responsibility underlined by the rise of inter-religious hatred and by international terrorism.

Looking back over this history, one cannot but be struck by the enormous diversity of churches and by the vastly different experiences their members have undergone. The Christian churches have proved immensely adaptive and resourceful but also incapable time and again of rising above self-interest or narrowness of vision. Theirs was a history of terror and hope, of persecution and perseverance, of failure and fulfilment. All of the great traditions of the Christian Church faced significant internal dissent at the end of the century, which seemed to have grown just at the same time as the traditions were at last beginning to understand one another. This was eloquent about the roots of Christian experience in local communities, with their intense loyalties and personal commitments, but it was also eloquent about the difficulty of cultivating and yet transcending the particularity of local perspectives in the interest of supporting the worldwide community of faith – that, perhaps, looked set to be the hardest challenge of all for the Christian Church in the third millennium.

Notes

Introduction. The Church and the World on the Eve of War

1. W.H. Temple Gairdner, *Edinburgh 1910: An Account and Interpretation of the World Missionary Conference* (London and Edinburgh: Oliphant, Anderson and Ferrier, 1910), p 50.
2. C. Peter Williams, 'British Religion and the Wider World: Mission and Empire, 1800–1940', in S. Gilley and W.J. Sheils (eds), *A History of Religion in Britain: Practice and Belief from Pre-Roman Times to the Present* (Oxford: Blackwell, 1994), p 402.
3. John R. Mott, *The Decisive Hour of Christian Mission* (London: CMS, 1910), p 29.
4. Temple Gairdner, *Edinburgh 1910*, p 10.
5. World Missionary Conference, *Report of Commission I. Carrying the Gospel to All the Non-Christian World* (London and Edinburgh: Oliphant, Anderson and Ferrier, 1910), p 25.
6. J.M. Roberts, *The Penguin History of the Twentieth Century* (London: Penguin, 1999), p 168.
7. W.O. Chadwick, *A History of the Popes 1830–1914* (Oxford: Oxford University Press, 1998), p 176.
8. I.S. Belliustin, *Description of the Clergy in Rural Russia: The Memoir of a Nineteenth-Century Parish Priest*, ed and trans G.L. Freeze (Ithaca and London: Cornell University Press, 1985), p 171.
9. D.B. Barrett, G.T. Kurian and T.M. Johnson (eds), *World Christian Encyclopedia: A Comparative Survey of Churches and Religions in the Modern World* (Oxford and New York: Oxford University Press, 2nd ed., 2001), p 4.
10. See T.M. Johnson and S.Y. Chung, 'Tracking Global Christianity's Statistical Centre of Gravity, AD33–AD2100', *International Review of Mission* 93 (2004), pp 166–81.

Chapter 1. From Imperial Wars to Wars of Ideology

1. J. Fontana, *Les Catholiques français pendant la Grande Guerre* (1990), p 68. My translation.
2. E. Busch, *Karl Barth: His Life from Letters and Autobiographical Texts*

(London: SCM, 1976), p 81.

3. E. Bethge, *Dietrich Bonhoeffer* (London: Fount, 1977), p 106.

Chapter 2. The Catholic Church: Triumphant and Resistant 1914–45

1. E. Duffy, *Saints and Sinners: A History of the Popes* (New Haven and London: Yale University Press, 1997), p 337.
2. These figures are from H. Jedin (ed), *History of the Church, Vol. X. The Church in the Modern Age* (London: Burns and Oates, 1981), p 8.
3. E. Duffy, *Faith of Our Fathers: Reflections on Catholic Tradition* (London: Continuum, 2004), p 34.
4. W.A. Christian, *Person and God in a Spanish Valley* (Princeton: Seminar Press, 1972), p 44.

Chapter 3. The Orthodox Churches

1. Sergei Bulgakov, *A Bulgakov Anthology*, ed J. Pain and N. Zernov (Philadelphia: Westminster Press, 1976), p 3.
2. P. Ramet, *Eastern Christianity and Politics in the Twentieth Century* (Durham, NC, and London: Duke University Press, 1988), p 186.

Chapter 4. Worldwide Protestantism

1. E. Troeltsch, *The Social Teaching of the Christian Churches* (1912; London: Allen and Unwin: ET, 1931), vol. 2, p 461.
2. *Ibid.*, pp 468–9.
3. G. Dorrien, 'American Liberal Theology: Crisis, Irony, Decline, Renewal, Ambiguity', *Cross Currents* 55 (Winter 2005–6).

Chapter 5. Christian Internationalism: Mission and Ecumenism

1. *The Statistical Atlas of World Mission* (1910), p 21.
2. Quoted in K. Cracknell, *Justice, Courtesy and Love: Theologians and Missionaries Encountering World Religions, 1846–1914* (London: Epworth, 1995), p 200.
3. *Ibid.*, p 199.
4. R.C.D. Jasper, *George Bell* (London: Oxford University Press, 1967), p 59.
5. Toronto Statement, at http://wcc-coe.org/wcc/what/ecumenical/ts-e.html.
6. S.C. Neill, *A History of Christian Missions* (1964), p 450.

Chapter 6. Nuclear Powers and Decolonization

1. Cited in P. Hebblethwaite, *John XXIII* (London: Continuum, new ed, 2000), p 121.

Chapter 7. The Catholic Church: Inner Transformation

1. Quoted in H. Küng, *My Struggle for Freedom* (2002), p 102.
2. Hebblethwaite, *John XXIII*, p 213.

3. A. Ngindi Mushete, in R. Gibellini, *Paths of African Theology* (London: SCM, 1994), p 24.

Chapter 8. The Orthodox Churches

1. Michael A. Meerson, in P. Ramet (ed), *Eastern Christianity and Politics in the Twentieth Century* (Durham, NC, and London: Duke University Press, 1988), p 129.

Chapter 9. Protestant Unsettlement

1. C.G. Brown, *The Death of Christian Britain: Understanding Secularisation* (London and New York: Routledge, 2001), p 1.
2. G. Davie, *Religion in Britain since 1945: Believing without Belonging* (Oxford: Blackwell, 1994), p 1.
3. Barrett, Kurian and Johnson (eds), *World Christian Encyclopedia*, p 28.

Chapter 10. Independent Churches and New Religious Movements

1. M. Northcott, 'A Survey of the Rise of Charismatic Christianity in Malaysia', *Asia Journal of Theology* 4 (1990), p 274.
2. E. Barker, *The Making of a Moonie: Choice or Brainwashing?* (Oxford: Blackwell, 1984).

Chapter 11. From Oil Crisis to Oil Wars

1. A speech in January 1990, quoted in G. Weigel, *The Final Revolution: The Resistance Church and the Collapse of Communism* (Oxford: Oxford University Press, 1992), p 37.

Chapter 12. The Catholic Church

1. G. O'Connor, *Universal Father: A Life of Pope John Paul II* (London: Bloomsbury, 2005), p 214.
2. For example, by Peter Hebblethwaite, in 'A Fundamentalist Pope?', in H. Küng and J. Moltmann (eds), *Fundamentalism as an Ecumenical Challenge: A Concilium Special* (London: SCM, 1992), p 87.

Chapter 13. The Orthodox Churches

1. K. Ware, 'Orthodox Theology in the New Millennium: What is the Most Important Question?', *Sobornost* 26:2 (2004), p 8.

Chapter 14. Protestantism and Its Tribulations

1. The full text can be found at http://www.warc.ch/24gc/tatt/ab2004.pdf.
2. Emerito P. Nacpil, President of Union Theological Seminary, Manila, in 1971, quoted at http://www.religion-online.org/showarticle.asp?title=1574, from an article that originally appeared in *Christian Century* in 1974.
3. From http://www.confessingchurch.homestead.com/index.html.

Chapter 15. Pentecostalism

1. Walter J. Hollenweger, *Pentecostalism: Origins and Developments Worldwide* (Peabody, MA: Hendrickson, 1997), pp 18–19.
2. David Martin, *Forbidden Revolutions: Pentecostalism in Latin America, Catholicism in Eastern Europe* (London: SPCK, 1996), p 26.
3. The report of Wilhelmina (Wilma) Davies, cited in Allan Anderson, *An Introduction to Pentecostalism* (Cambridge: Cambridge University Press, 2004), p 6.
4. Allan Anderson, 'African Pentecostalism and the Ancestor Cult: Confrontation or Compromise?', *Missionalia* 21 (1993), p 33.
5. Harvey Cox, *Fire from Heaven: The Rise of Pentecostal Spirituality and the Reshaping of Religion in the Twenty-First Century* (London: Cassell, 1996), p 81.
6. *Ibid.*, p 82.
7. *Ibid.*, p 244.
8. Martyn Percy, *Words, Wonders and Power: Understanding Contemporary Christian Fundamentalism and Revivalism* (London: SPCK, 1996), p 79.

Bibliography

This is only a select list of books most likely to be useful to students setting out in the field. Much of the material on which this book is based came from specialist journals; a final category lists the journals I found most helpful.

General twentieth-century histories

Best, Anthony, Hanhimaki, Jussi M., Maiolo, Joseph A., and Schulze, Kirsten E., *International History of the Twentieth Century* (London: Routledge, 2003)

Betts, Raymond F., *Decolonization* (London: Routledge, 2nd ed, 2004)

Grenville, J.A.S., *A History of the World from the 20th to the 21st Century* (London: Routledge, 2nd ed, 2004)

Hobsbawm, Eric, *The Age of Extremes* (London: Michael Joseph, 1994)

Howard, Michael, and Louis, William Roger (eds), *The Oxford History of the Twentieth Century* (Oxford: Oxford University Press, 1998)

Judd, Denis, *The Lion and the Tiger: The Rise and Fall of the British Raj* (Oxford: Oxford University Press, 2004)

Mazlish, Bruce and Iriye, Akira (eds), *The Global History Reader* (New York and London: Routledge, 2005)

Roberts, J.M., *The Penguin History of the Twentieth Century* (London: Penguin, 1999)

General histories and discussions of Christianity

Avis, Paul, *The Christian Church: An Introduction to the Major Traditions* (London: SPCK, 2002)

Barrett, David (ed), *World Christian Encyclopedia* (Oxford and New York: Oxford University Press, 1982; 2nd ed, also ed by G.T Kurian and T.M. Johnson, 2001)

Fisher, Mary Pat, *Religion in the Twenty-First Century* (London: Routledge, 1999)

Hastings, Adrian (ed), *A World History of Christianity* (London: Geoffrey Chapman, 1999)

Hoover, A.J., *God, Germany, and Britain in the Great War: A Study in Clerical Nationalism* (New York: Praeger, 1989)

Jenkins, Philip, *The Next Christendom: The Coming of Global Christianity* (Oxford and New York: Oxford University Press, 2002)

Johnson, Todd M., and Chun, Sun Yung, 'Tracking Global Christianity's Statistical Centre of Gravity, AD33–AD2100', *International Review of Mission* 93 (2004)

Küng, Hans, *A Global Ethic for Global Politics and Economics* (London: SCM, 1997)

Northcott, Michael, *Life after Debt: Christianity and Global Justice* (London: SPCK, 1999)

Roman Catholicism

Butler, Christopher, *The Theology of Vatican II* (London: DLT, 1967; rev. ed, 1981)

Conway, Martin, *Catholic Politics in Europe, 1918–1945* (London: Routledge, 1997)

Duffy, Eamon, *Saints and Sinners: A History of the Popes* (New Haven and London: Yale University Press, 1997; new ed, 2001)

Flannery, Austin (ed), *Vatican Council II: The Conciliar and Post Conciliar Documents* (Leominster: Gracewing, new ed, 1992)

Hastings, Adrian (ed), *Modern Catholicism: Vatican II and After* (London: SPCK, 1991)

Hebblethwaite, Peter, *John XXIII* (London: Continuum, new ed, 2000)

Jedin, Hubert (ed), *History of the Church, Vol. X. The Church in the Modern Age* (London: Burns and Oates, 1981)

Pollard, John, *The Unknown Pope: Benedict XV (1914–1922) and the Pursuit of Peace* (London: Geoffrey Chapman, 1998)

Weigel, George, *Witness to Hope: The Biography of Pope John Paul II* (London: Cliff Street Books, 2001)

Orthodoxy

Binns, John, *An Introduction to the Christian Orthodox Churches* (Cambridge: Cambridge University Press, 2002)

Burgess, Michael, *The Eastern Orthodox Churches: Concise Histories* (Jefferson, NC: McFarland, 2005)

Curtiss, John Shelton, *The Russian Church and the Soviet State 1917–1950* (Boston: Little, Brown and Company, 1954)

Ellis, Jane, *The Russian Orthodox Church: A Contemporary History* (London: Croom Helm, 1986)

—, *The Russian Orthodox Church: Triumphalism and Defensiveness* (Basingstoke: Macmillan, 1996)

Pospielovsky, Dimitry, *The Russian Church under the Soviet Regime, 1917–1982*, 2 vols. (New York: St Vladimir's Press, 1984)

Ramet, Pedro (ed), *Eastern Christianity and Politics in the Twentieth Century* (Durham, NC and London: Duke University Press, 1988)

Shevzov, Vera, *Russian Orthodoxy on the Eve of Revolution* (Oxford: Oxford University Press, 2004)

Walters, Philip (ed), *World Christianity: Eastern Europe* (Eastbourne: MARCC, 1988)

Ware, Kallistos, *The Orthodox Church* (Harmondsworth: Penguin, new ed, 1980)

Zernov, Nicolas, *The Russian Religious Renaissance of the Twentieth Century* (London: DLT, 1963)

Protestantism

Davies, Rupert E. (ed), *The Testing of the Churches 1932–1982* (London: Epworth, 1982)

Freston, Paul, *Evangelicals and Politics in Asia, Africa and Latin America* (Cambridge: Cambridge University Press, 2001)

Hope, Nicholas, *German and Scandinavian Protestantism 1700–1918* (Oxford: Oxford University Press, 1995)

Jacob, W.M., *The Making of the Anglican Church Worldwide* (London: SPCK, 1997)

Sachs, W.L., *The Transformation of Anglicanism: From State Church to Global Communion* (Cambridge: Cambridge University Press, 1993)

Schrorring, Jens Holger, Kumari, Presanna, and Hjelm, Norman A. (eds), *From Federation to Communion: The History of the Lutheran World Federation* (Minneapolis: Fortress Press, 1997)

Sell, Alan, *A Reformed, Evangelical, Catholic Theology: The Contribution of the World Alliance of Reformed Churches, 1875–1982* (Grand Rapids, MI: Eerdmans, 1991)

Turner, J.M., *Conflict and Reconciliation: Studies in Methodism and Ecumenism 1740–1982* (London: Epworth, 1985)

Willis, David, and Welker, Michael (eds), *Toward the Future of the Reformed Theology* (Grand Rapids, MI: Eerdmans, 1999)

Independent churches and New Religious Movements

Anderson, Allan, *Zion and Pentecost: The Spirituality and Experience of Pentecostal/Apostolic Churches in South Africa* (Pretoria: UNISA, 2000)

—, *African Reformation: African Initiated Christianity in the 20th Century* (Trenton, NJ, and Asmara, Eritrea: Africa World Press, 2001)

Arweck, Elisabeth, *New Religious Movements in the West: Constructions and Controversies* (London: Routledge, 2004)

Borowik, I., and Babinski, G. (eds), *New Religious Phenomena in Central and Eastern Europe* (Krakow: Nomos, 1997)

Clarke, Peter B., *New Religions in Global Perspective* (London: Routledge, 2004)

Lucas, P.C., and Robbins, T. (eds), *New Religious Movements in the 21st Century: Legal, Political and Social Challenges in Global Perspective* (London: Routledge, 2004)

Sundkler, Bengt, *Bantu Prophets in South Africa* (London: Lutterworth, 1948)
—, *Zulu Zion and Some Swazi Zionists* (London and New York: Oxford University Press, 1976)

Pentecostalism

Anderson, Allan, *An Introduction to Pentecostalism* (Cambridge: Cambridge University Press, 2004)
Brewster, P.S. (ed), *Pentecostal Doctrine* (Cheltenham: Greenhurst Press, 1976)
Burgess, S.M., McGee, G.B., and Alexander, P.H. (eds), *The Dictionary of Pentecostal and Charismatic Movements* (Grand Rapids, MI: Zondervan, 1988)
Coleman, S., *The Globalization of Charismatic Christianity: Spreading the Gospel of Prosperity* (Cambridge: Cambridge University Press, 2001)
Cox, Harvey, *Fire from Heaven: The Rise of Pentecostal Spirituality and the Reshaping of Religion in the 21st Century* (London: Cassell, 1996)
Harris, Harriet A., *Fundamentalism and Evangelicals* (Oxford: Clarendon, 1998)
Hollenweger, Walter J., *Pentecostalism: Origins and Developments Worldwide* (Peabody, MA: Hendrickson, 1997)
Martin, David, *Tongues of Fire: The Explosion of Protestantism in Latin America* (Oxford: Blackwell, 1990)
—, *Pentecostalism: The World Their Parish* (Oxford: Blackwell, 2001)
Percy, Martyn, *Words, Wonders and Power: Understanding Contemporary Christian Fundamentalism and Revivalism* (London: SPCK, 1996)

Missionary movements

Cracknell, K., *Justice, Courtesy and Love: Theologians and Missionaries Encountering World Religions 1846–1914* (London: Epworth Press, 1995)
Stanley, Brian, *The Bible and the Flag: Protestant Missions and British Imperialism in the Nineteenth and Twentieth Centuries* (Leicester: Apollos, 1990)
Sundkler, Bengt, *The World of Mission* (London: Lutterworth, 1965)
Walls, Andrew, *The Missionary Movement in Christian History* (Maryknoll, NY: Orbis, 1996)
—, *The Cross-Cultural Process in Christian History* (Maryknoll, NY: Orbis, 2002)
Yates, Timothy, *Christian Mission in the Twentieth Century* (Cambridge: Cambridge University Press, 1994)

The ecumenical movement

Briggs, John, Oduyoye, Mercy Amba, and Tsetsis, Georges (eds), *A History of the Ecumenical Movement. Vol. 3. 1968–2000* (Geneva: WCC, 2004)
Clements, Keith, *Faith on the Frontier: A Life of J.H. Oldham* (Edinburgh: T and T Clark, 1999)
Fey, Harold E., *A History of the Ecumenical Movement: The Ecumenical Advance 1948–1968* (Geneva: WCC, 2nd ed, 1986)
Lossky, Nicholas et al, *Dictionary of the Ecumenical Movement* (Geneva: WCC, 2002)

Nurser, John, *For All Peoples and All Nations: The Ecumenical Church and Human Rights* (Washington, DC: Georgetown University Press, 2005)

Raiser, Konrad, *Ecumenism in Transition: A Paradigm Shift in the Ecumenical Movement?* (Geneva: WCC, 1991)

Rouse, Ruth, and Neill, Stephen (eds), *A History of the Ecumenical Movement 1517–1968* (Geneva: WCC, 3rd ed, 1986)

Wainwright, Geoffrey, *The Ecumenical Movement: Crisis and Opportunity for the Church* (Grand Rapids, MI: Eerdmans, 1983)

Women and the churches

Bendroth, Margaret Lamberts, and Brereton, Virginia Lieson (eds), *Women and Twentieth-Century Protestantism* (Chicago: University of Illinois Press, 2002)

Darling, Pamela W., *New Wine: The Story of Women Transforming Leadership and Power in the Episcopal Church* (Cambridge, MA: Cowley Publications, 1994)

Gill, Sean, *Women and the Church of England: From the Eighteenth Century to the Present* (London: SPCK, 1994)

Greaves, Richard L. (ed), *Triumph over Silence: Women in Protestant History* (Westport, CT: Greenwood Press, 1986)

Lindley, Susan Hill, *You Have Stept Out of Your Place: A History of Women and Religion in America* (Louisville: Westminster John Knox, 1996)

O'Brien, Anne, *God's Willing Workers: Women and Religion in Australia* (Sydney: University of New South Wales Press, 2005)

Prelinger, Catherine (ed), *Episcopal Women: Gender, Spirituality and Commitment in an American Mainline Denomination* (New York and Oxford: Oxford University Press, 1992)

Raab, Kelley A., *When Women Become Priests: The Catholic Women's Ordination Debate* (New York: Columbia University Press, 2000)

Rowbotham, Sheila, *A Century of Women: The History of Women in Britain and the United States* (London: Viking, 1997)

Ruether, Rosemary Radford, and Keller, Rosemary S. (eds), *Women and Religion in America: A Documentary History* (New York: HarperCollins, 3 vols., 1981–6)

Theological history

Barth, Karl, *How I Changed My Mind* (Edinburgh: St Andrew Press, 1969)

Baum, Gregory (ed), *The Twentieth Century: A Theological Overview* (London: Chapman, 1999)

Busch, Eberhard, *Karl Barth: His Life from Letters and Autobiographical Texts* (London: SCM, 1976)

Cone, James, *A Black Theology of Liberation* (Maryknoll, NY: Orbis, new ed, 1990)

Davidson, Robert, and Leaney, A.R.C., *Biblical Criticism: The Pelican Guide to Modern Theology, Vol. 3* (Harmondsworth: Penguin, 1970)

Edwards, David L. (ed), *The Honest to God Debate* (London: SCM, 1963)

Ford, David, and Muers, Rachel (eds), *The Modern Theologians* (Oxford: Blackwell, 3rd ed, 2005)

Gutiérrez, Gustavo, *A Theology of Liberation: History, Politics and Culture* (Maryknoll, NY: Orbis, 1973)

Küng, Hans, *My Struggle for Freedom* (London: Continuum, 2003)

Nicholls, William, *Systematic and Philosophical Theology: The Pelican Guide to Modern Theology, Vol. 1* (Harmondsworth: Penguin, 1969)

Nichols, Aidan, *From Newman to Congar: The Idea of Doctrinal Development from the Victorians to the Second Vatican Council* (Edinburgh: T and T Clark, 1990)

—, *Catholic Thought since the Enlightenment* (Leominster: Gracewing, 1998)

Schmemann, Akexander, *Russian Theology 1920–1972* (Virginia: Union Theological Seminary, 1969)

Secularization

Bibby, Reginald, *Fragmented Gods* (Toronto: Stoddart, 1990)

Brown, Callum G., *The Death of Christian Britain* (London: Routledge, 2001)

Bruce, Steve (ed), *Religion and Modernization: Sociologists and Historians Debate the Secularization Thesis* (Oxford: Clarendon, 1992)

—, *Religion in the Modern World: From Cathedrals to Cults* (Oxford: Oxford University Press, 1996)

Davie, Grace, Heelas, Paul, and Woodhead, Linda, *Predicting Religion: Christian, Secular and Alternative Futures* (Aldershot: Ashgate, 2004)

Gilbert, Alan, *The Making of Post-Christian Britain* (London: Longman, 1980)

Africa

Bediako, Kwame, *Christianity in Africa: The Renewal of a Non-Western Religion* (Maryknoll, NY: University of Edinburgh and Orbis Books, 1995)

Dedji, Valentin, *Reconstruction and Renewal in African Christian Theology* (Nairobi: Acton: 2003)

Gibellini, Rosino, *Paths of African Theology* (London: SCM, 1994)

Gifford, Paul, *African Christianity: Its Public Role* (London: Hurst, 1998)

Hastings, Adrian, *A History of African Christianity 1950–1975* (Cambridge: Cambridge University Press, 1979)

—, *The Church in Africa 1450–1950* (Oxford: Oxford University Press, 1994)

Magesa, Lauenti, *African Religion: The Moral Traditions of Abundant Life* (Maryknoll, NY: Orbis, 1997)

Muzorewa. Gwinyai, *The Origins and Development of African Theology* (Maryknoll, NY: Orbis 1987)

Oduyoye, Mercy, *Hearing and Knowing: Theological Reflections on Christianity in Africa* (Maryknoll, NY: Orbis Books 1986)

Sanneh, Lamin, *Encountering the West: Christianity and the Global Cultural Process: The African Dimension* (London: Marshall Pickering, 1993)

—, and Carpenter, Joel A. (eds), *The Changing Face of Christianity: Africa, the West, and the World* (Oxford: Oxford University Press, 2005)

Sundkler, Bengt, and Steed, Christopher, *A History of the Church in Africa* (Cambridge: Cambridge University Press, 2000)

Asia

Billington Harper, S., *In the Shadow of the Mahatma: Bishop V. S. Azariah and the Travails of Christianity in British India* (Grand Rapids, MI, and Cambridge: Eerdmans, 2000)

Buswell, R.E., and Lee, T.S., *Christianity in Korea* (Honolulu: University of Hawaii Press, 2005)

Covell, Ralph R., *The Liberating Gospel in China: The Christian Faith among China's Minority Peoples* (Grand Rapids, MI: Baker Books, 1995)

Cox, Jeffrey, *Imperial Fault Lines: Christianity and Colonial Power in India, 1818–1940* (Stanford, CA: Stanford University Press, 2002)

Fox, Thomas C., *Pentecost in Asia: A New Way of Being Church* (Maryknoll, NY: Orbis, 2002)

Hunter, Alan, and Kim-Kwong, Chan, *Protestantism in Contemporary China* (Cambridge: Cambridge University Press, 1993)

Reid, David, *New Wine: The Cultural Shaping of Japanese Christianity* (Berkeley: Asian Humanities Press, 1991)

Sundkler, Bengt, *Church of South India: The Movement towards Union 1900–1947* (London: Lutterworth, 1954)

Sunquist, Scott (ed), *A Dictionary of Asian Christianity* (Grand Rapids, MI: Eerdmans, 2001)

Whyte, Bob, *Unfinished Encounter: China and Christianity* (London: Fount, 1988)

Wickeri, Philip, *Seeking the Common Ground: Protestant Christianity and China's United Front* (Maryknoll, NY: Orbis, 1988)

Australasia and the Pacific

Breward, Ian, *A History of the Churches in Australasia* (Oxford and New York: Oxford University Press, 2000)

Carey, Hilary M., *Believing in Australia: A Cultural History of Religions* (Sydney: Allen and Unwin, 1996)

Davidson, Allan K., *Christianity in Aotearoa: A History of Church and Society in New Zealand* (Wellington: Education for Ministry, 2nd ed, 1997)

Forman, Charles, *The Island Churches of the South Pacific: Emergence in the Twentieth Century* (Maryknoll, NY: Orbis, 1982)

O'Farrell, Patrick, *Catholic Church and Community: An Australian History* (Sydney: University of New South Wales Press, new ed, 1992)

Piggin, Stuart: *Evangelical Christianity in Australia: Spirit, Word and World* (Melbourne: Oxford University Press, 1996)

Europe

Buchanan, Tom, and Conway, Martin (eds), *Political Catholicism in Europe, 1918–1965* (Oxford: Clarendon, 1996)

Chadwick, Owen, *The Christian Church in the Cold War* (Harmondsworth: Penguin, 1992)

Davie, Grace, *Europe: The Exceptional Case: Parameters of Faith in the Modern World* (London: DLT, 2002)

Fulton, J., and Gee, P. (eds), *Religion in Contemporary Europe* (Lewiston, NY, and Lampeter: Edwin Mellen Press, 1994)

Gehler, Michael, and Kaiser, Wolfram (eds), *Christian Democracy in Europe since 1945* (London: Routledge, 2004)

Kerkhofs, J. (ed), *Europe without Priests* (London: SCM, 1995)

McLeod, D.H., *Religion and the People of Western Europe 1789–1990* (Oxford: Oxford University Press, new ed, 1997)

—, and Ustorf, W. (eds), *The Decline of Christendom in Western Europe, 1750–2000* (Cambridge: Cambridge University Press, 2003)

Remond, René, *Religion and Society in Modern Europe* (Oxford: Blackwell, 1999)

Robbers, G. (ed), *State and Church in the European Union* (Baden-Baden: Nomos Verlagsgesellschaft, 1996)

Weigel, George, *The Final Revolution: The Resistance Church and the Collapse of Communism* (Oxford: Oxford University Press, 1992)

North America

Dolan, Jay P., *The American Catholic Experience: A History from Colonial Times to the Present* (Notre Dame, IN: University of Notre Dame Press, new ed, 1992)

Finke, R., and Stark, R., *The Churching of America, 1776–2005: Winners and Losers in Our Religious Economy* (Chapel Hill, NC: Rutgers University Press, rev. ed, 2005)

Lincoln, C.E., and Mamiya, L.H., *The Black Church in the African American Experience* (Durham, NC: Duke University Press, 1990)

Marty, M.E., *Modern American Religion: Under God Indivisible, 1941–1960* (Chicago: University of Chicago Press, 3 vols., 1996)

McLoughlin, W.G., *Revivals, Awakenings and Reform: An Essay on Religion and Social Change in America, 1607–1977* (Chicago: University of Chicago Press, 1978)

Noll, Mark A., *A History of Christianity in the United States and Canada* (London: SPCK, 1992)

Wills, D.W., *Christianity in the United States: A Historical Survey and Interpretation* (Notre Dame, IN: University of Notre Dame Press, 2005)

Wuthnow, Robert, *The Restructuring of American Religion: Society and Faith since World War II* (Princeton: Princeton University Press, 1988)

Latin America

Cleary, Edward L. (ed), *Born of the Poor: The Latin American Church since Medellin* (Notre Dame, IN: University of Notre Dame Press, 1990)

—, and Stewart-Gambino, Hannah (eds), *Conflict and Competition: The Latin American Church in a Changing Environment* (Boulder, CO, and London: Lynne Rienner, 1992)

Dussel, E. (ed), *The Church in Latin America: 1492–1992* (Tunbridge Wells: Burns and Oates, 1992)

Lehmann, David, *Struggle for the Spirit: Religious Transformation and Popular Culture in Brazil and Latin America* (Cambridge: Polity Press, 1996)

Mecham, Lloyd, *Church and State in Latin America* (Chapel Hill, NC: University of North Carolina Press, 1966)

Mignone, Emilio, *Witness to the Church: The Complicity of the Church and Dictatorship in Argentina* (Maryknoll, NY: Orbis, 1988)

Schmitt, K.M. (ed), *The Roman Catholic Church in Modern Latin America* (New York: Knopf, 1972)

Stoll, David, *Is Latin America Turning Protestant? The Politics of Evangelical Growth* (Berkeley, CA: University of California Press, 1990)

Useful journals

Catholic Historical Review
Journal of Contemporary History
Journal of Ecclesiastical History
Journal of Religion in Africa
Journal of Religious History
Religion, State and Society (formerly *Religion in Communist Lands*)
Sobornost

Index